The Art of Kelin B. Kiell

For information address mickiedaltonbooks@lycos.com

First Printing 2016

ISBN: 978-0-9944523-3-7

Published by The Mickie Dalton Foundation
NSW
Australia

Dedicated to my dear Grandfather,
Thank you for showing such encouragement and pride in my work all these years...

Contents

Part 1 – Dragon's Throne

Dragon's Throne

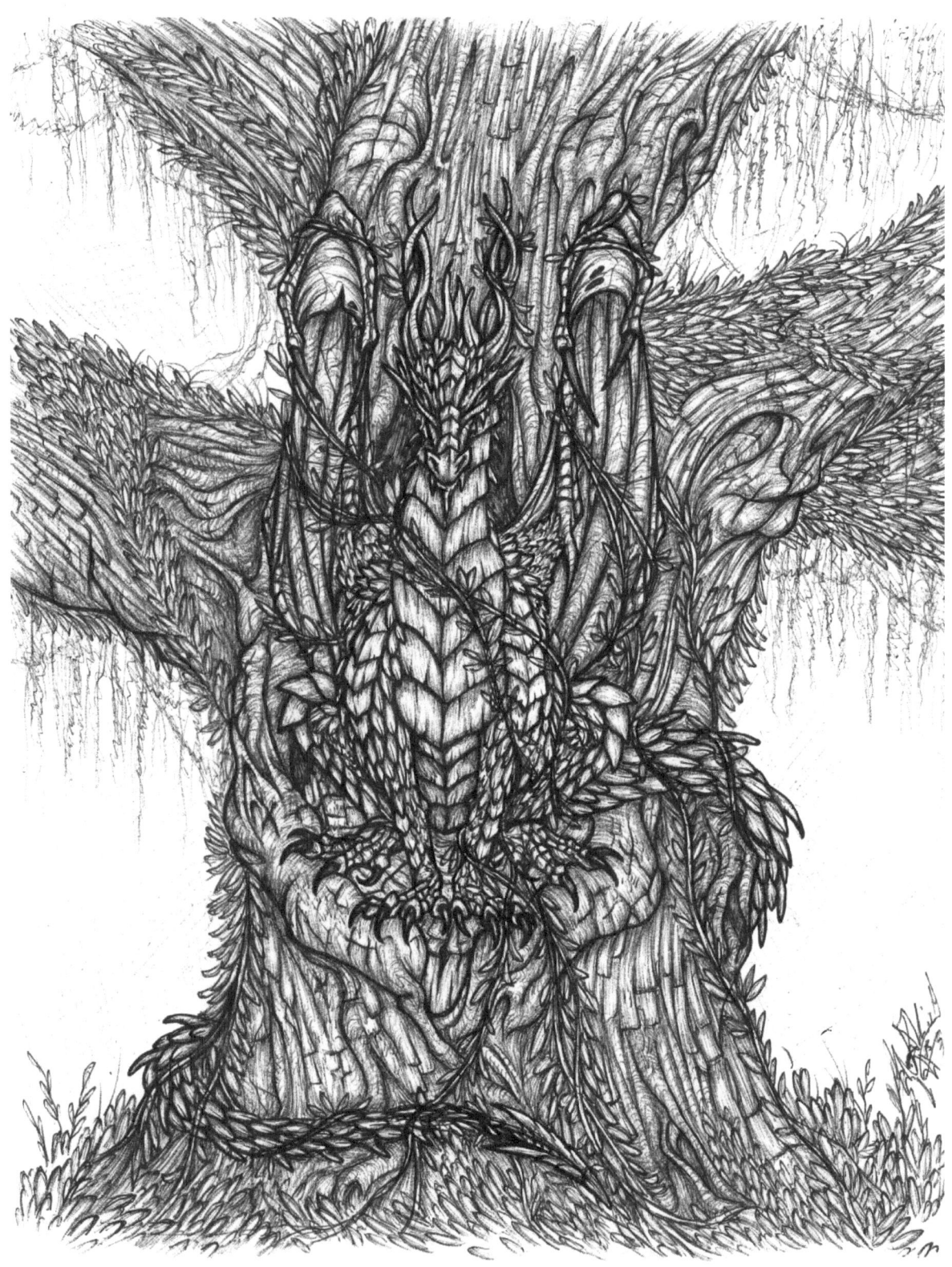

In a changing world, on ever shifting sands and flowing waters, empires are built and fall to the progressing storms of death and renewal.

Never stationary nomads seek fortunes in the open worlds, and wander astray in fear at the edges of older kingdoms. Kept from illuminations their austere secrets fester among the firm held roots. Deeper into the tangles of growth, sheltered from the open world dwells the aging past, no tree nor creature here forgets.

In the depths of the forest grows a testimony to the powers of the natural world and the past whence it came. A trunk of cracked skin, scaled as a great serpent, its claws dug deep into the earth, with mighty reaching arms bent with the weight of ages. Perched upon a shelf against a hollow of this ancient tree, a splendor sits, enfolded within great wings stiffened like stone, tail entwined round the twisting trunk.

Upon the throne of its kingdom, as ancient as the forest itself, it watches with glass eyes ever keen, yet wearied for all the wonders there. For it has watched for many centuries and all remains. Still the moons wax and wane, even change has lost its meaning with time.

Behind the glassy surface of the deep reflecting pools the eyes stare outwards to the moving shadows, no longer seeing but turned deep into the furrows of contemplation.

Over the years the vines of ivy creep and curl over the still form, lost in the dreams of thought.

Low creatures scurry past the throne without fear of the unmoving beast, even when the eyes focus to the world once more. The rustling of wind through the leaves brings a scent filtered from afar and carries the pleasant melodies of birdsong, until chill stings the air and freezes solid every limb.

The seasons renew.

With unwavering confidence that under the sheltered groves tradition remains strong, the beast returns to the solitary domain of thought.

Unchanged is the old kingdom.

Until, by chance, a change occurred.

With a whisper carried on the breeze and echoed in silence, strange footsteps fell and marked harshly the passing of unwelcome feet.

Stealing the sun ripened sweetness of berries and stained with their blood, a wanderer treads heavily the hidden paths in ignorance, paying no heed to the frenzied warnings from the boughs overhead.

At once the creatures flee from this stranger, their cries falling upon deafened ears. Through reverberations of distress they could feel what the stranger could not, a stirring in the depths.

Stumbling like a new colt over uneven ground, the wanderer progresses to an unknown destination. The roots of the treacherous trees seem to lift in purposeful hindrance, but do nothing to dissuade their curious quarry.

It was scent and sight that called to curiosity, the smell of trees, subtle against the damp musk of rain, or the dry pollen clouds as the bearing wind swept their dust over the fields. Beneath the eternal shade of the tall branches dark tales of the unknown sought to be proven, and mysteries yearned for answers. They urged the wandering feet in their own directions.

Thus pulled willingly along insidious and enlightening paths, the wanderer's eyes and ears obliged the teachings of the forest. And much did he learn. Much too did he forget, and wisdom was lost in bewilderment.

Full and fresh with many a query regarding every small thing, he gaily sang between gasps of astonishment. Crossing the glistening banks of a gently burbling stream he paused to drink from the silvery waters, and gaze down upon the vain visage of the reflected face. His laughter banished the absurdity of fears he could find no reason to dread, for the sounds of the wild were little more than a whistle and a rustle.

Little domes, soft and brightly spotted sat upon the fallen logs, hiding their poison in innocence. Beckoned with charm and promised delight, only the stranger was deceived.

On through the wood, through soggy pits and dense tangles, lengthening shadows enhanced the sinister glares of misshapen faces. Sunlight stabbed arrows through the curtains of green, brushed aside to view the ground laden with tiny flowers among the thick twisting roots and great cushions of emerald moss, a garden of singular beauty.

Above, the canopy of branches curled and tightened and narrowed into a peculiar passage. Following a call from far within, the wanderer tread the sea of violet blooms, crushing the fragile petals into the mossy rot.

The calls of distress from the creatures of the kingdom had reached beyond the path, and drawn from deep within, great eyes came to light and searched for the one who's presence shattered tranquility and provoked that which was long dormant. With patience eternal it waited for what it did not expect. When from the tangled shadows emerged a creature, the like of which had never strayed here before.

With confusion and surprise it looked upon the stranger, the theft of nature's bounty evident on reddened fingers. How abhorrent… how marvelous…

Coming to the clear the stranger blinked astonished eyes to a new sight. Here white flowers bloomed in a blanket of ivy that crept the ground and reached into a dominating shadow, to girdle the trunk of a marvelous tree, ensnaring the bending limbs in their many fingered grasp.

And there, upon a shelf of the ancient tree, he beheld the awesome beast.

As the stranger approached the throne he did not beseech the beast for mercy, nor flee in terror. Alight with the wonder of that which he had never seen, he stared rapt upon the statue and marveled at its age.

The beast could not recall a creature such as this, that breathed the very breath of change unforeseen, in years of contemplation of what was, what is, but never what could be.

The deep pools reflected the puzzlement of the young creature that approached with neither wisdom nor restraint, for its hand uplifted to brush fingers upon the relic, careless to its delicate nature.

The touch struck like a feather on stone, and traced the cracks of the weathered skin, like a trickle of water softly wearing away at a mountain.

Embraced with temptation, the young stranger took life with exhilaration and little respect.

But the beast did not recoil from the touch, it could not begrudge the youth his disrespect, for it was old and patient. Favoring new thoughts that came with the persistence of a plague, it turned inside once more.

Was the world still as it was in the long memory, an endless circle, or had the distant lands become as alien as the stars it only dreamed of. Does that which lies still and hidden within become a forgotten relic of the distant past, and live no more in the world.

Many centuries had passed since it came to rest in its dominion over the kingdom, and never conceived that it had stood upon a precarious balance that even the smallest touch could upset.

The touch that kindled uncertainty sparked the fires of fear and rage.

The beast shuddered, and all around trembled. Its wings had long grown rigid with only the distant memory of wind beneath their folds. They cracked and spread wide as the beast shook free of its bonds. Centuries of growth and decay fell to the earth, and from its jaws released a thunderous cry that shook the ground and traveled the sky like a storm.

The wanderer fell to his knees in terrified awe before the mighty dragon. With a cracking beat of thunder the great wings unleashed a furious gale, and the wanderer fell away from the terrible power, into a dream of endless darkness.

Awakened to birdsong and golden streams let down by the parted leaves, the stranger lay cradled in the curling ivy, with the gentle scent of white blooms. Bleary of mind as though fresh from a dream forgotten, leaving a lingering feeling of strangeness and unease.

The wanderer turned to regard the marvelous ancient tree, and ponder the vacant hollow. The shelf where once, he dreamt, a splendorous thing sat. All that remained was an empty throne.

By Kelin Kiell

Part 2
Penwork and Poetry

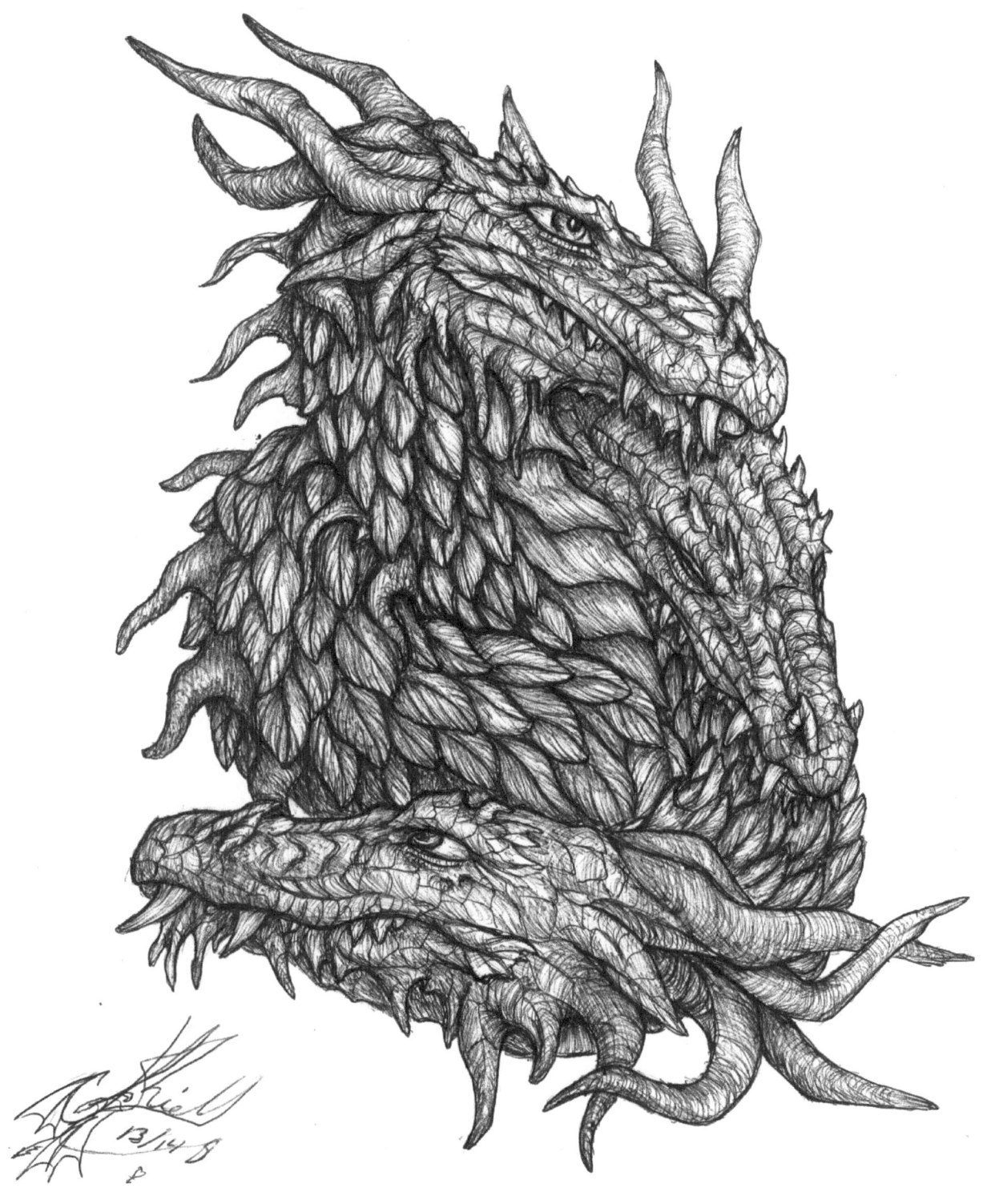

Past Present And Future

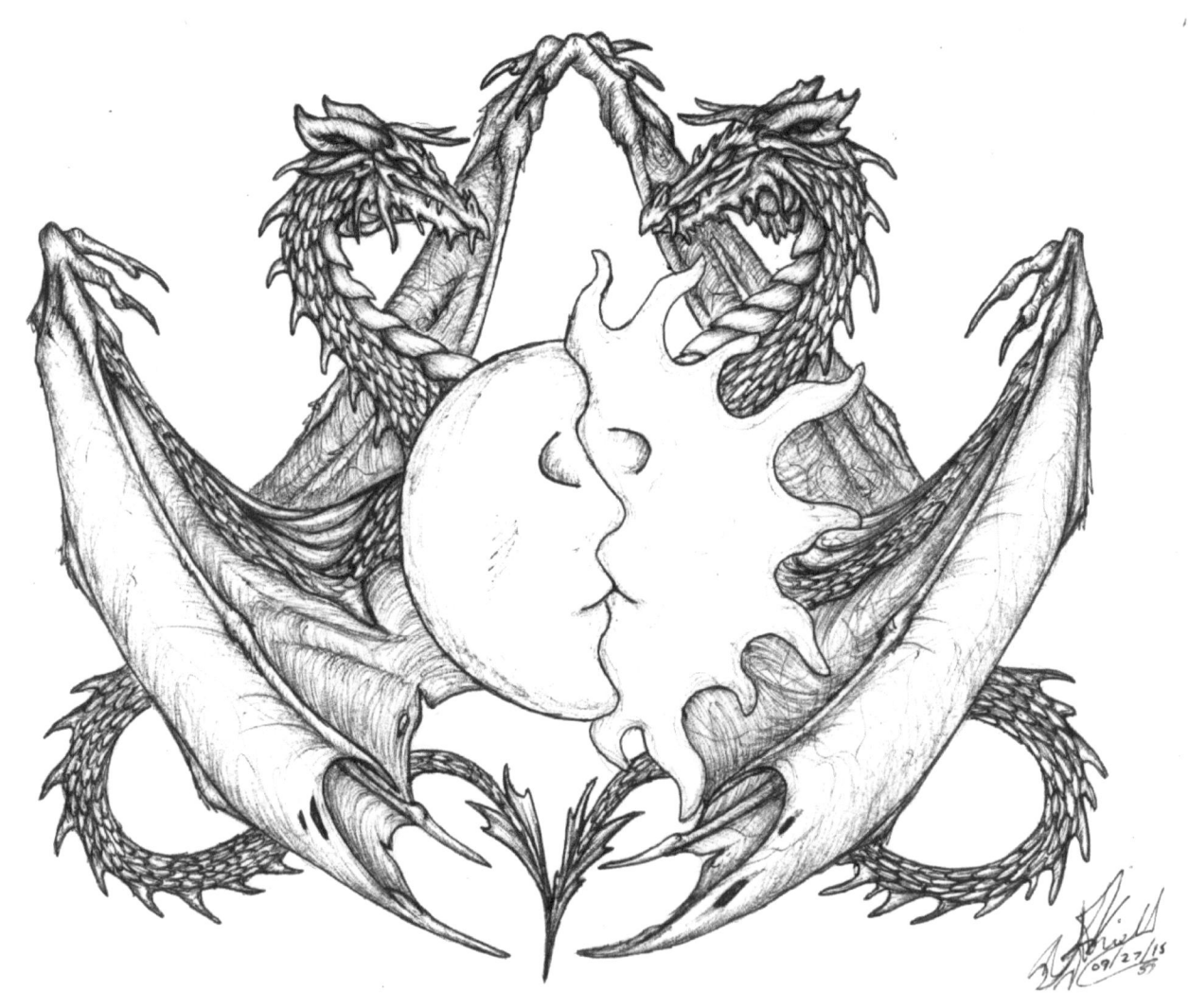

Emya and Ellya

Inspired by and drawn on the night of the lunar eclipse of 2015

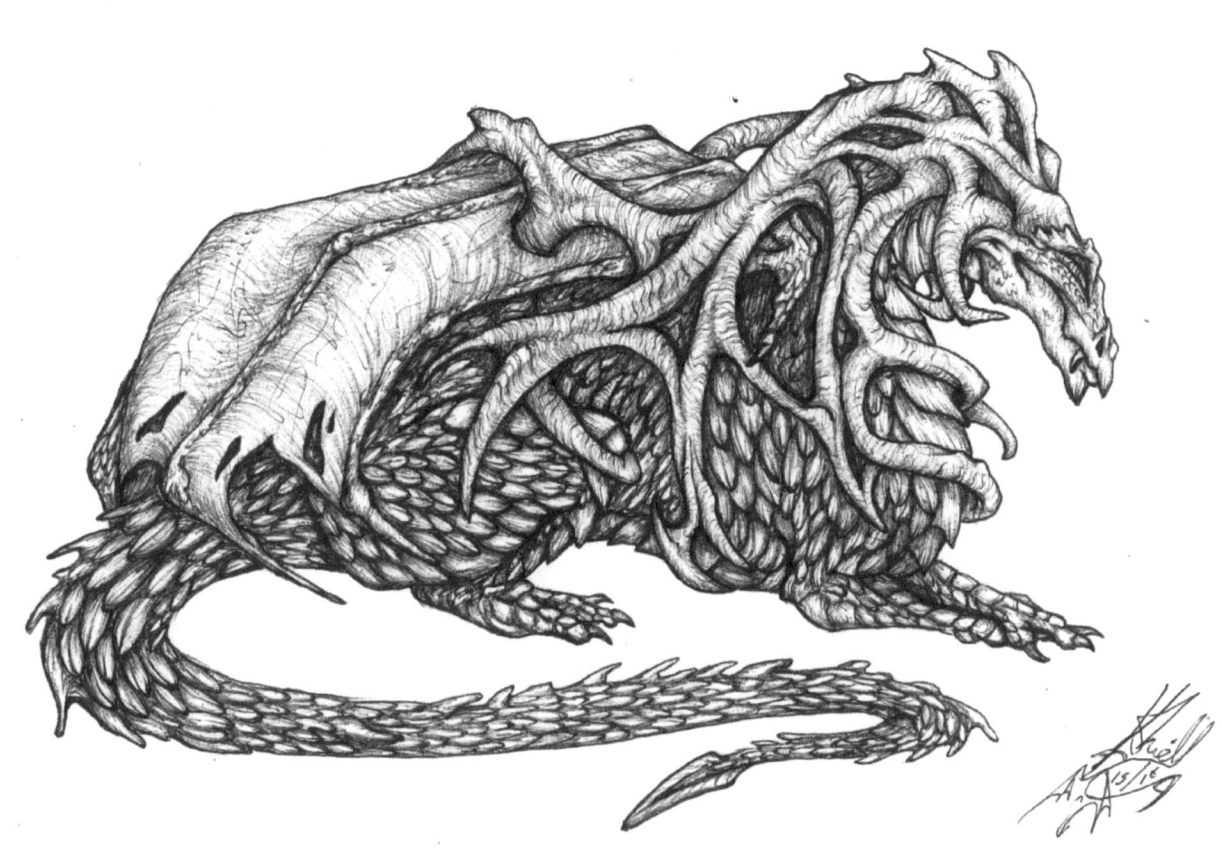

Tangled Growth

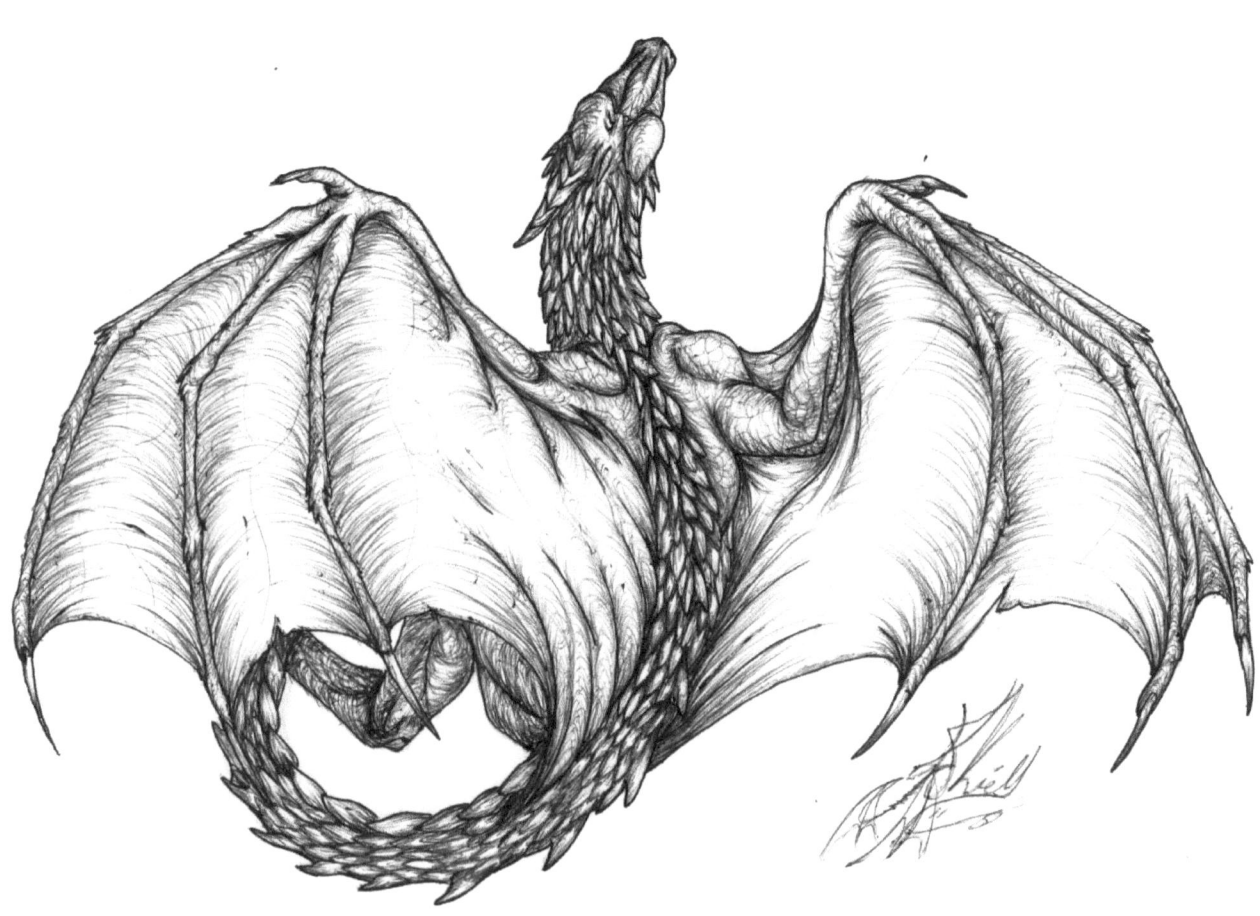

Drake

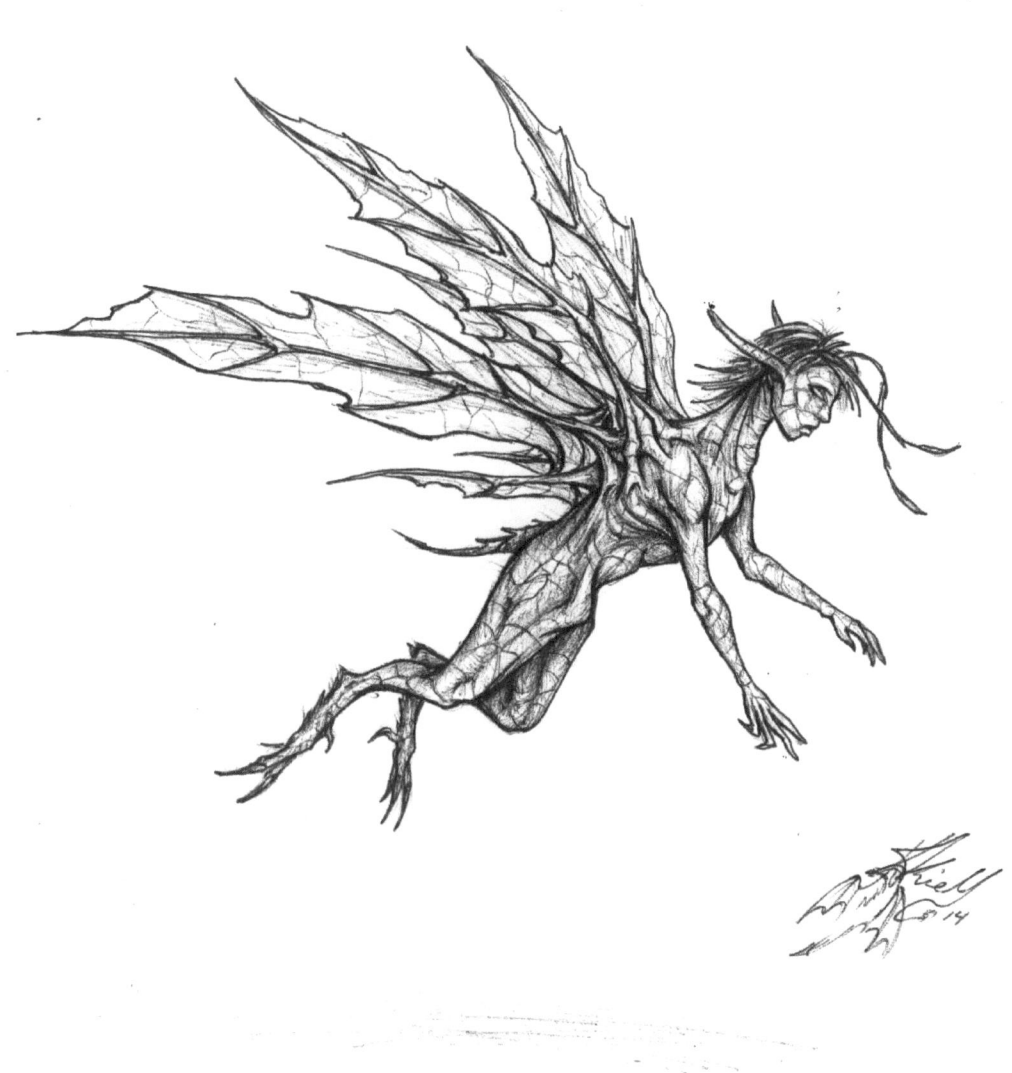

Draken Fairy

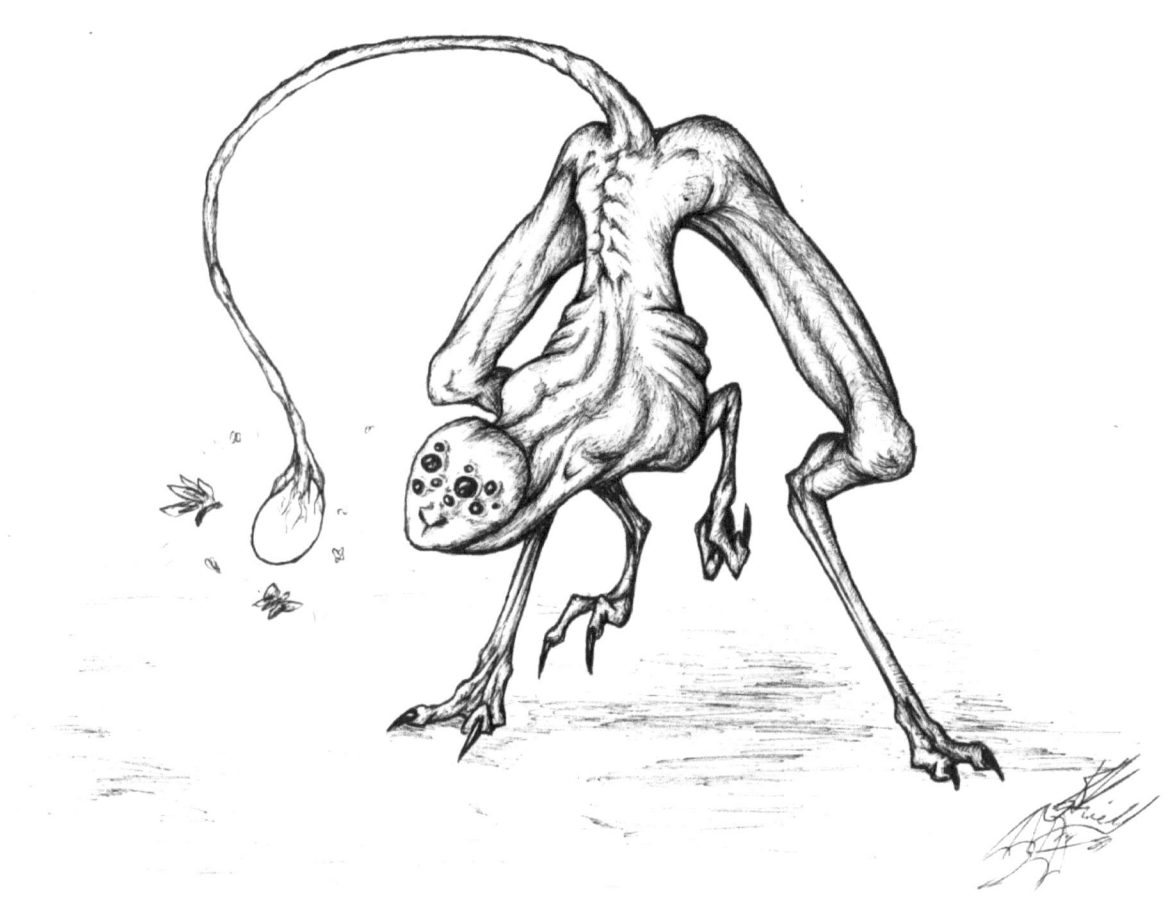

Creeping Lantern

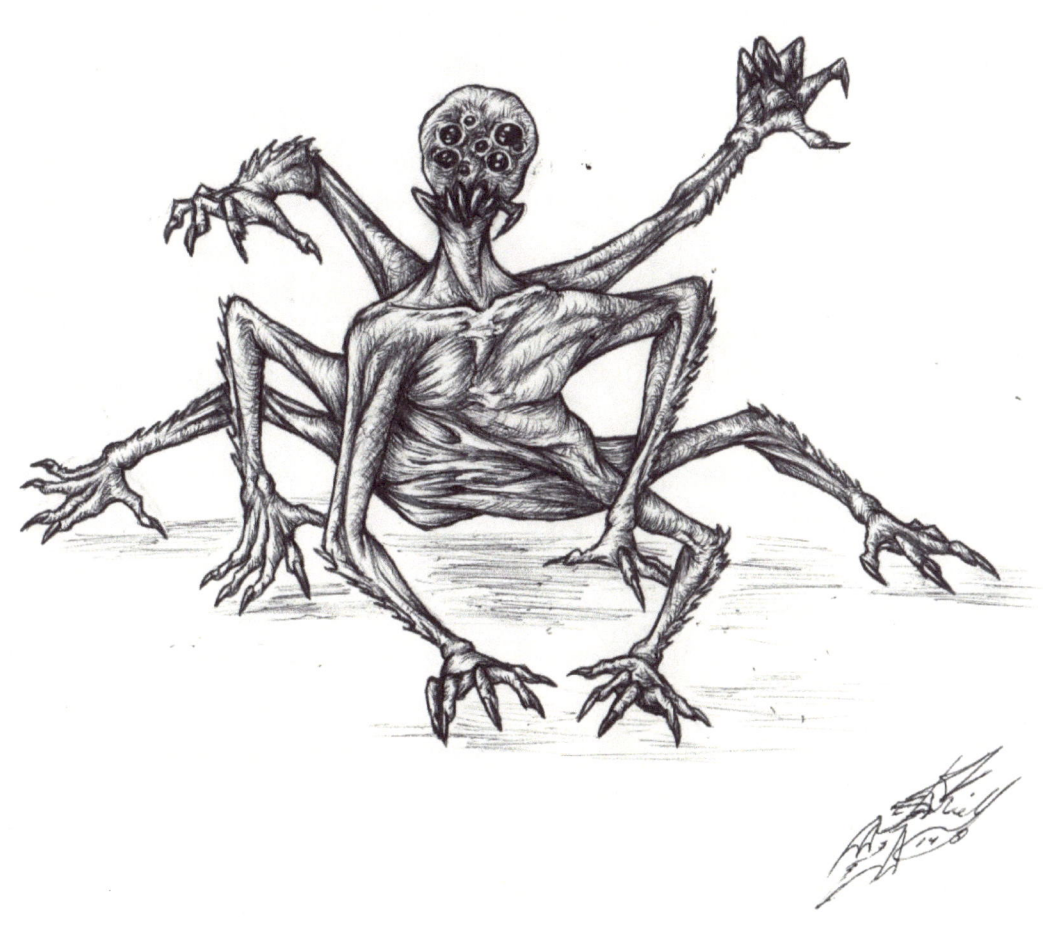

Creeper

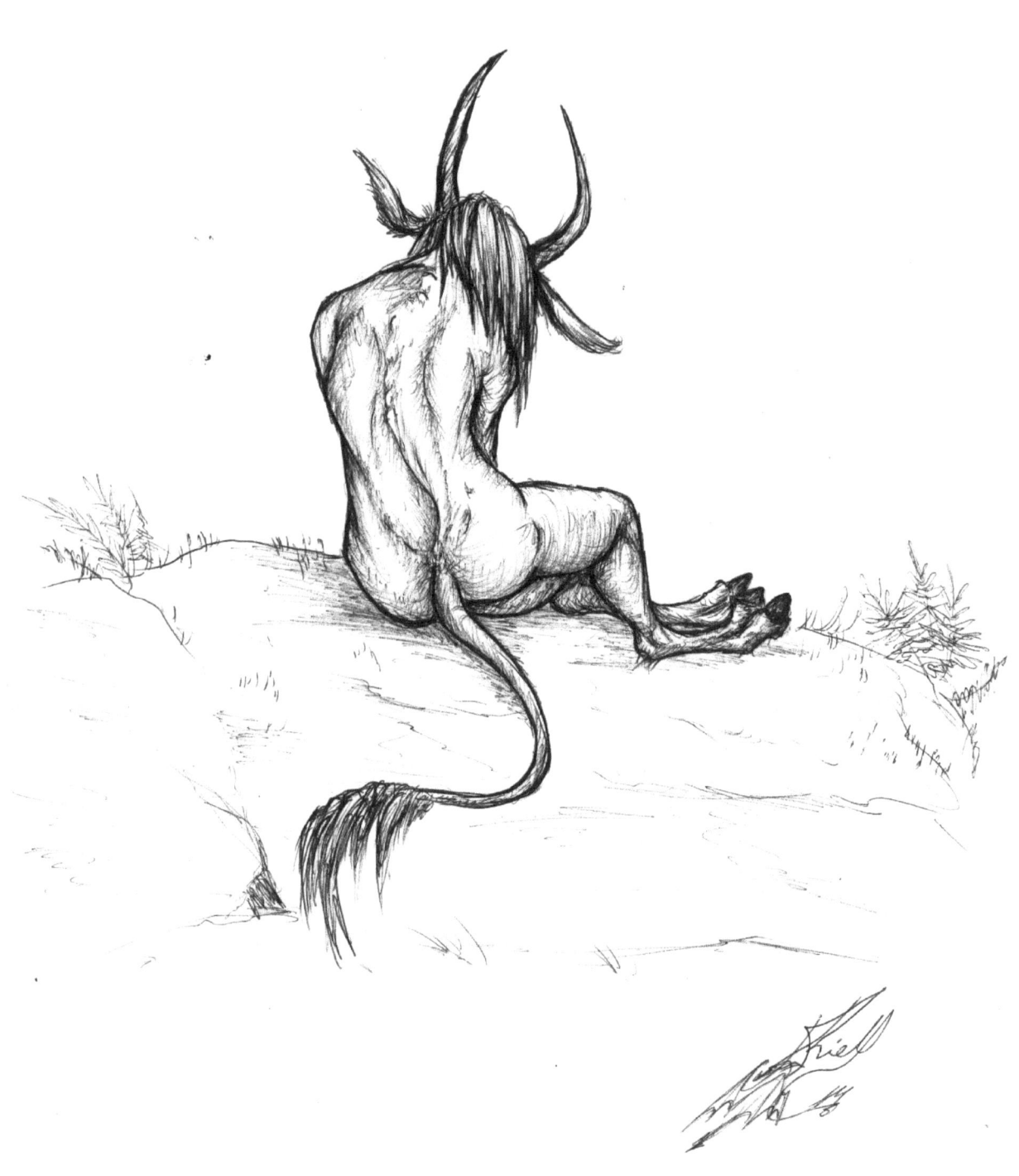

Faun

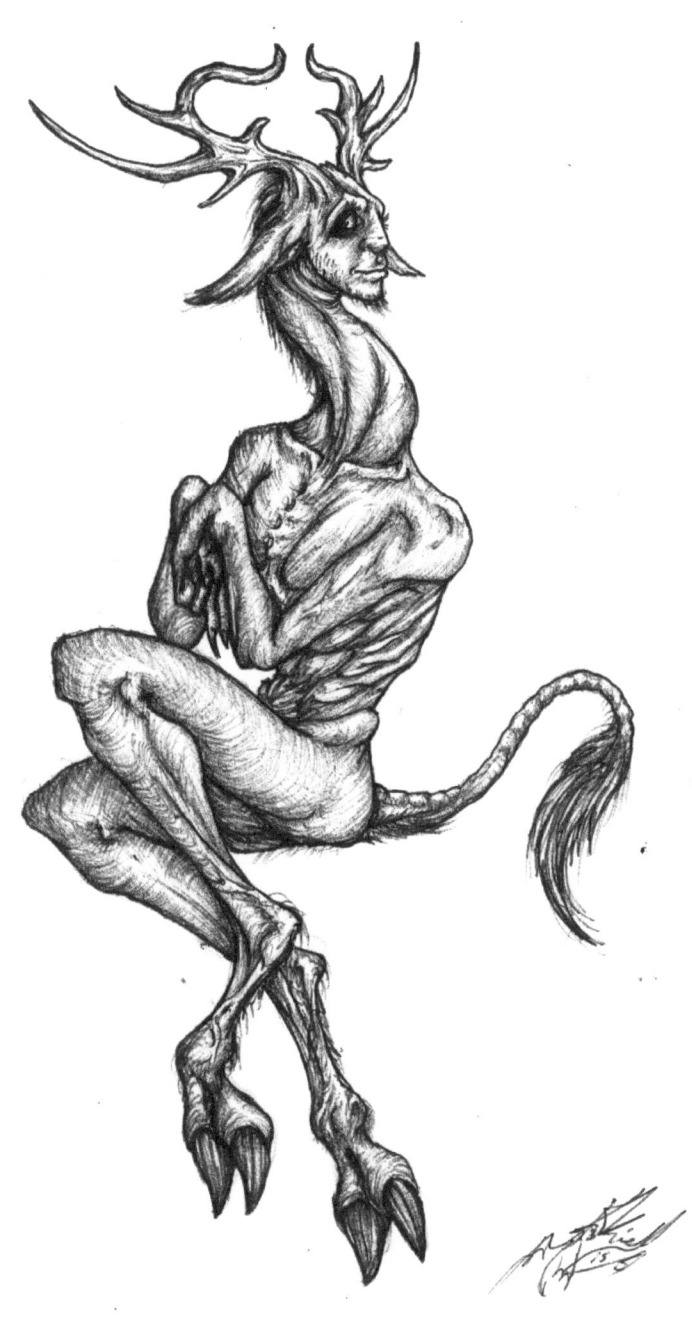

Satyr

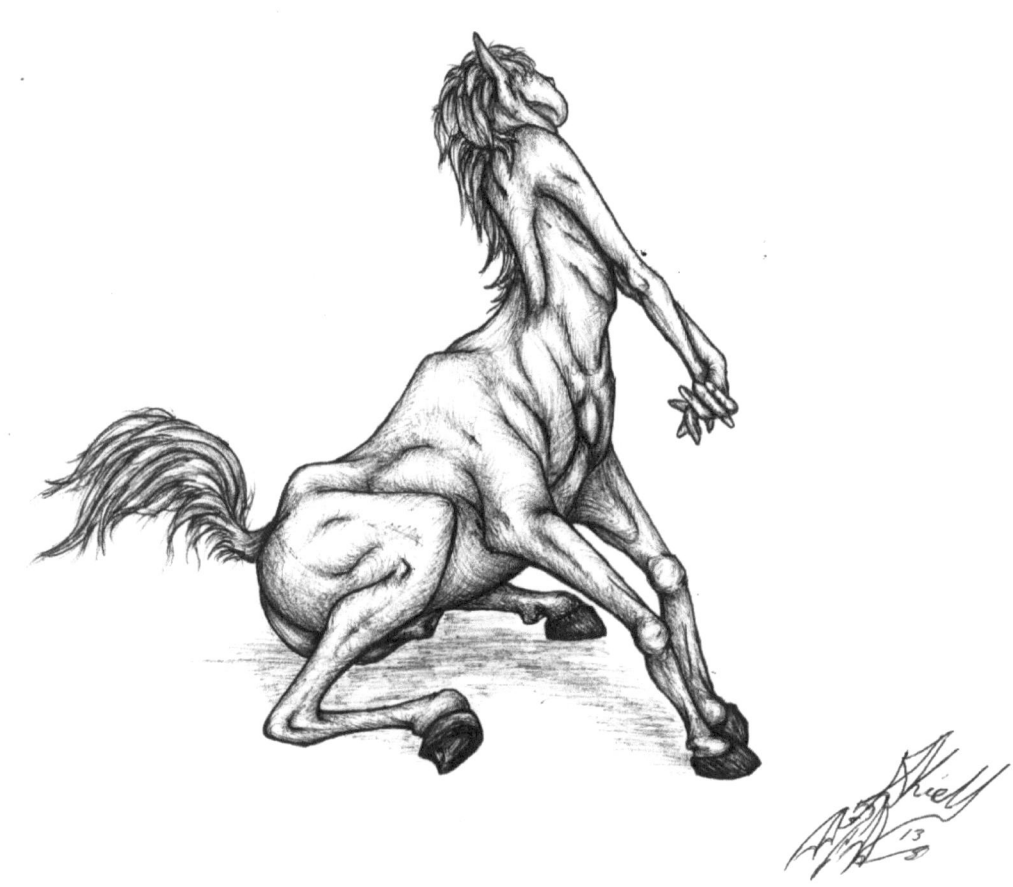

Centaurus Strenuus

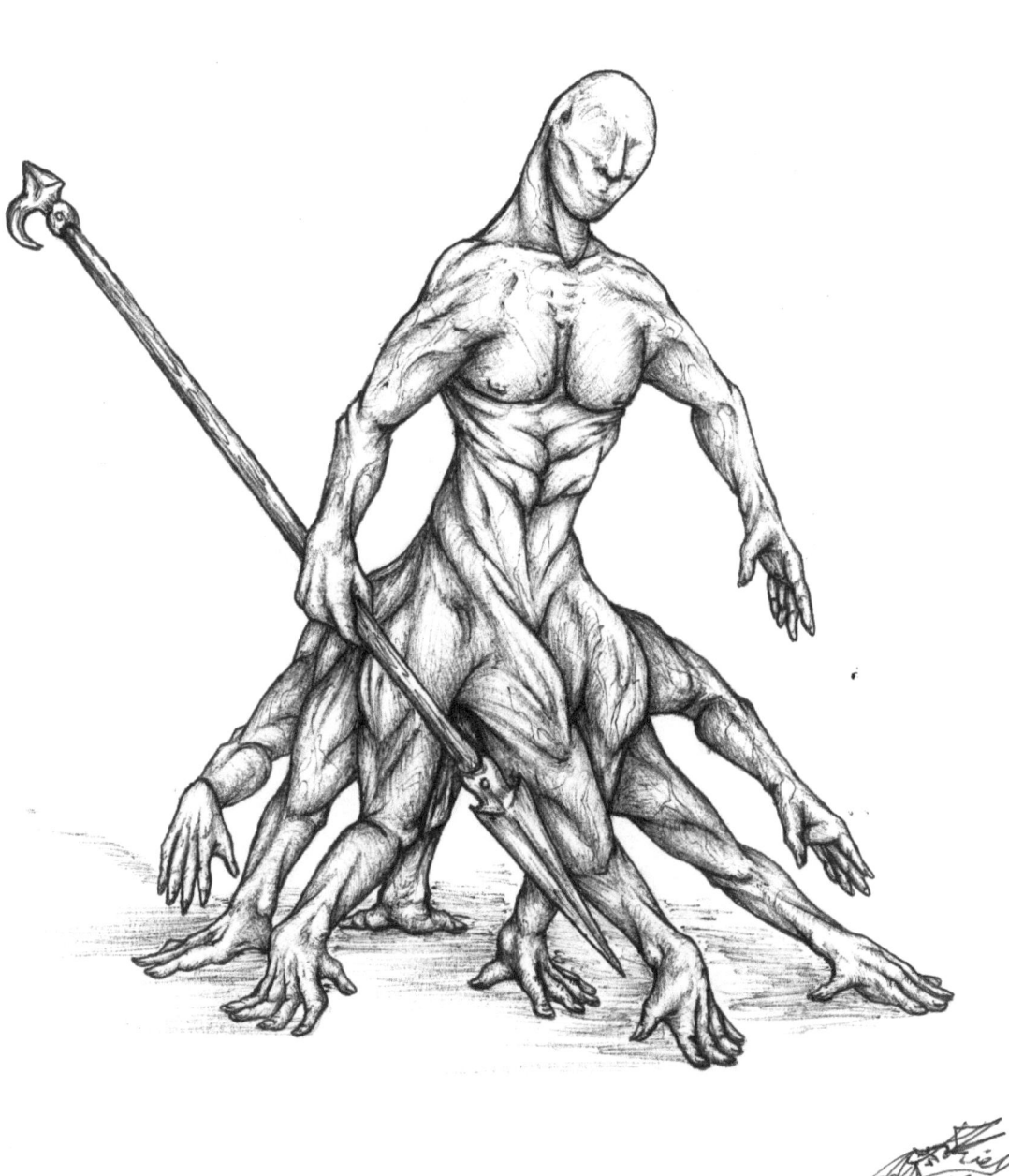

Hand Walker

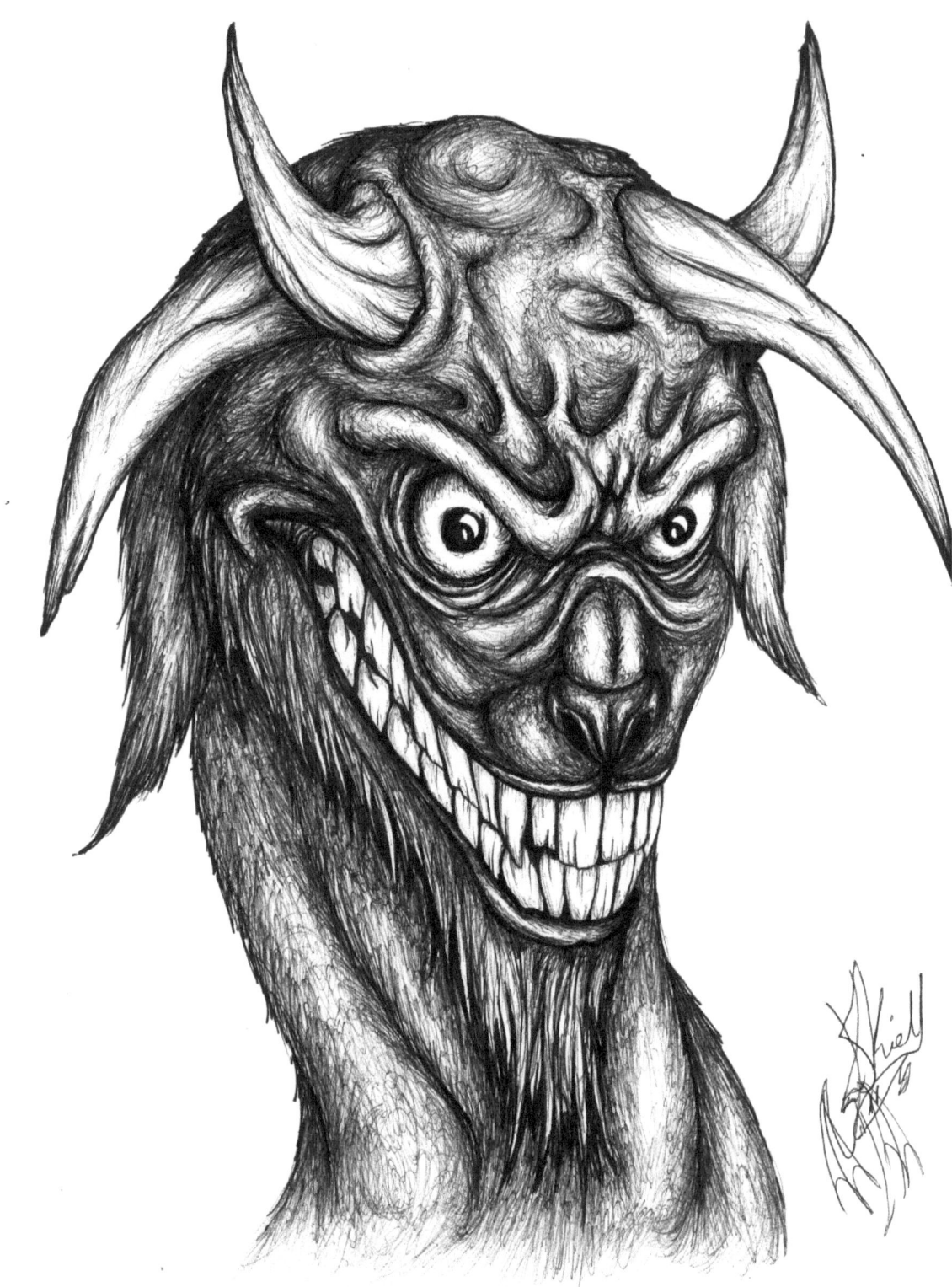

Creep

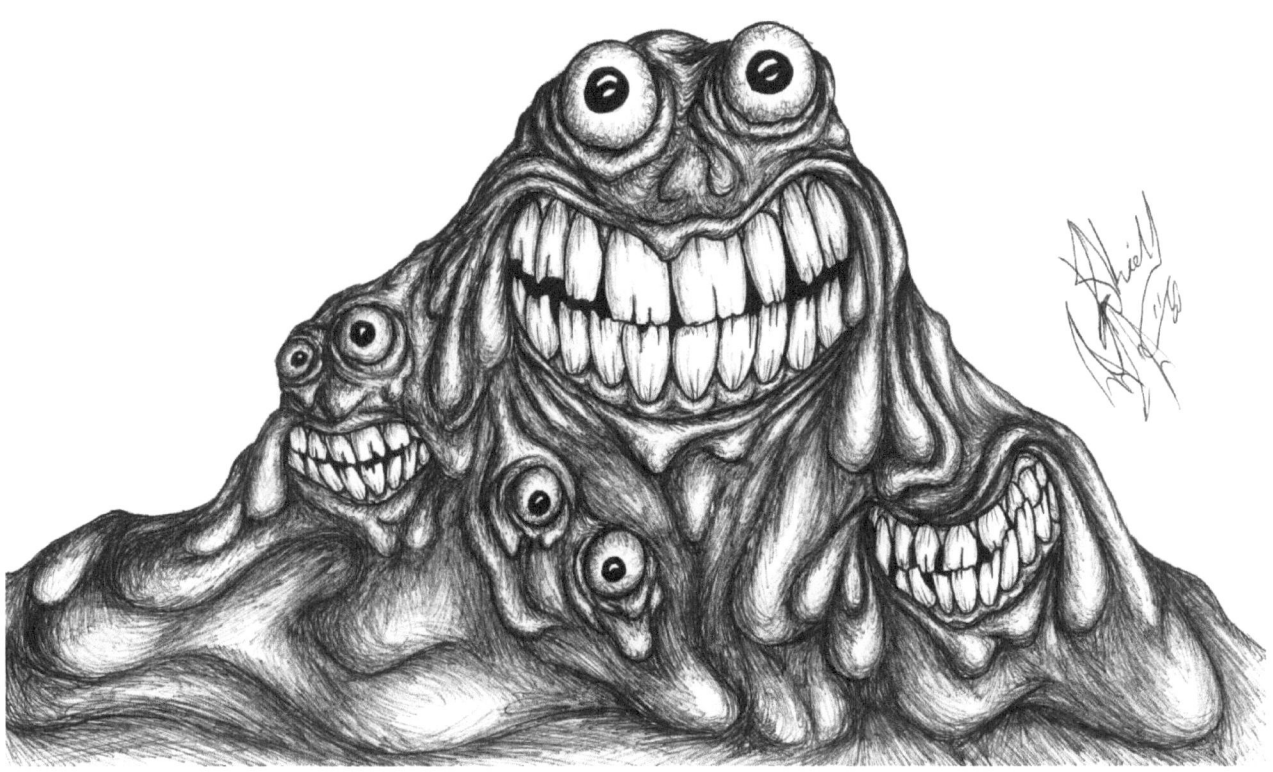

Blob

The Season of Rot

Wind chills the bone,

Trees shiver and shed,

Life begins to sleep,

The ground becomes littered with the dead,

As the skin of the world peels at the loss of springs flower to the underworld,

To become a blessed mess,

The season of rot is upon us.

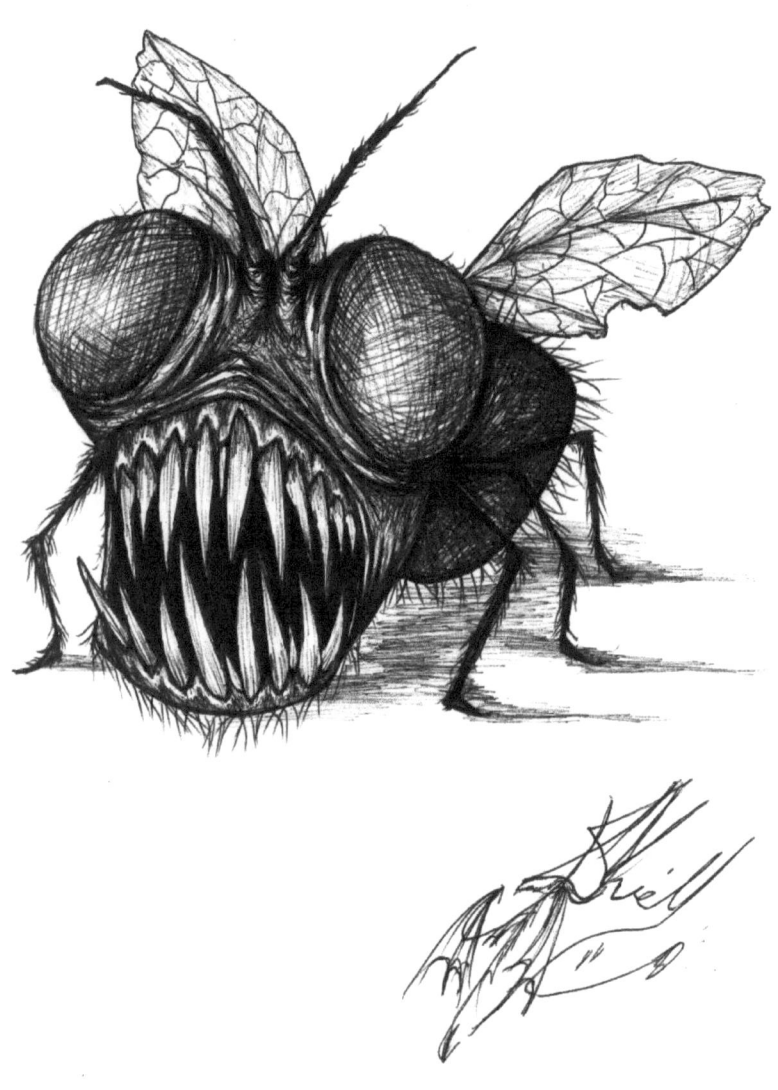

Black Fly

Did you ever wonder how such a small creature could take such a large bite out of you...

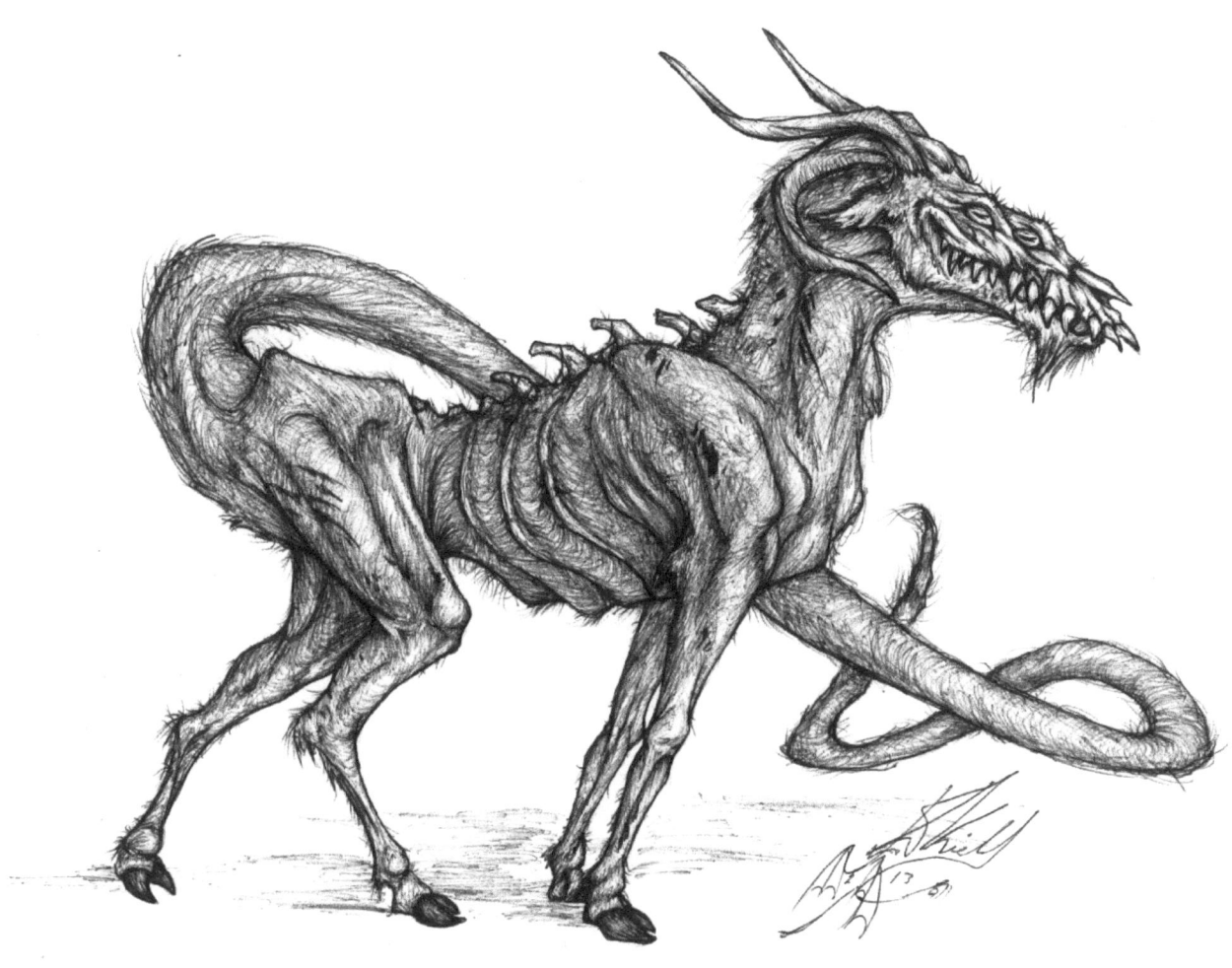

Demon Goat

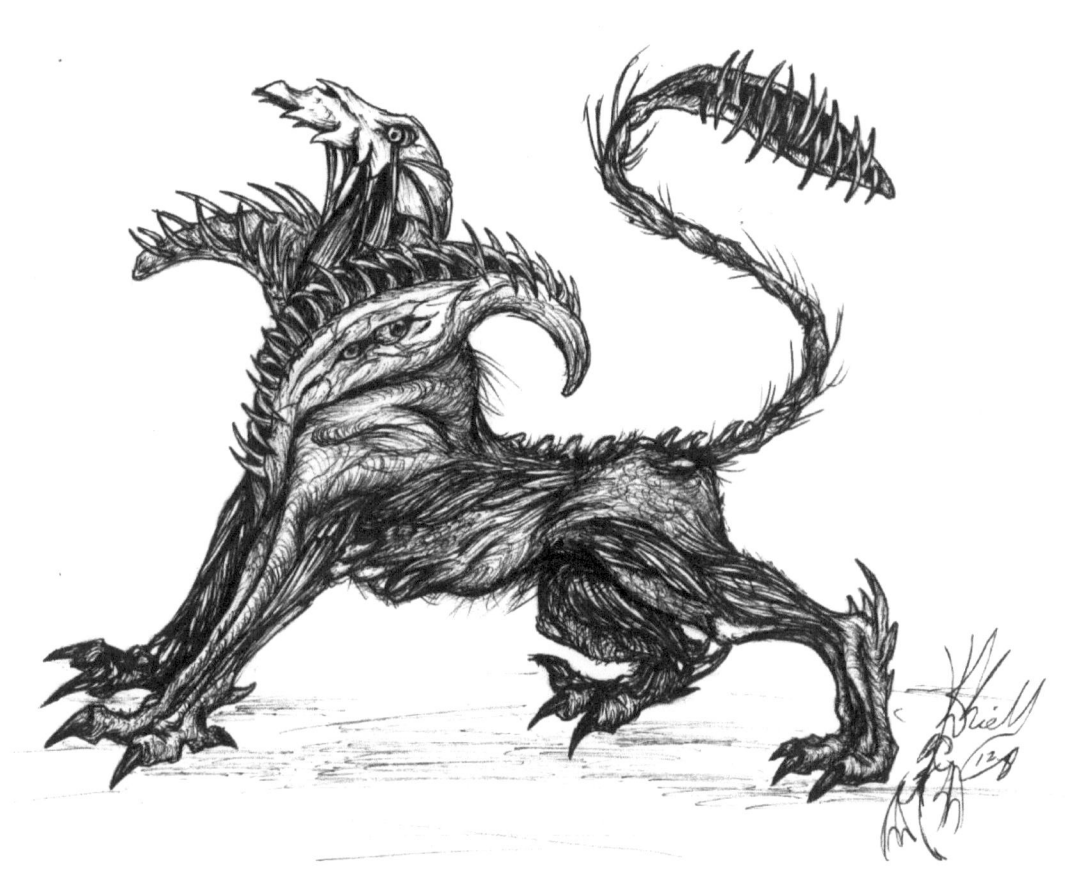

Necro Hund

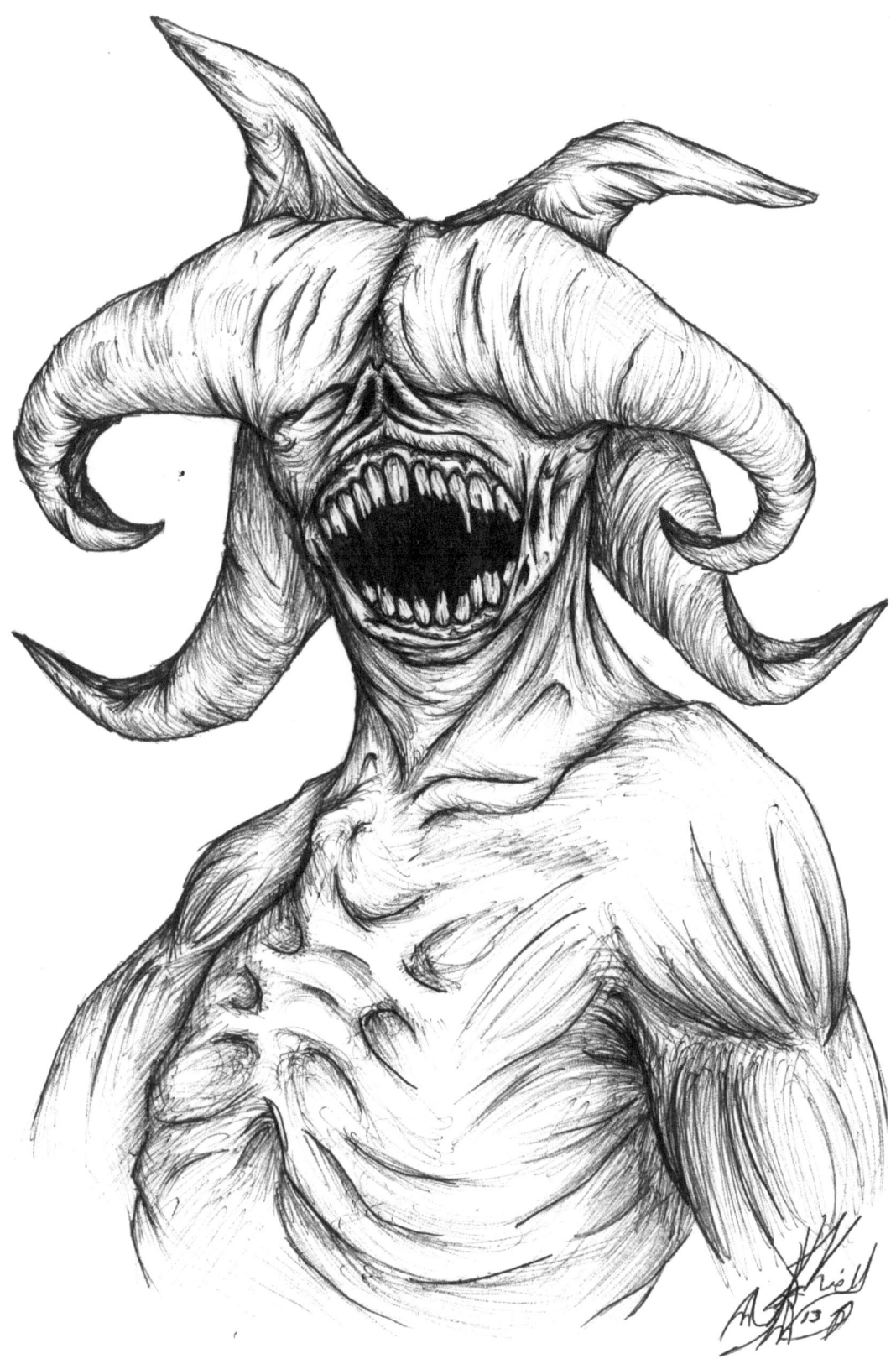

Necromantic Minion

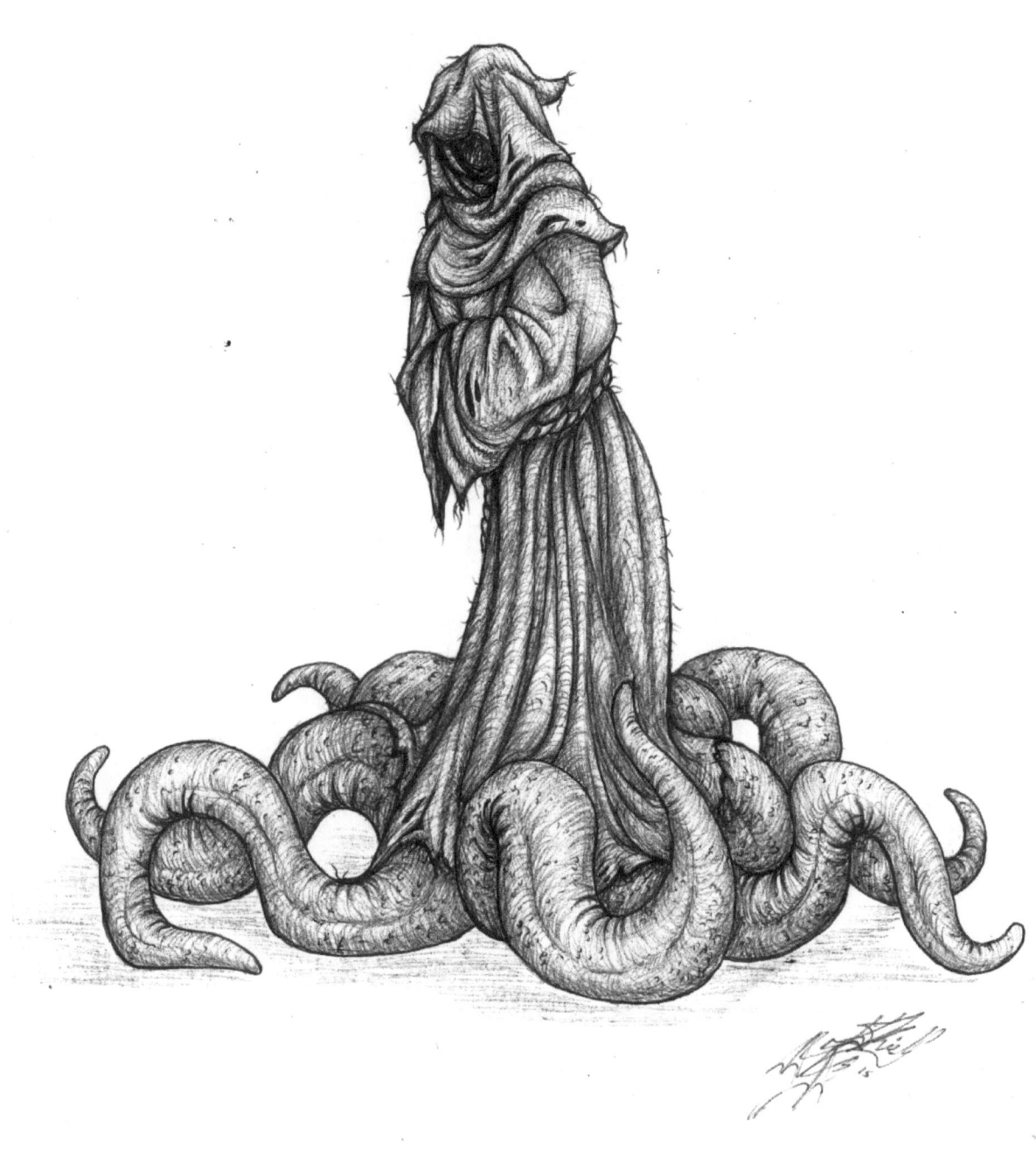

Cthulu Priest

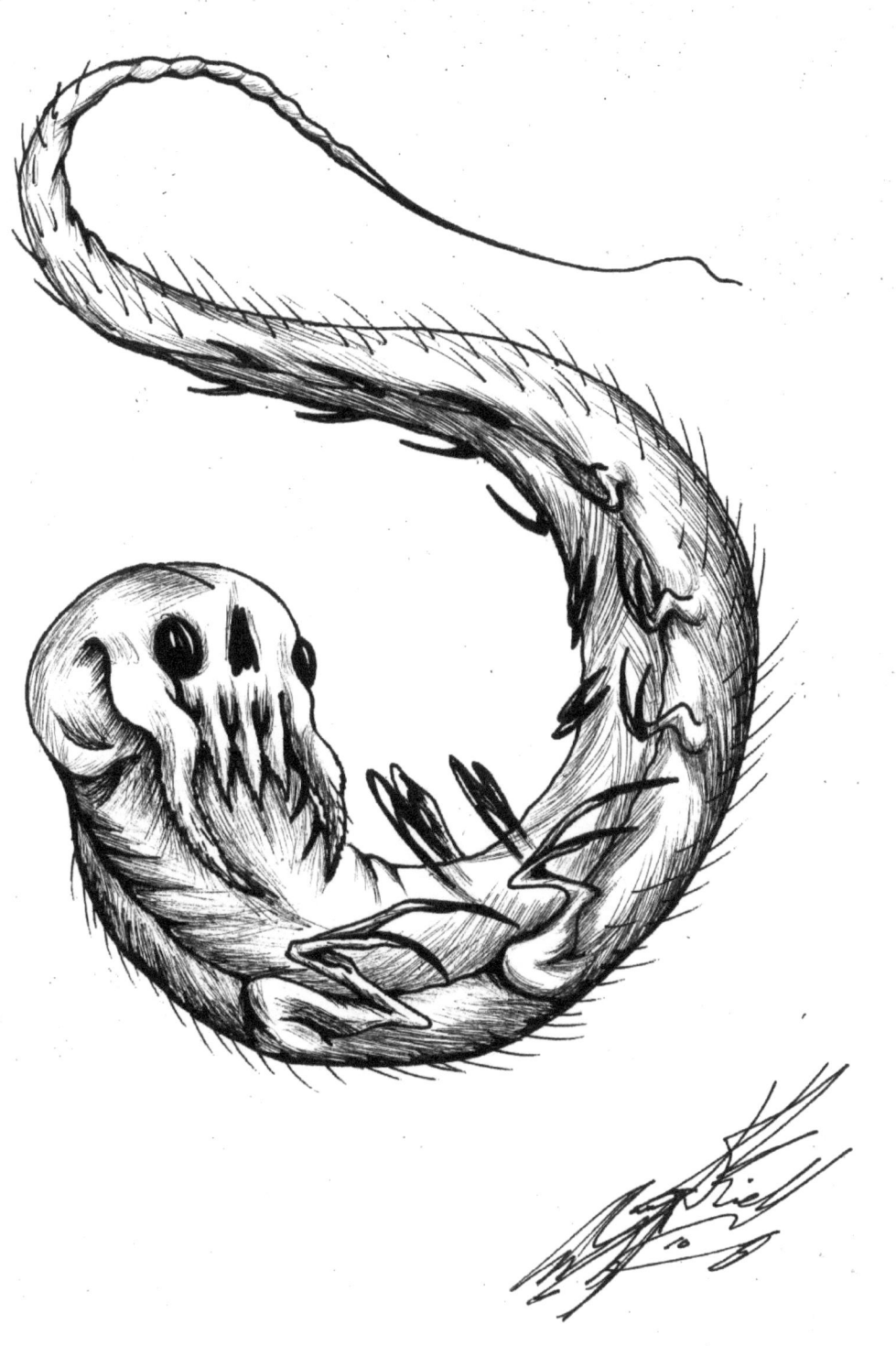

Parasite

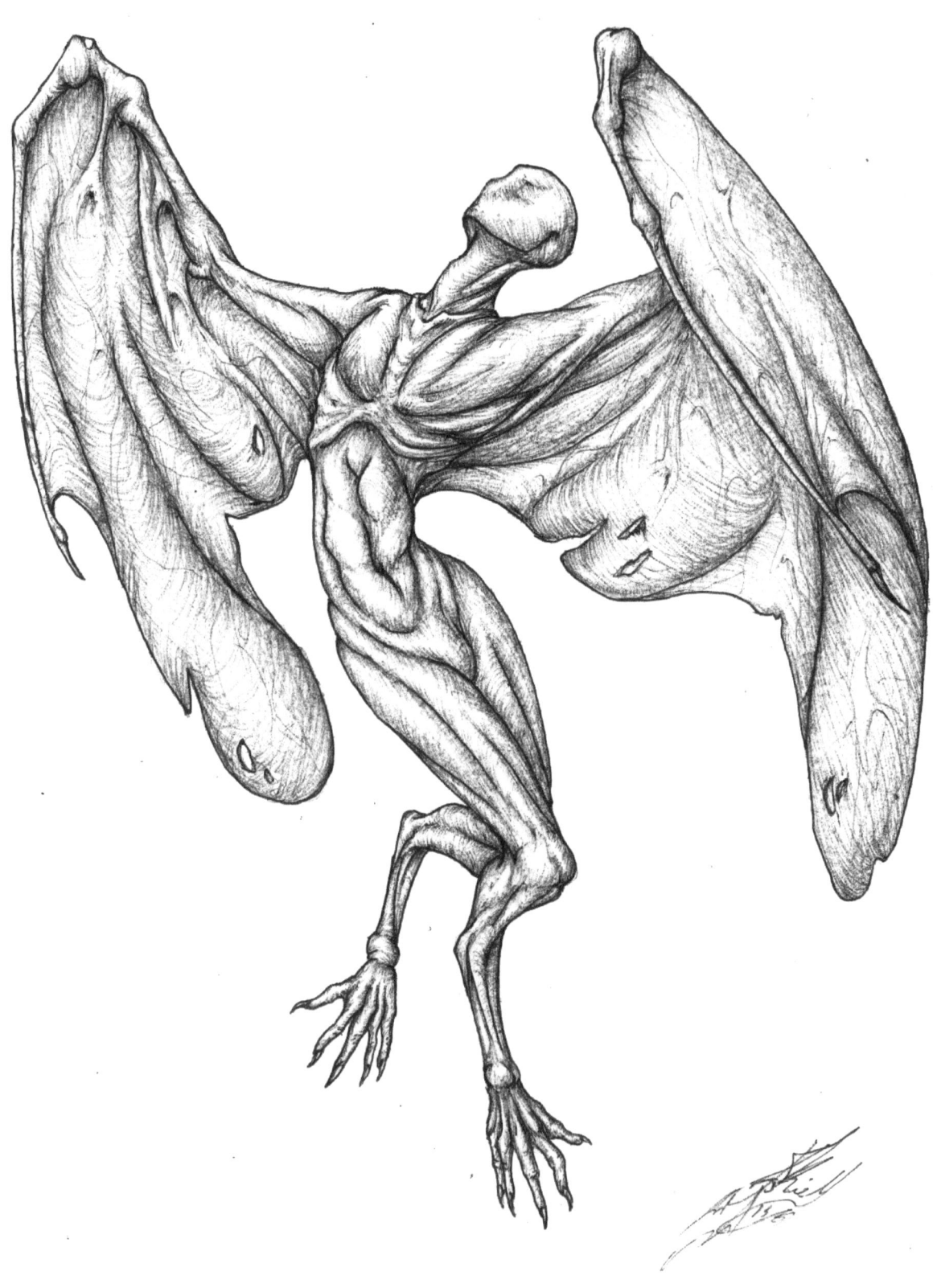

Gaunt

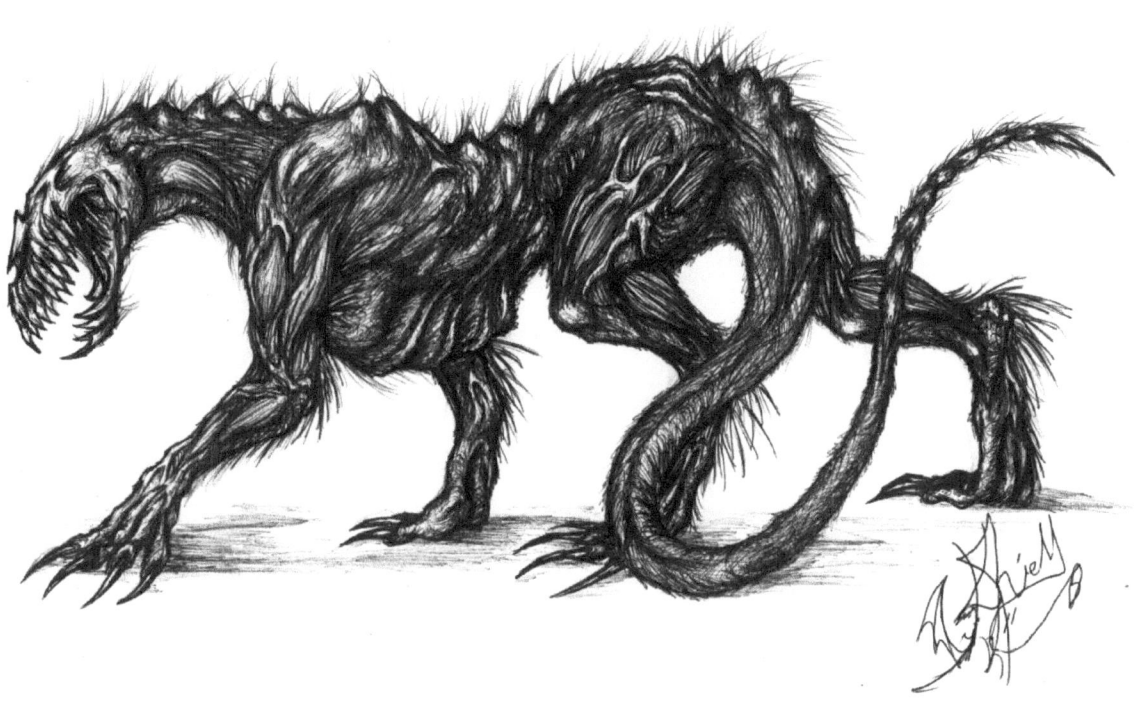

Flesh Eater

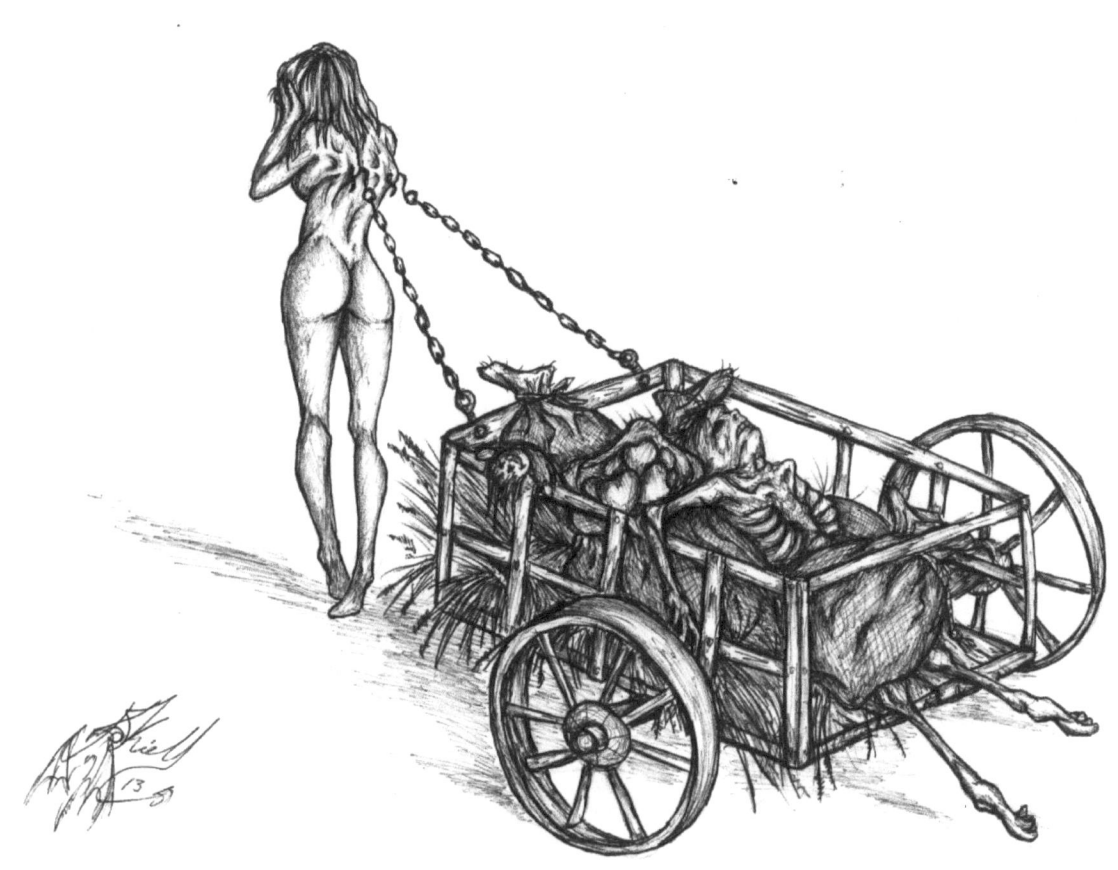

Beast of Burden

Heavy of mind, my doll of madness in a house of falsehood and beggary,

Fruitless pride of my heart to dust and poisoned soil,

Keep not your thoughts in passing, but place them here forever.

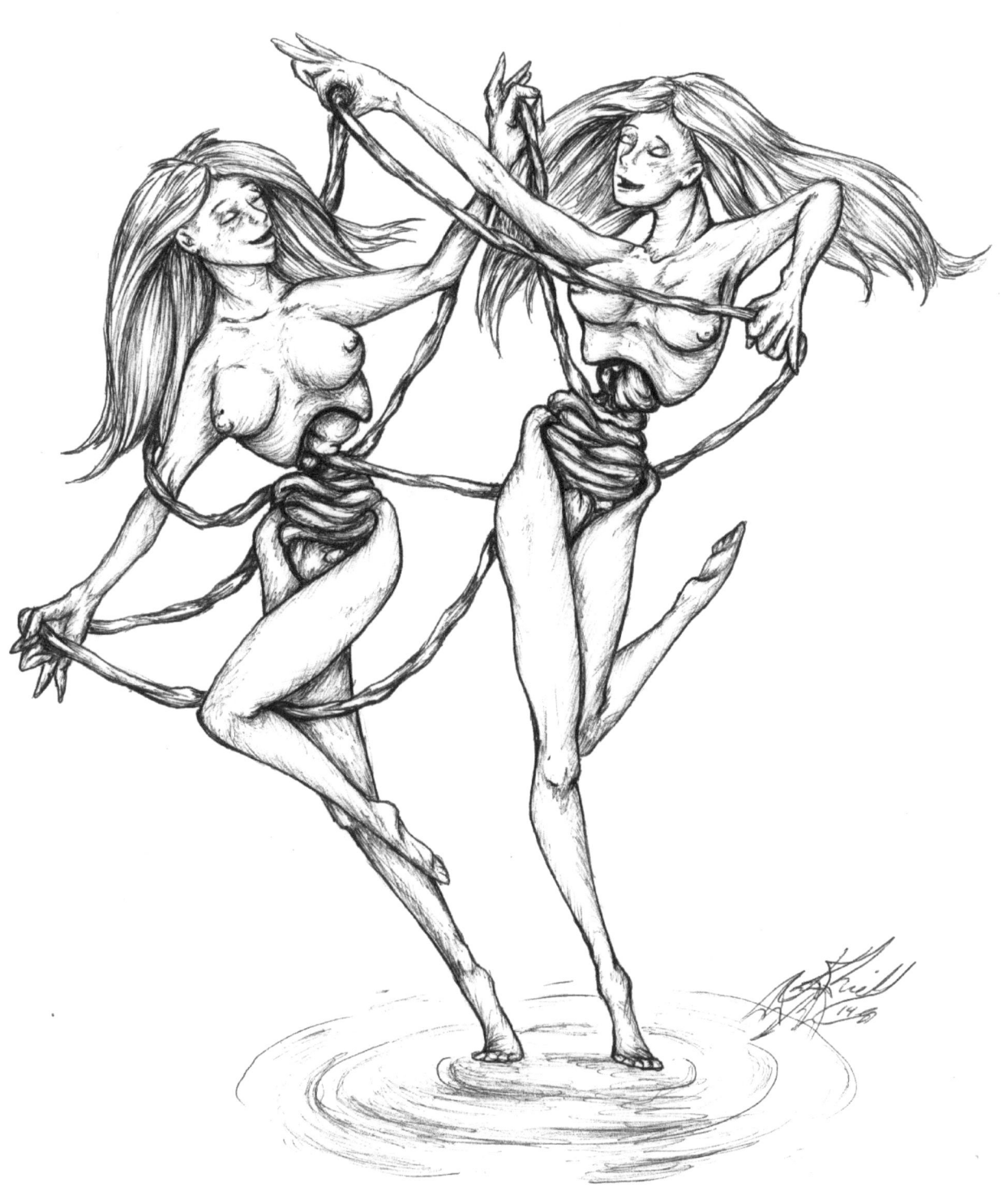

Mutual Sadism

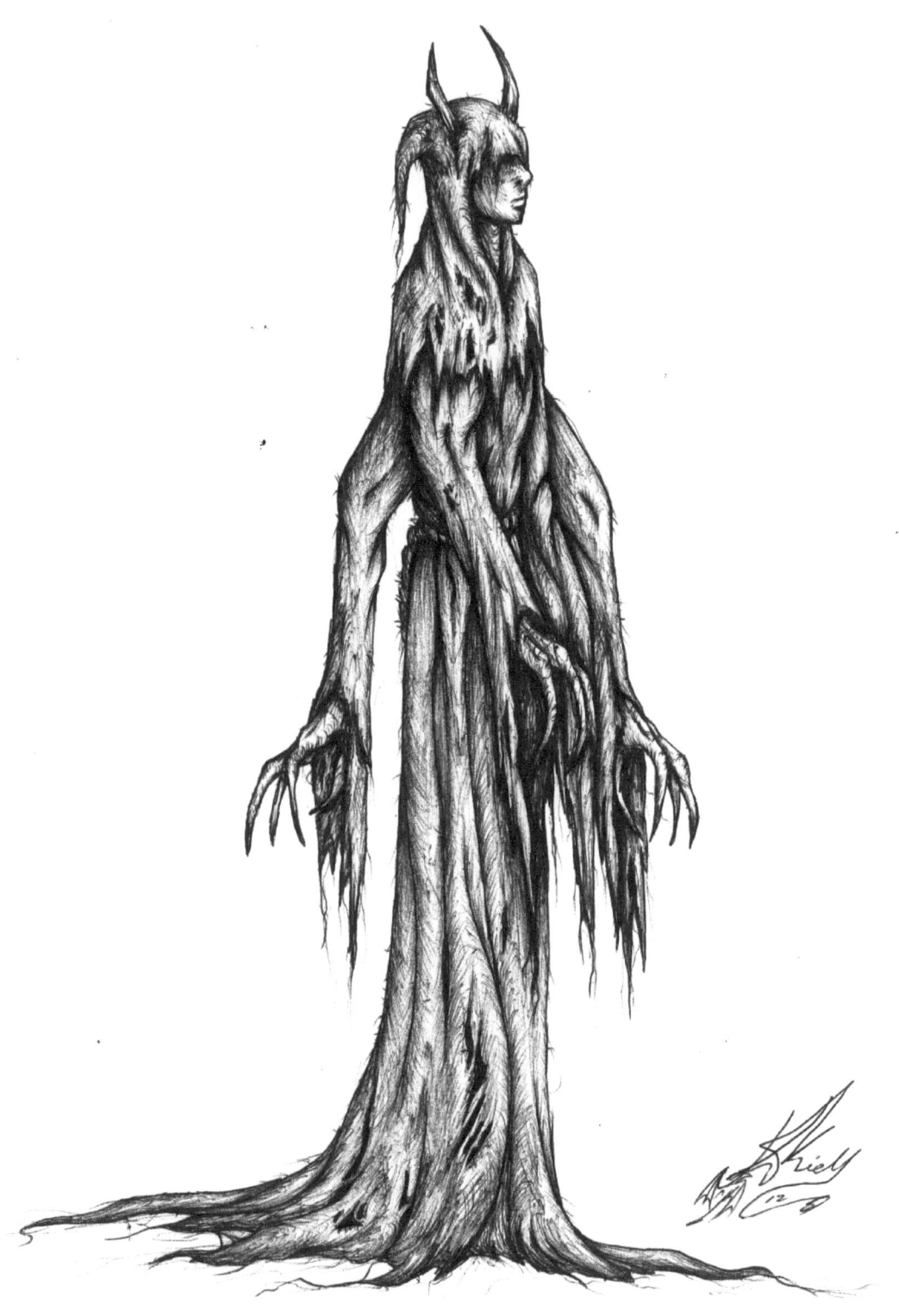

The Stranger

Beware the Stranger, he walks in dreams and leaves nightmares in his wake....

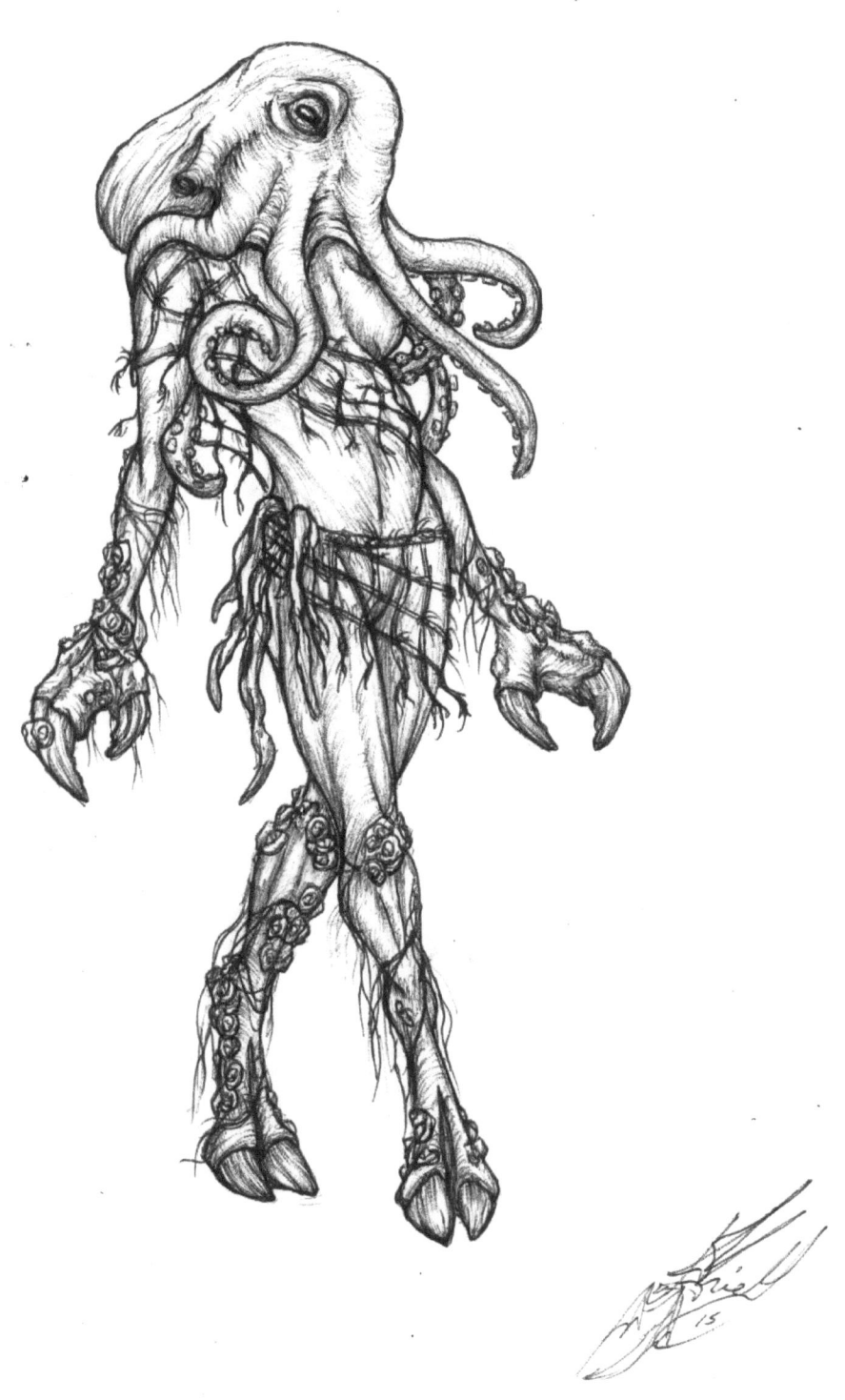

Cthulian Maiden

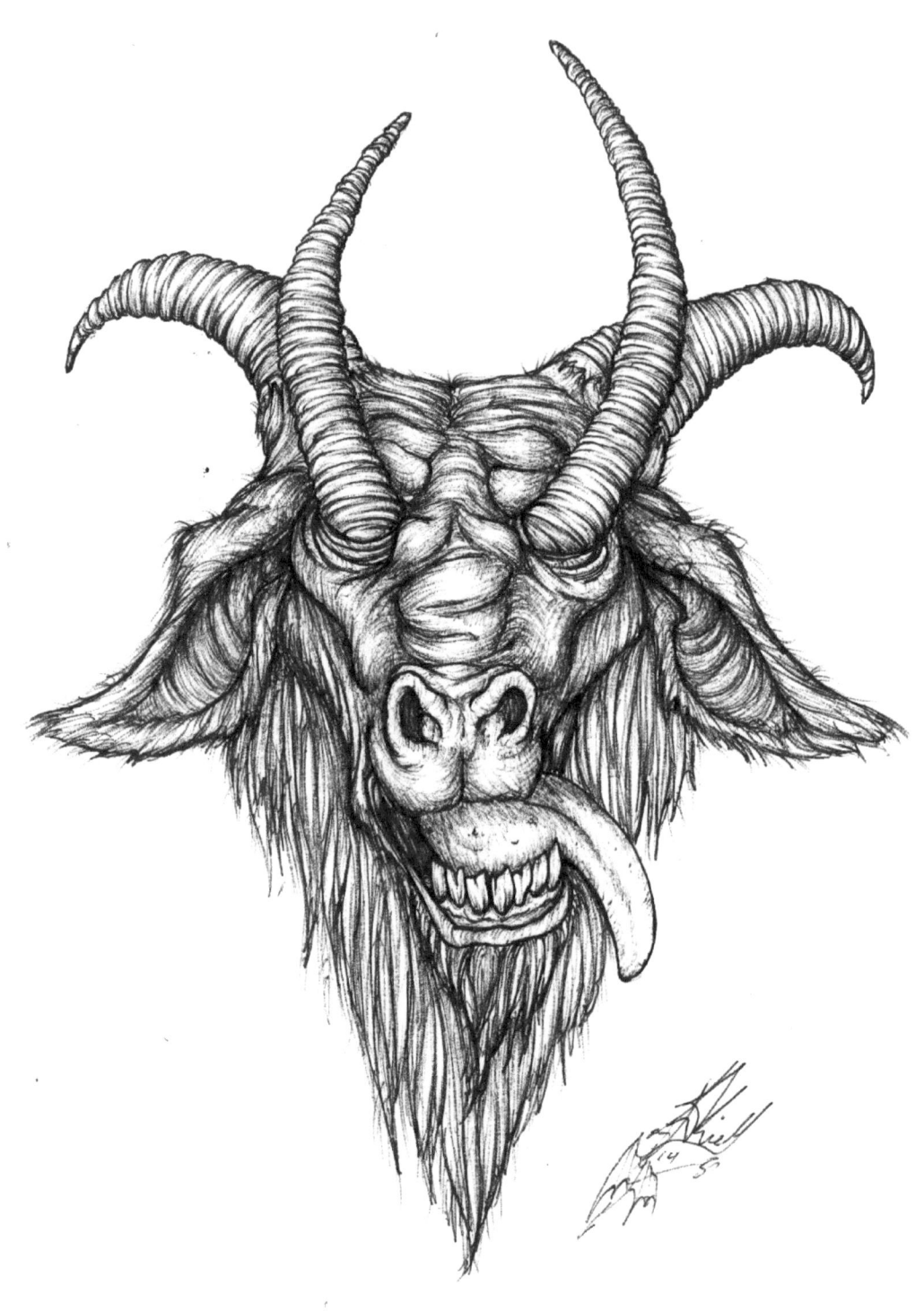

Horn Eye

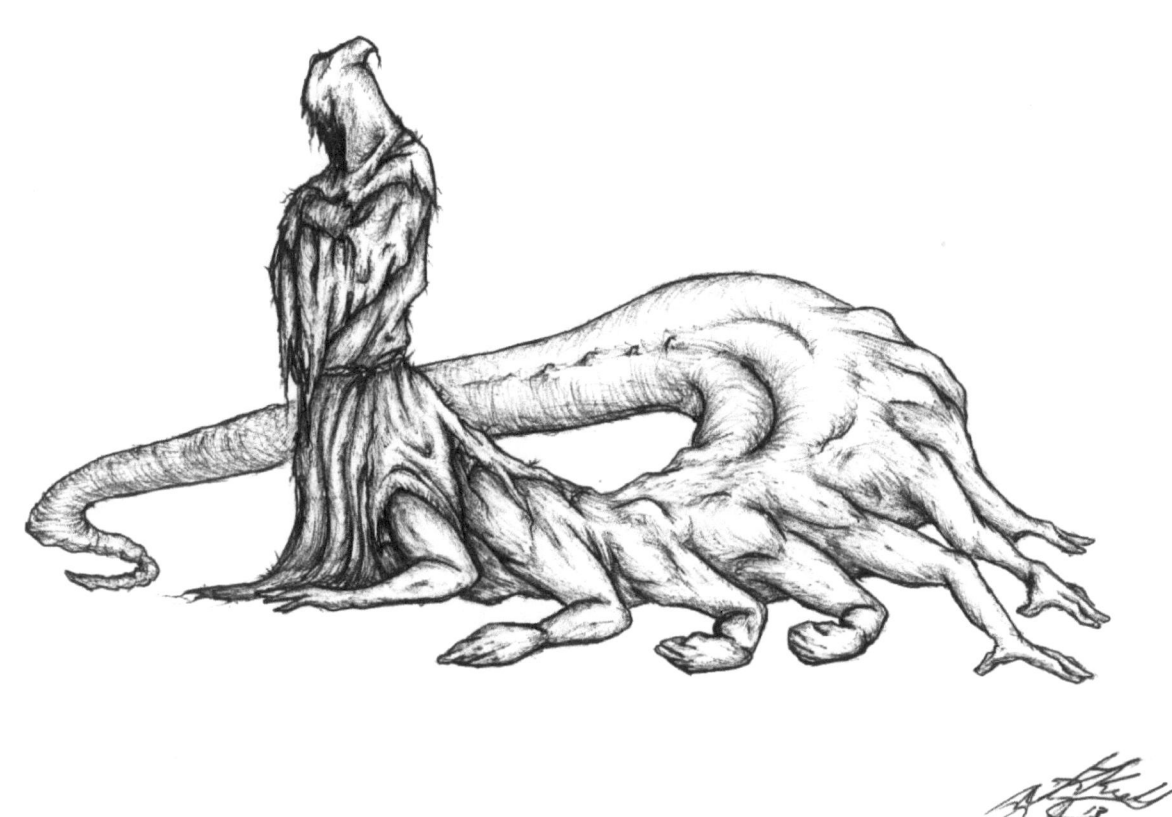

Prayer Hands

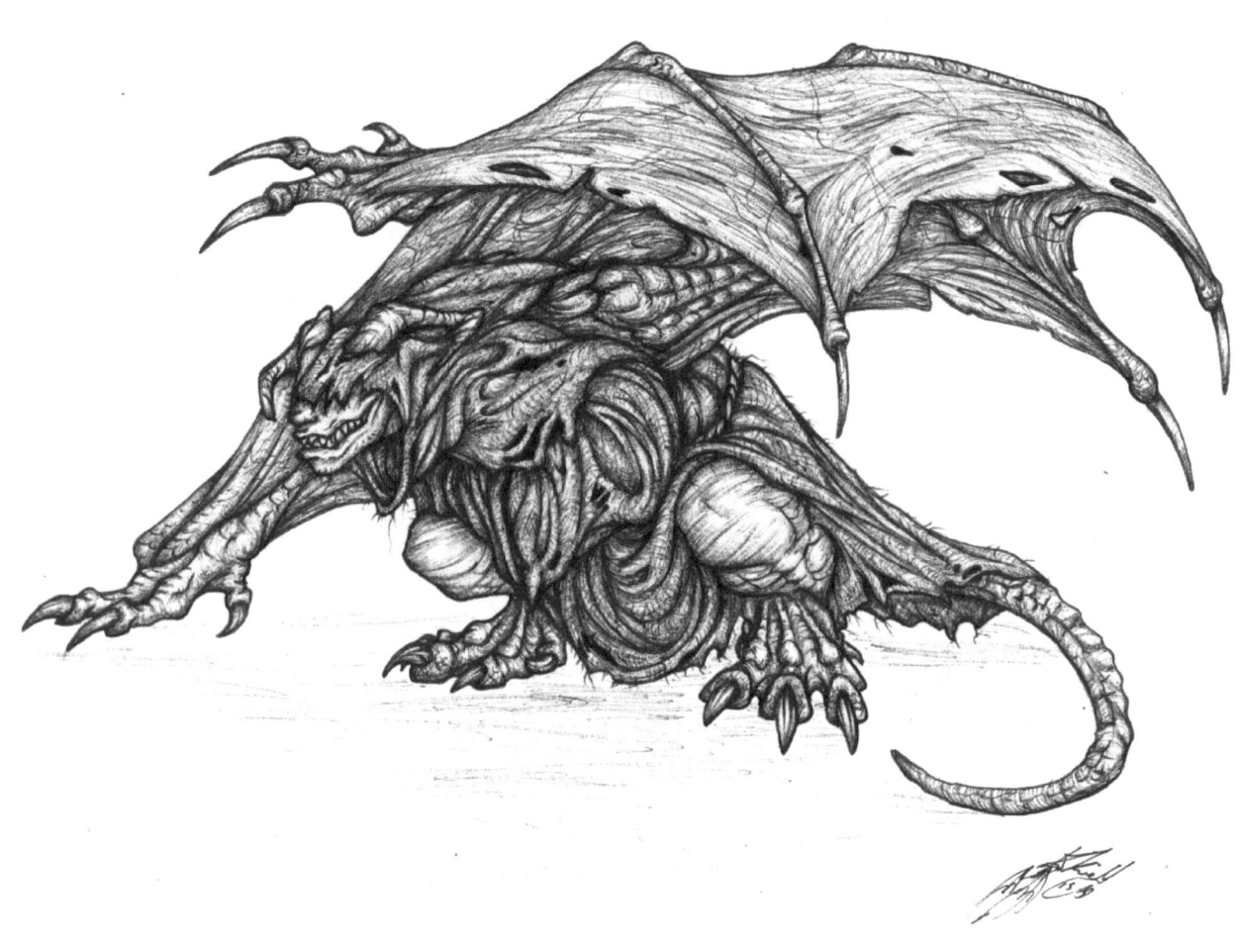

Ascended Dragon Cultist

Worshippers of the great dragons, ascended to a higher existence, their humanity is lost, but neither are they the great beasts themselves, but a perversion of both.

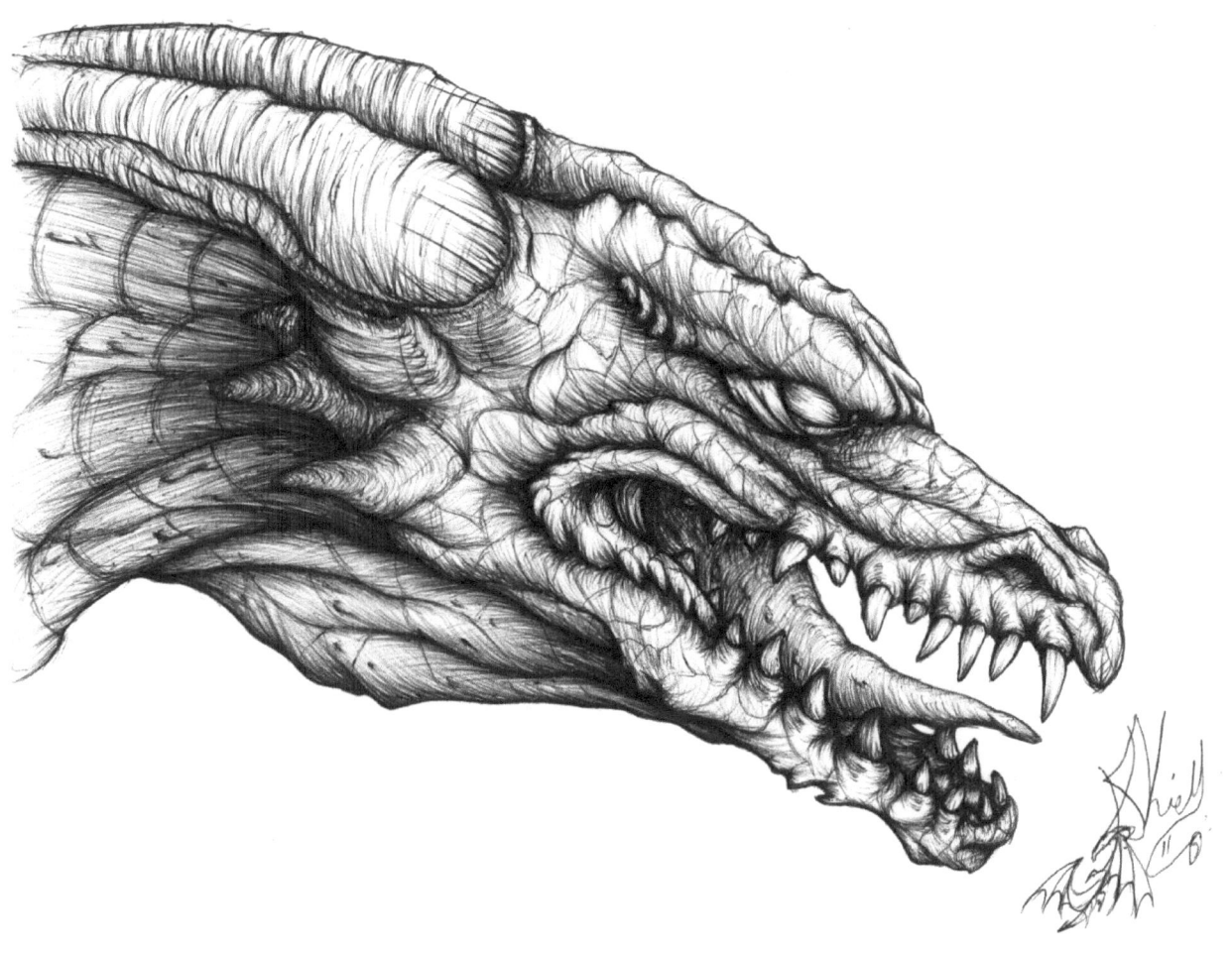

Dragon Head

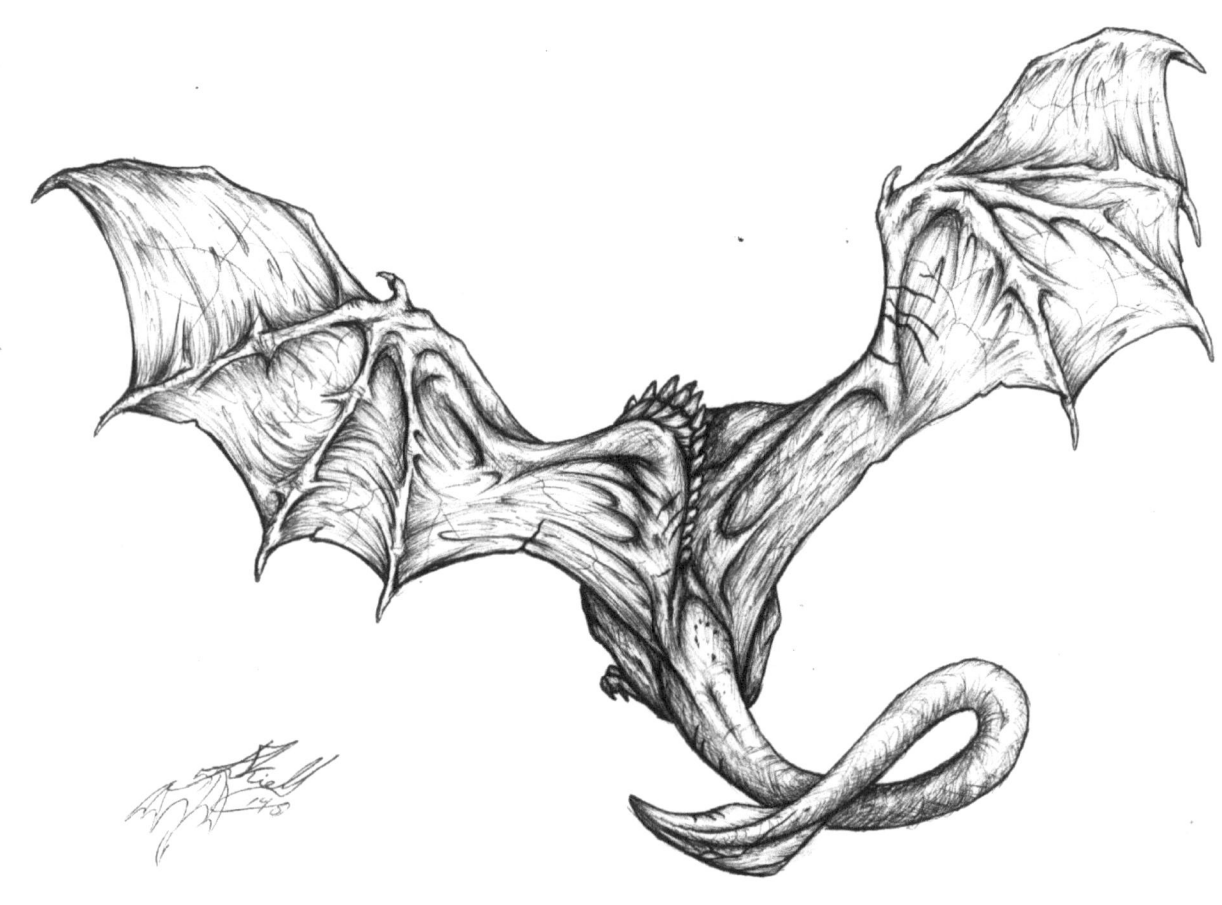

Dragon Back

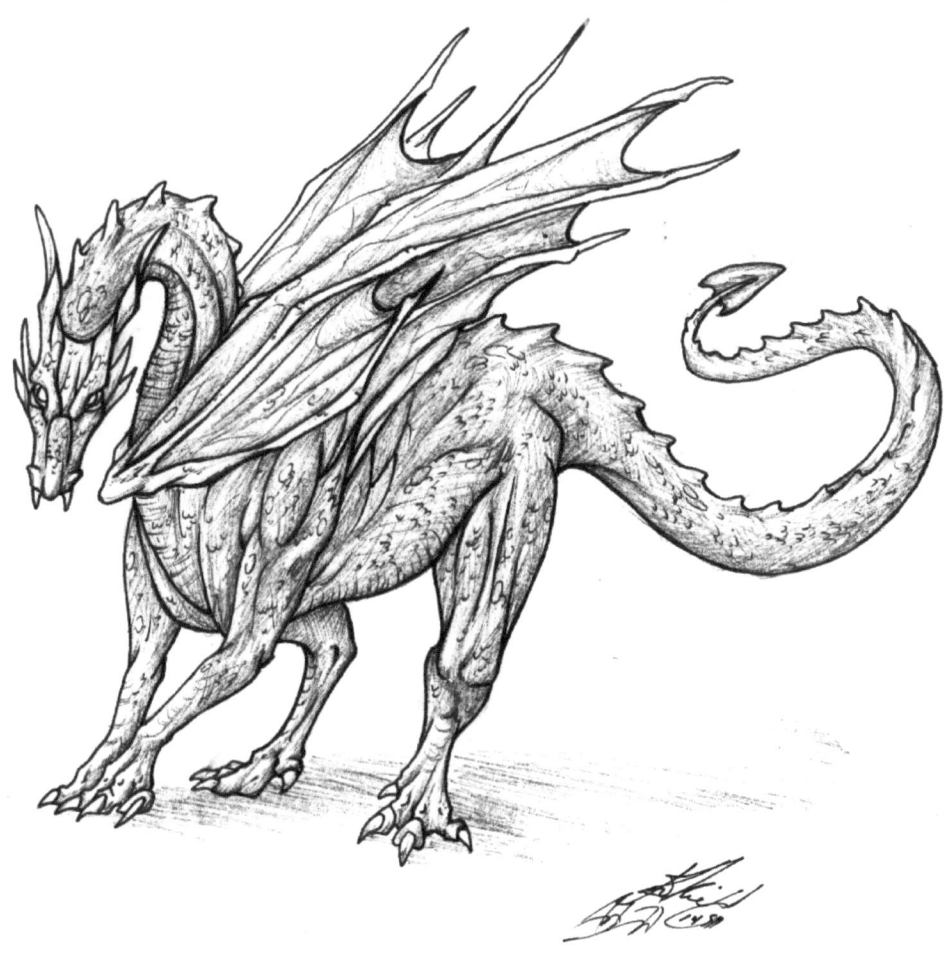

Golden Dragon

Resplendence

Ne'er in nature is seen,

Such vivid scales of iridescent sheen,

Her wings luminated by rays from above,

Cast their dappled pattern o'er the earth,

Like mottled stained glass,

Shone upon the altar of a holy chapel.

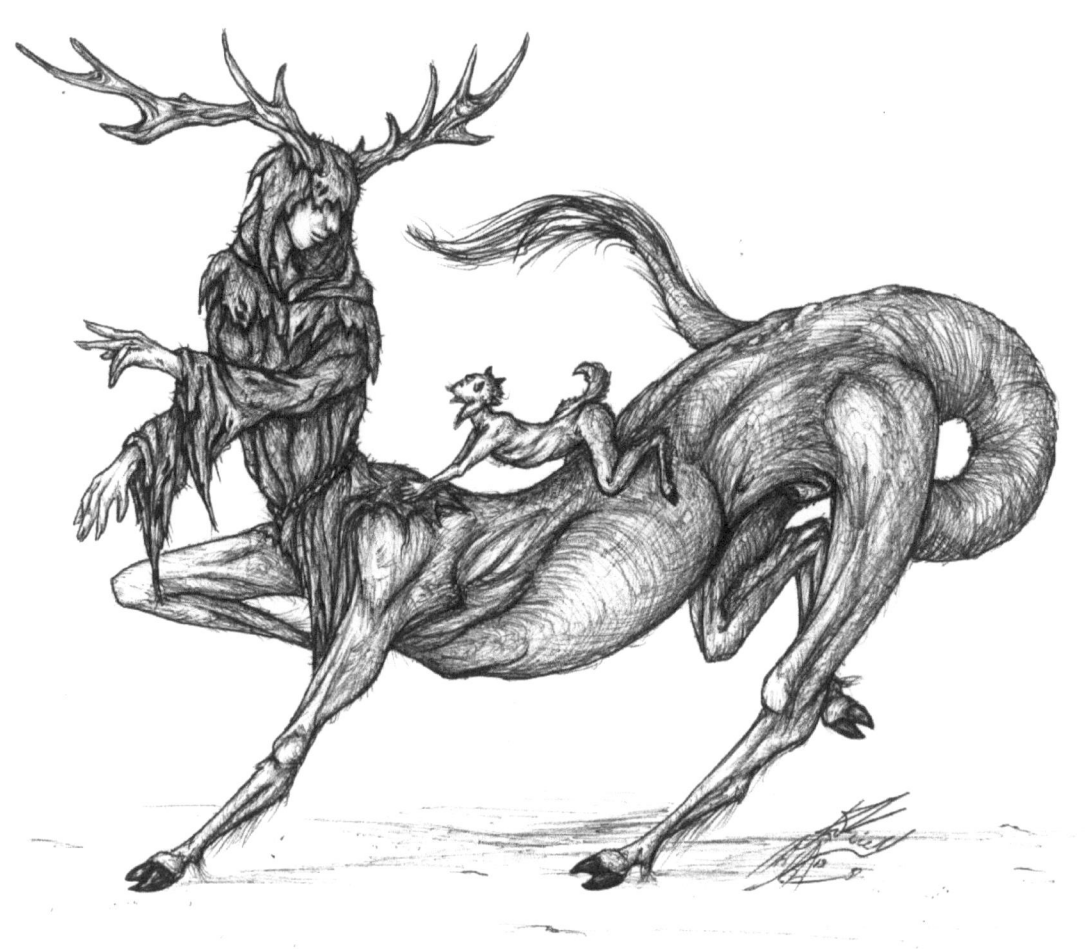

Playful Forest Spirit

Tree Whistler

As I walk through the forest I whistle to the trees,

A tune high and sweet,

Tapping words to their bark,

Life's heart beat,

This is who I am and who I forever will be.

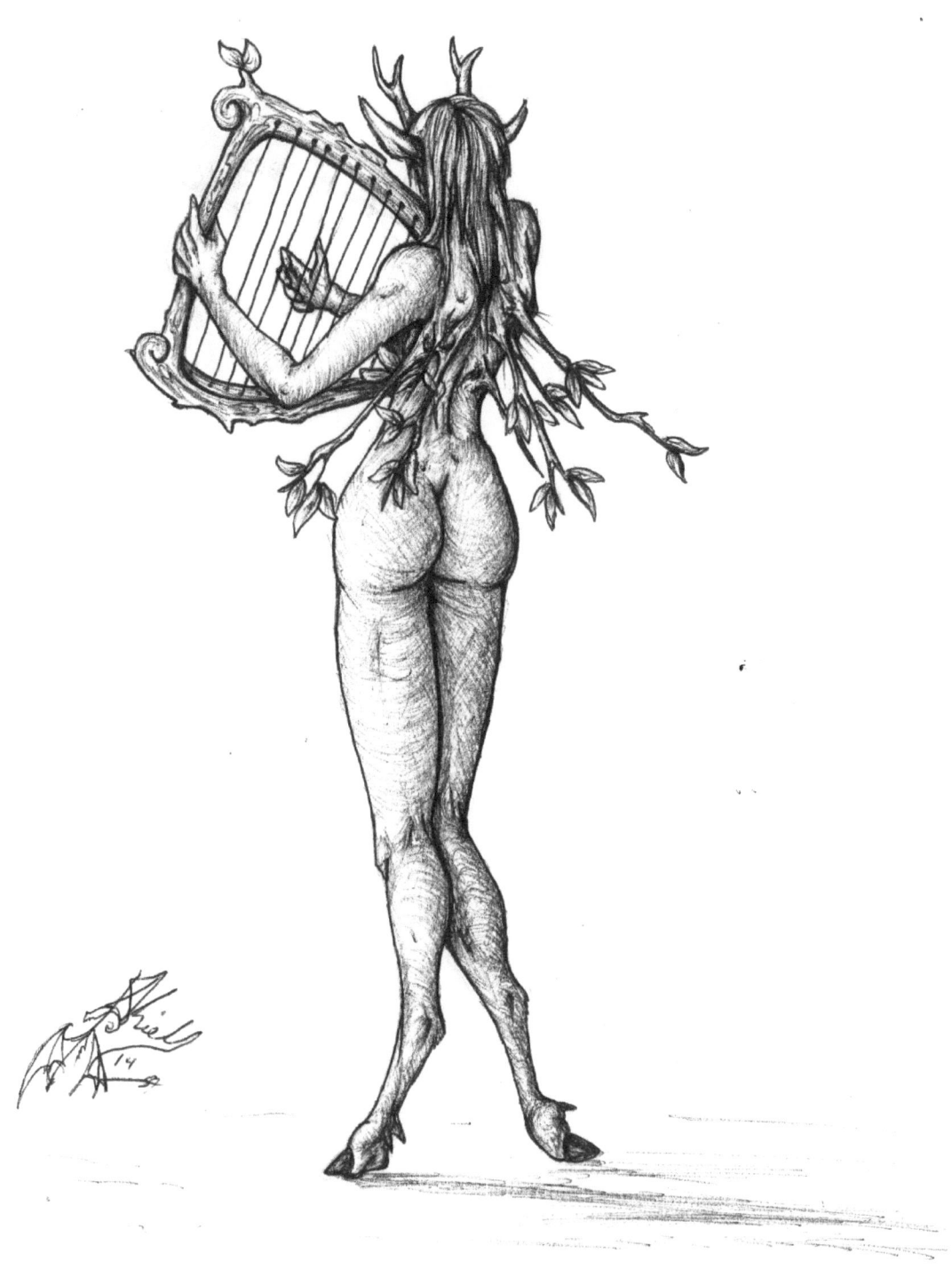

Forest Song Maiden

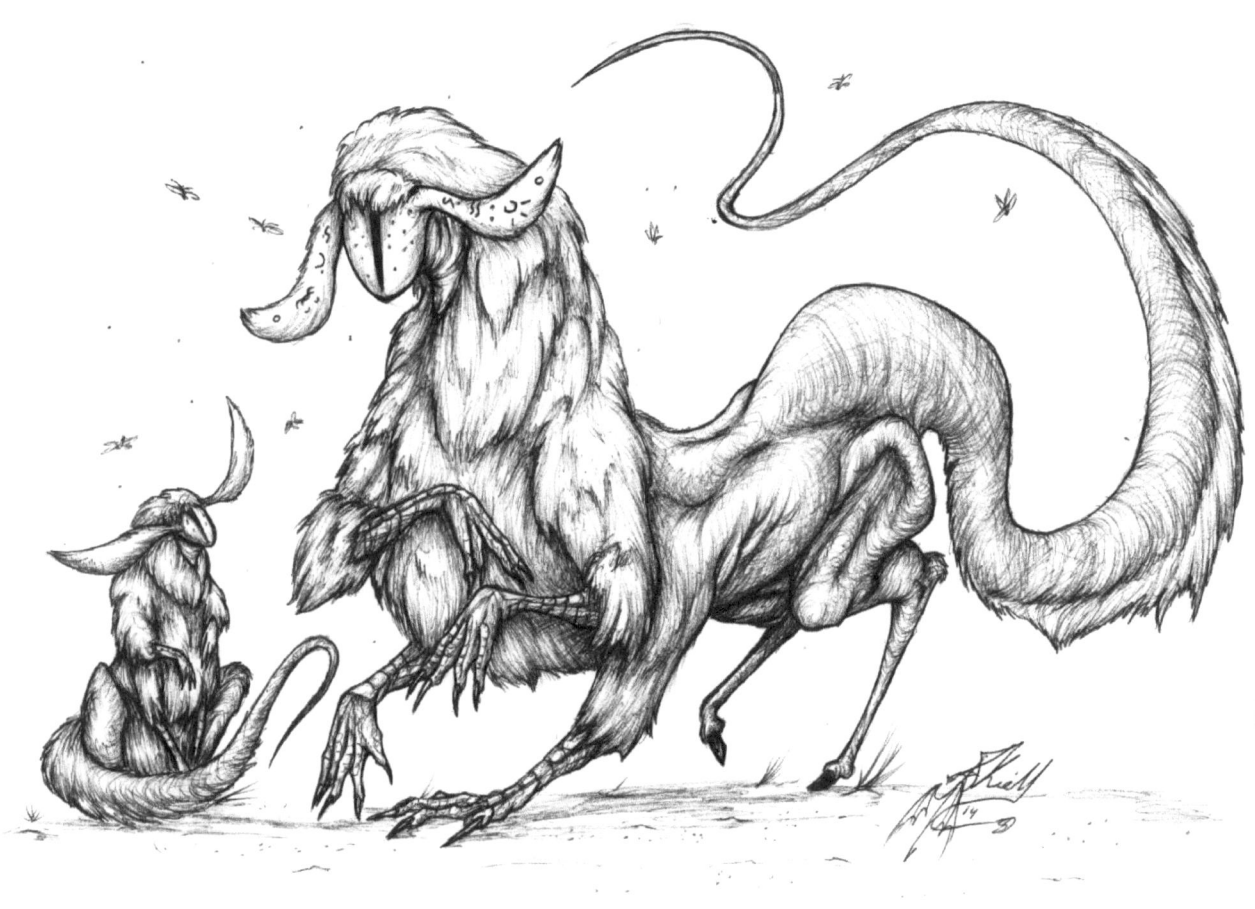

Somni Solaris

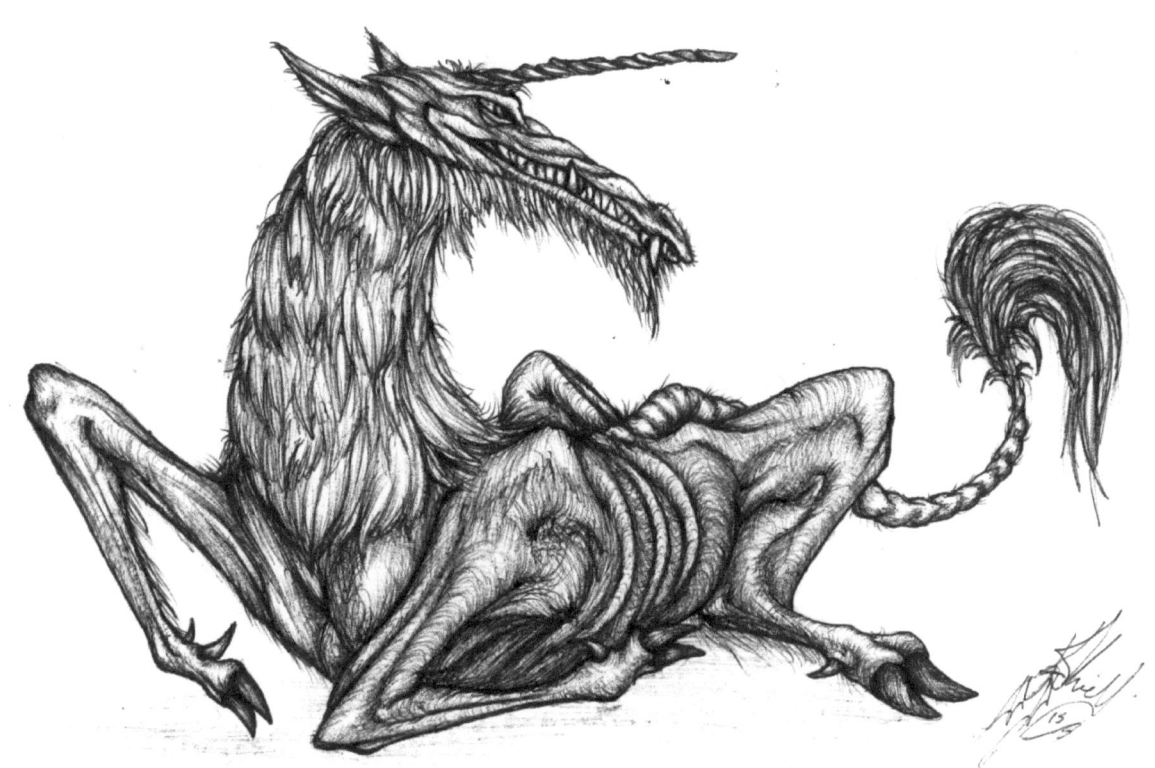

Unicorn

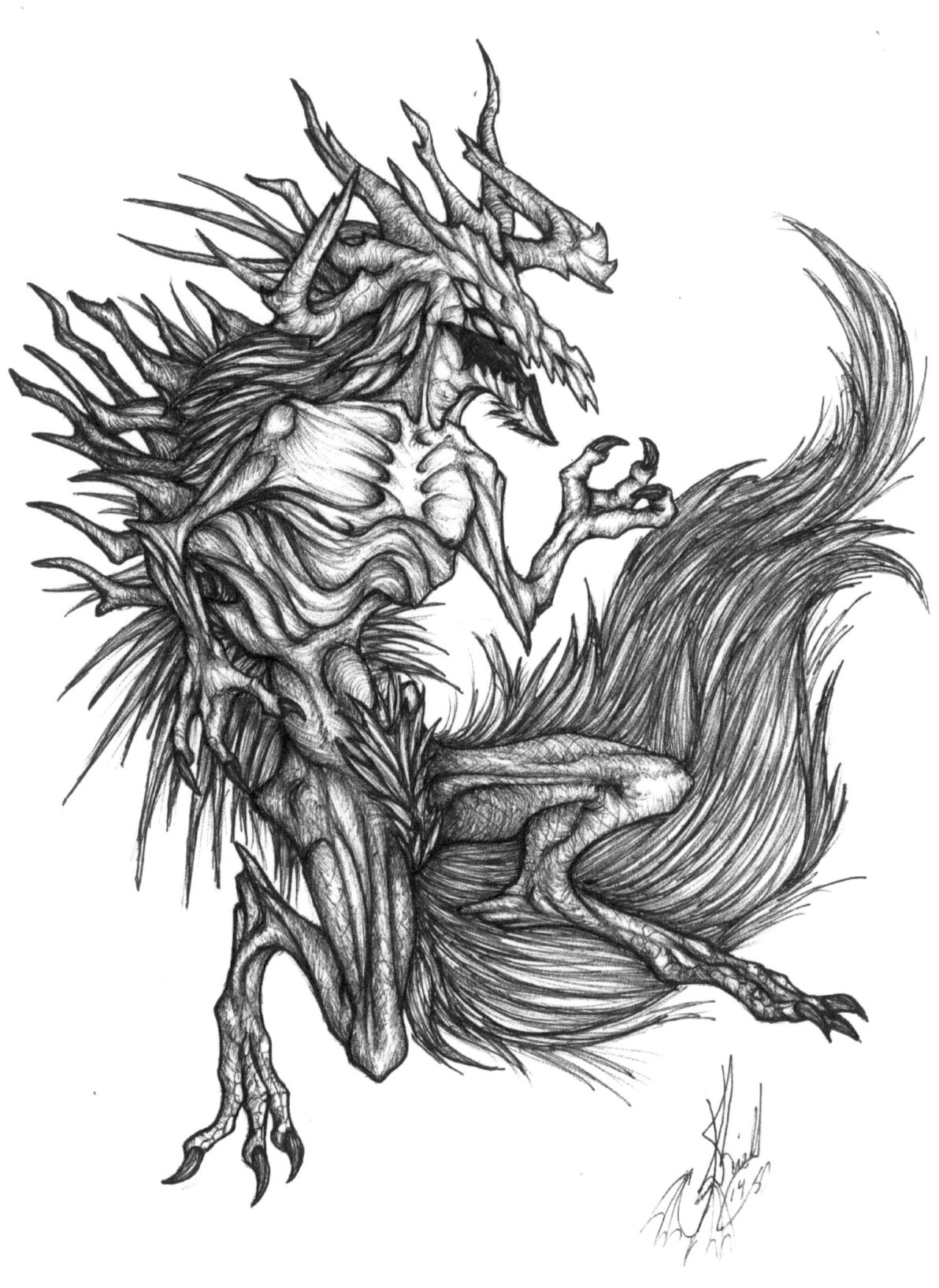

Scudishlougen

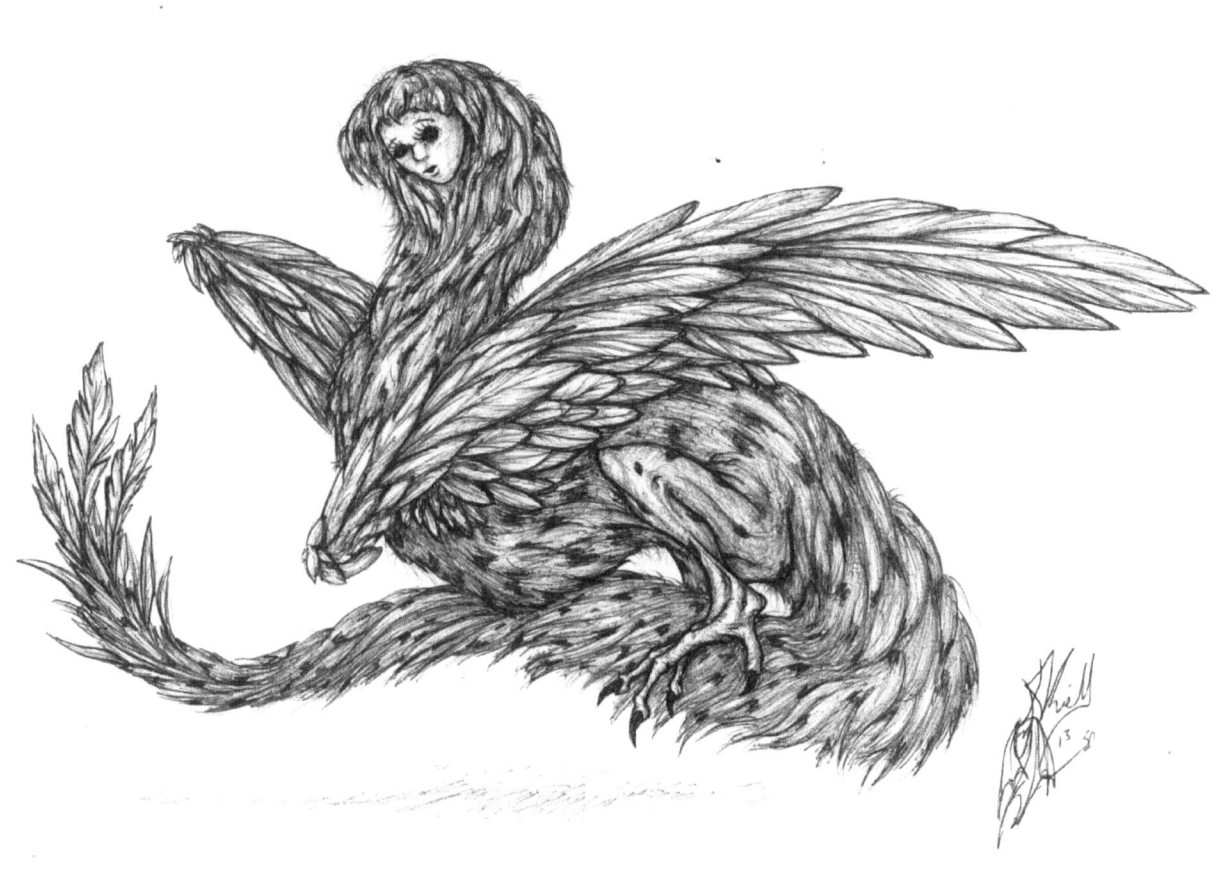

Spotted Angelia

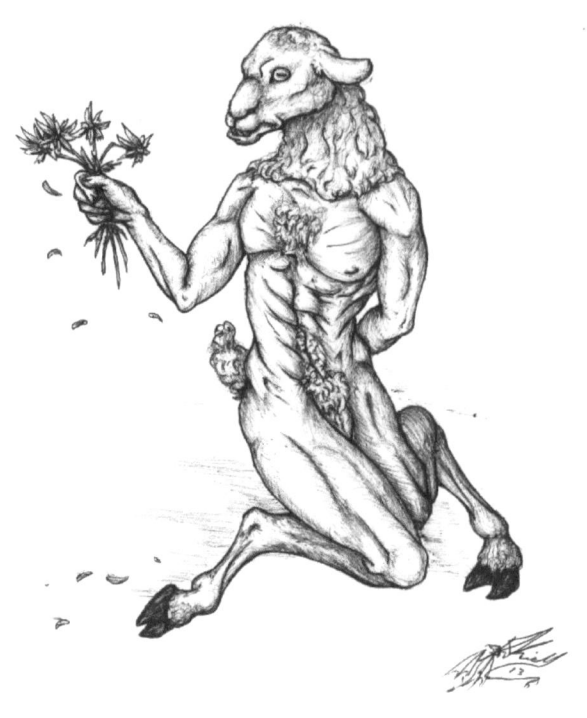

The Lamb

In the fields the lamb waits,

White fleece soft and pure as clouds,

innocent, gay and proud.

Cloven prints in the mud lead away into strange dreams,

where new love buds.

Glean the grass from his teeth,

Cradle the dead and dying stems and weep,

Count the silent sheep and sleep.

In the meadow the lamb waits still,

With empty eyes to fill.

He has flowers for you,

But oh, they've all been chewed...

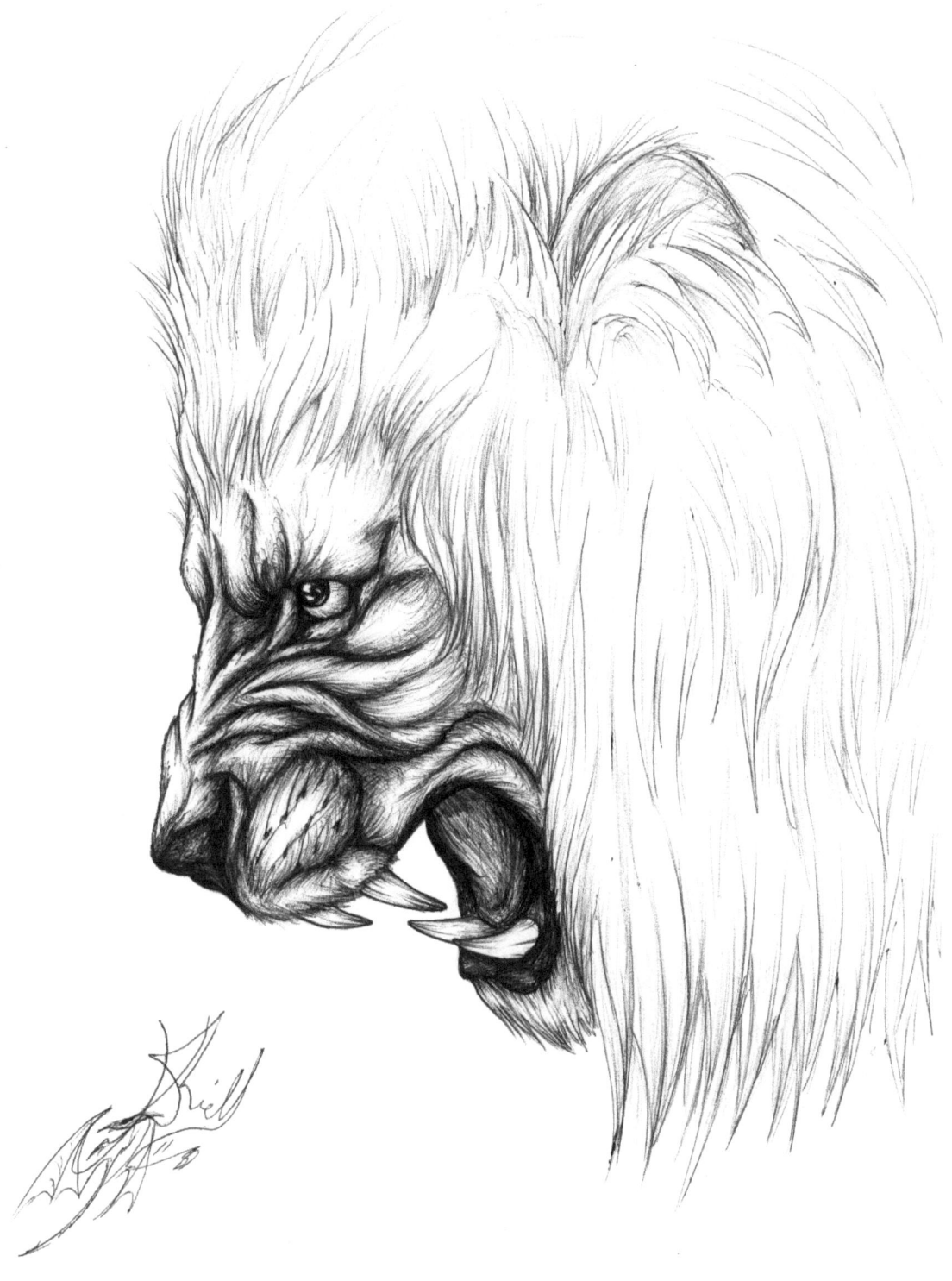

Lion

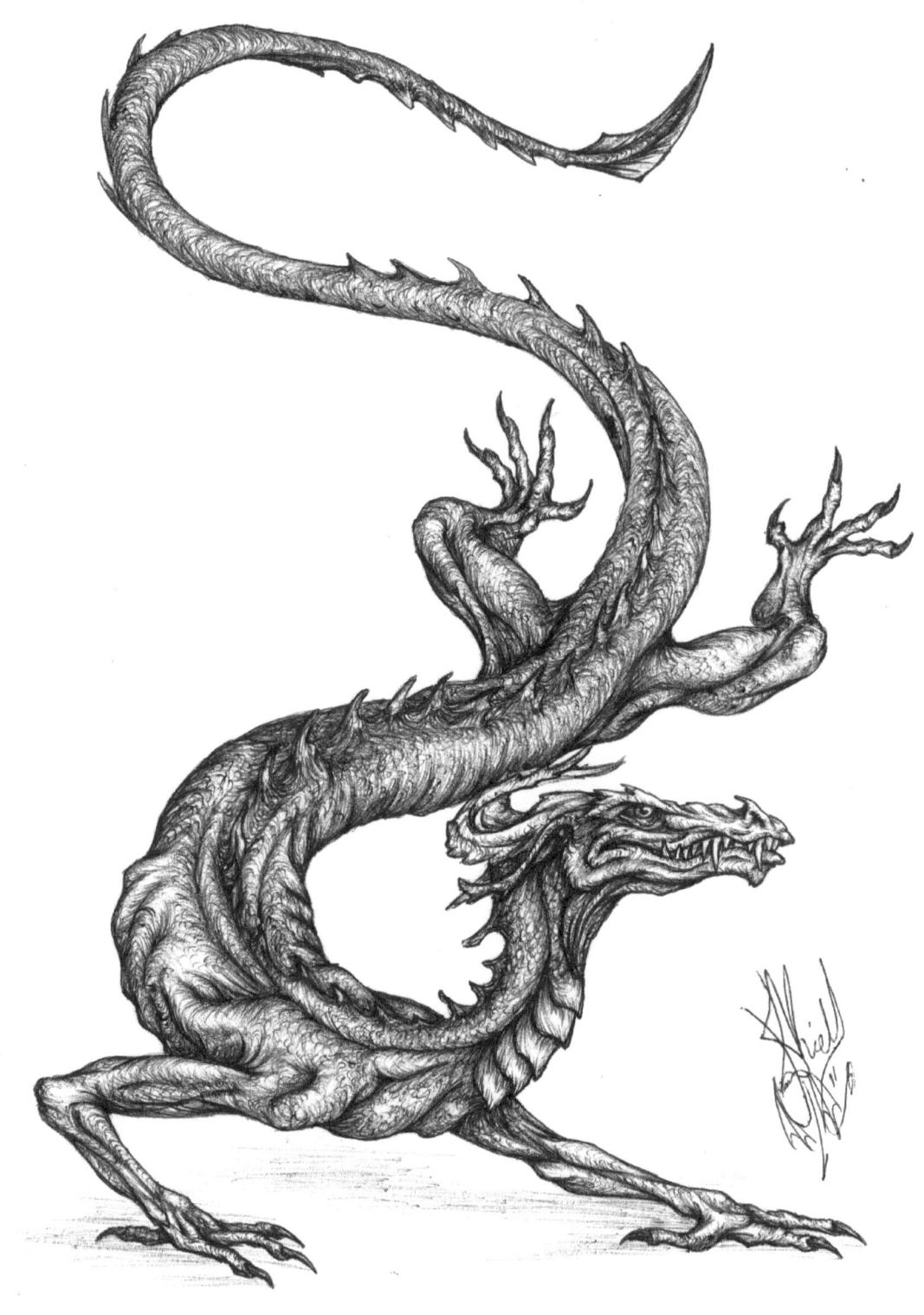

Wolfen Drak

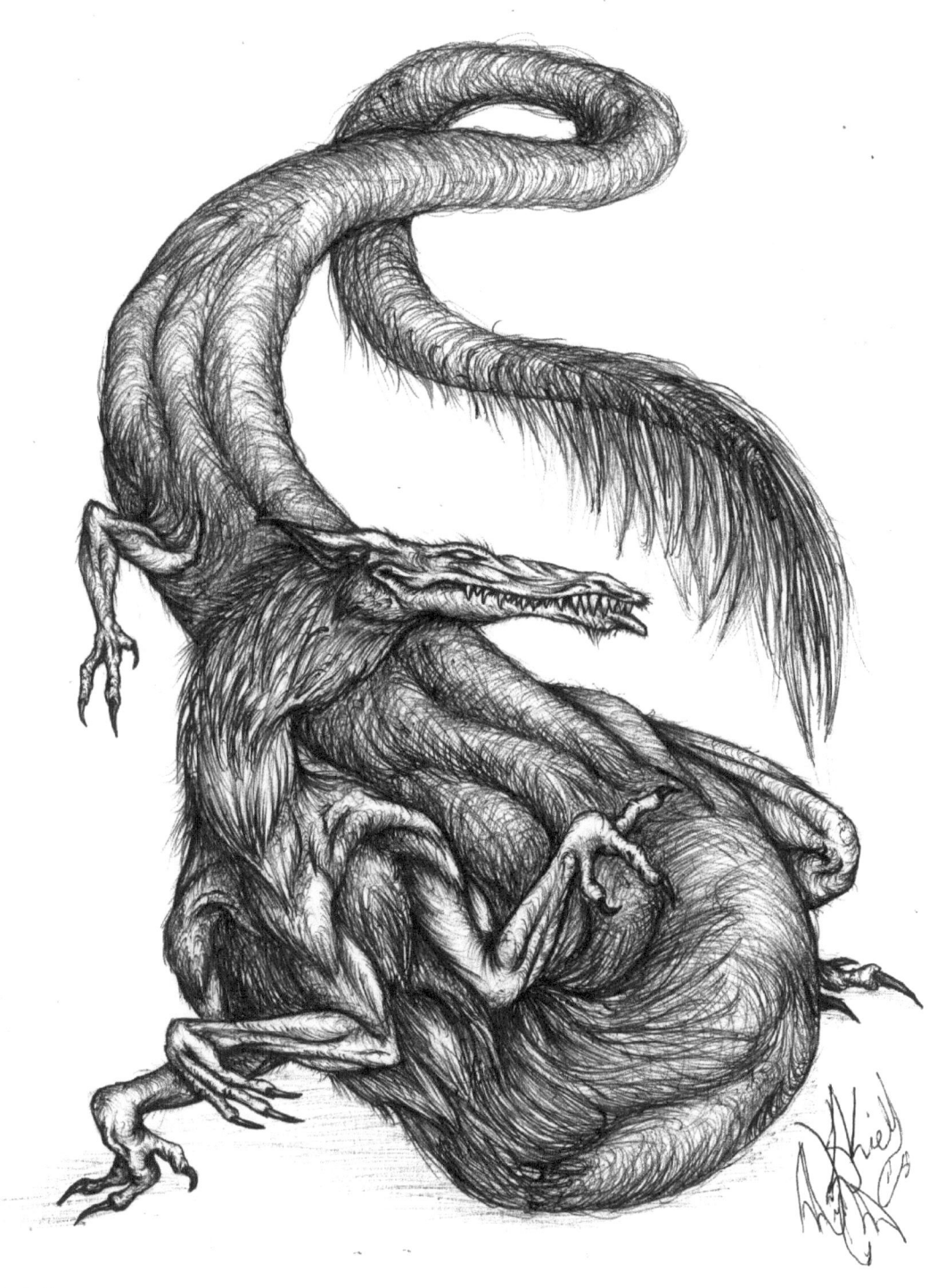

Shlider Wolfen

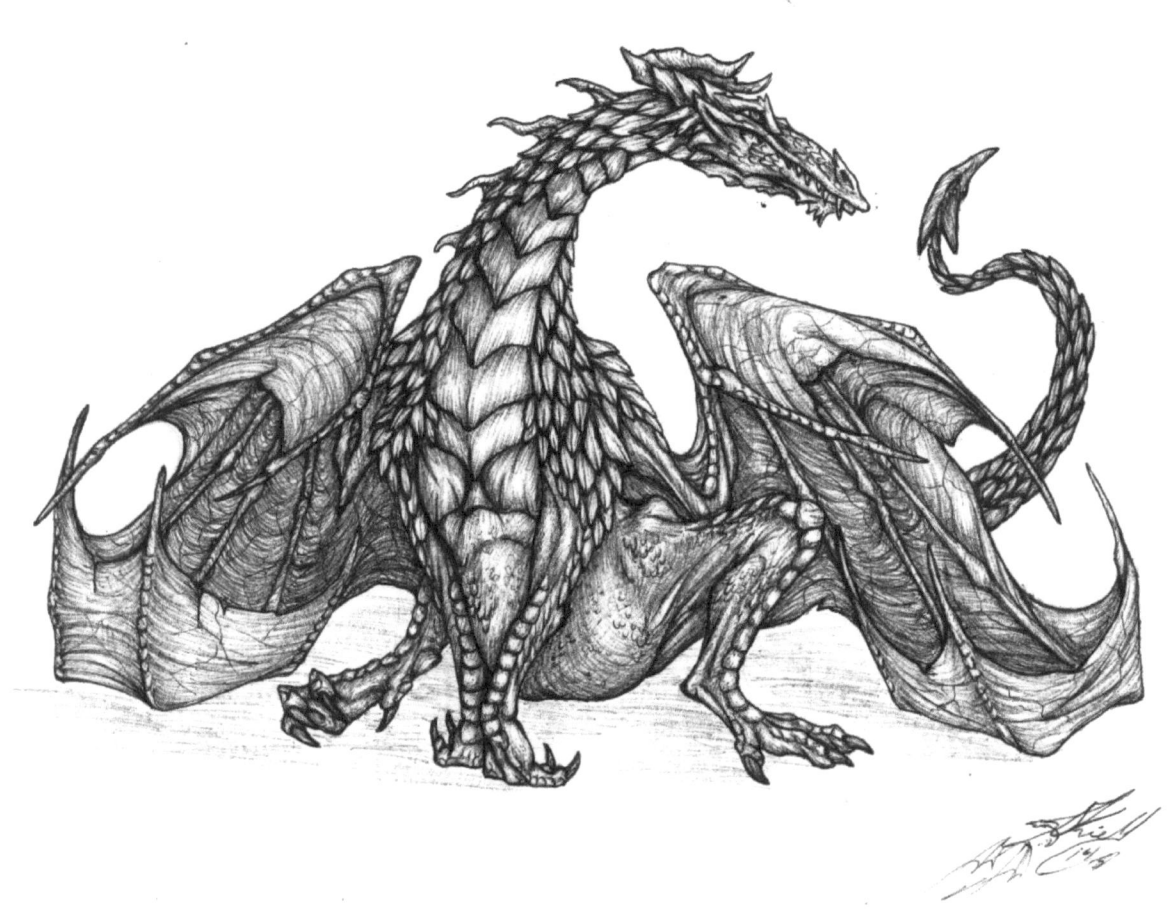

Sitting Dragon

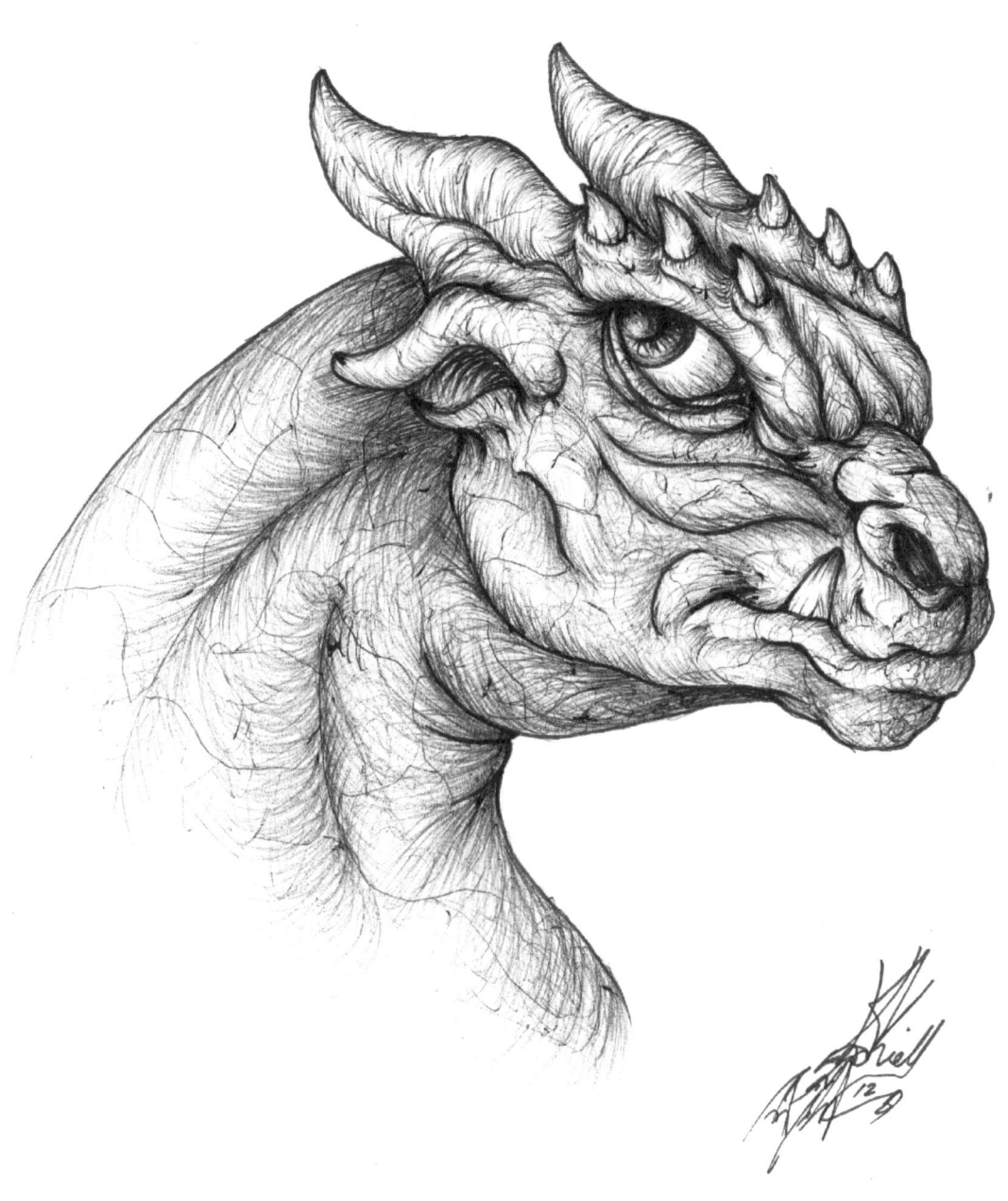

Pig the Dragon

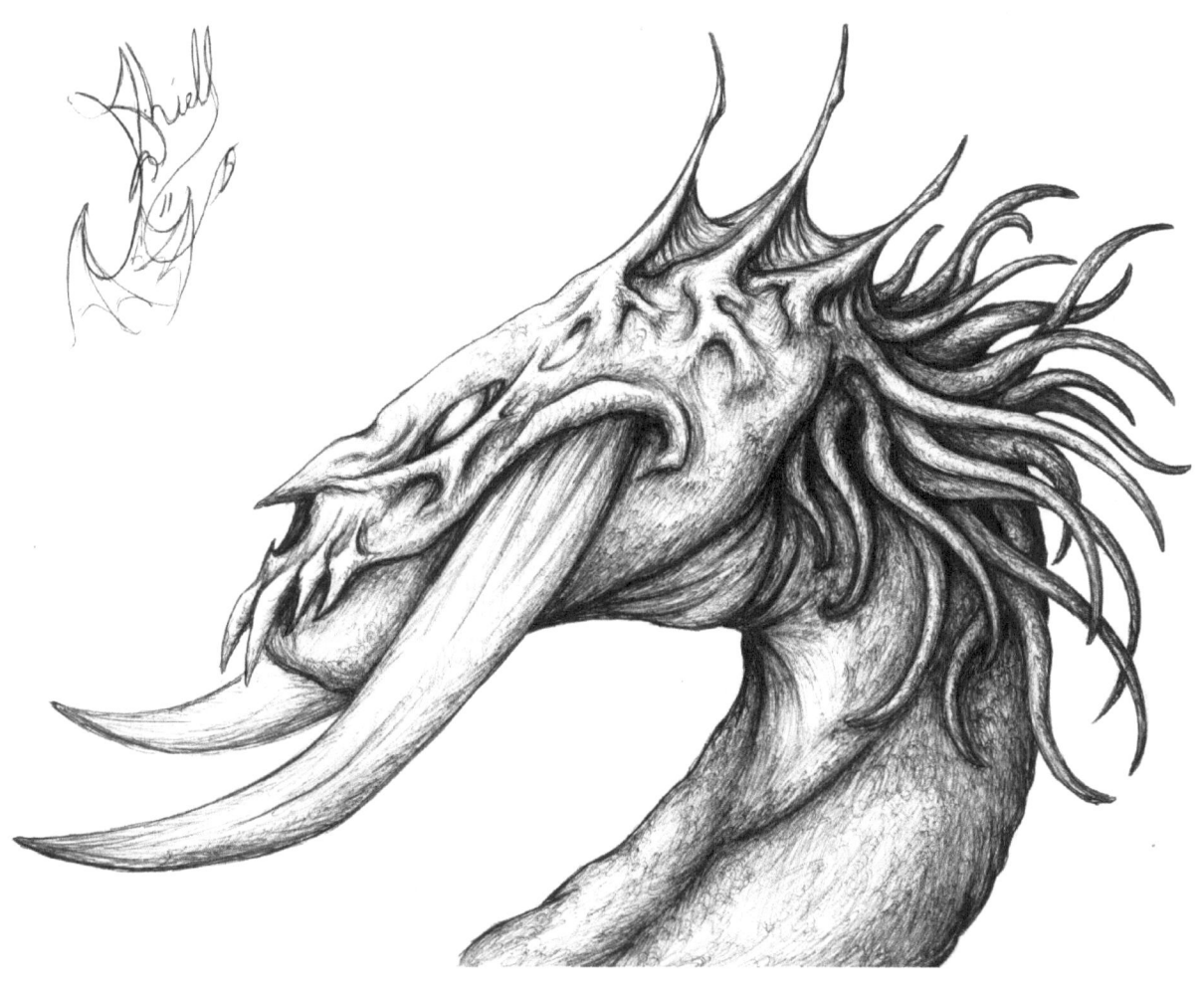

Saber Drak

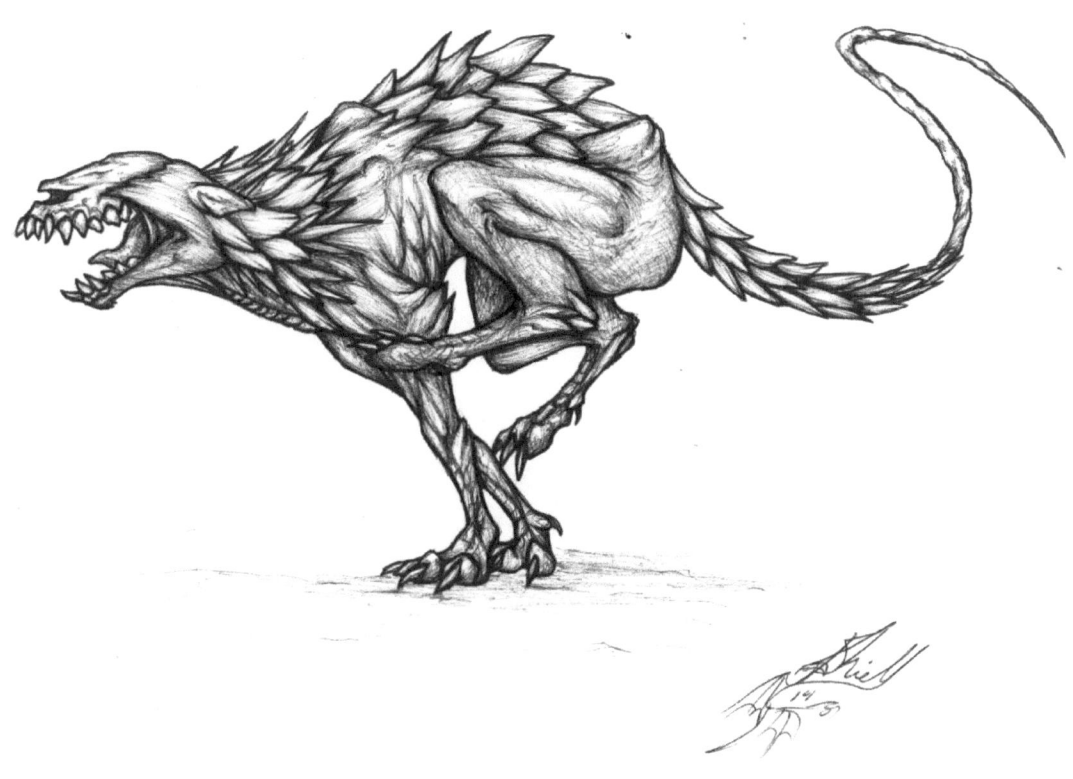

Scaleback Runner

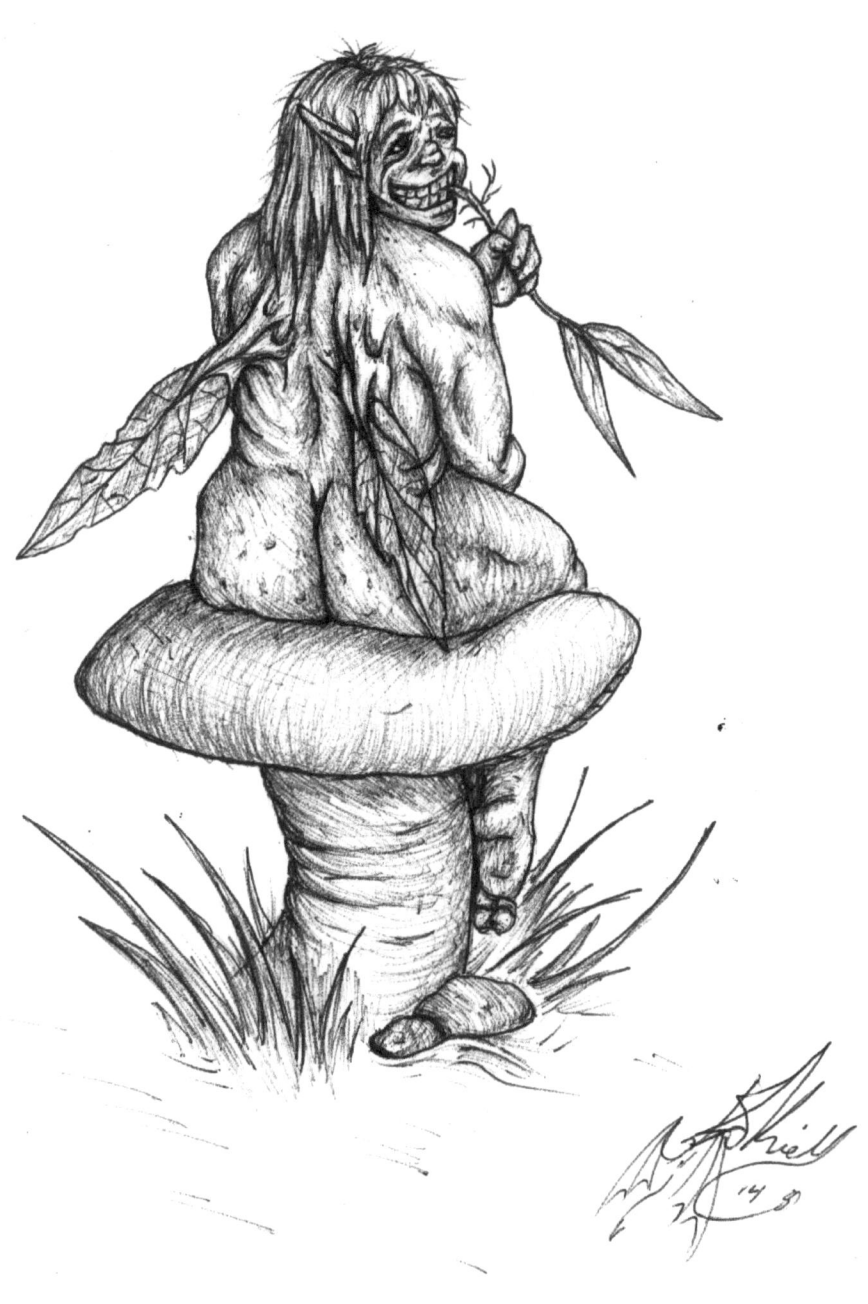

Saggy

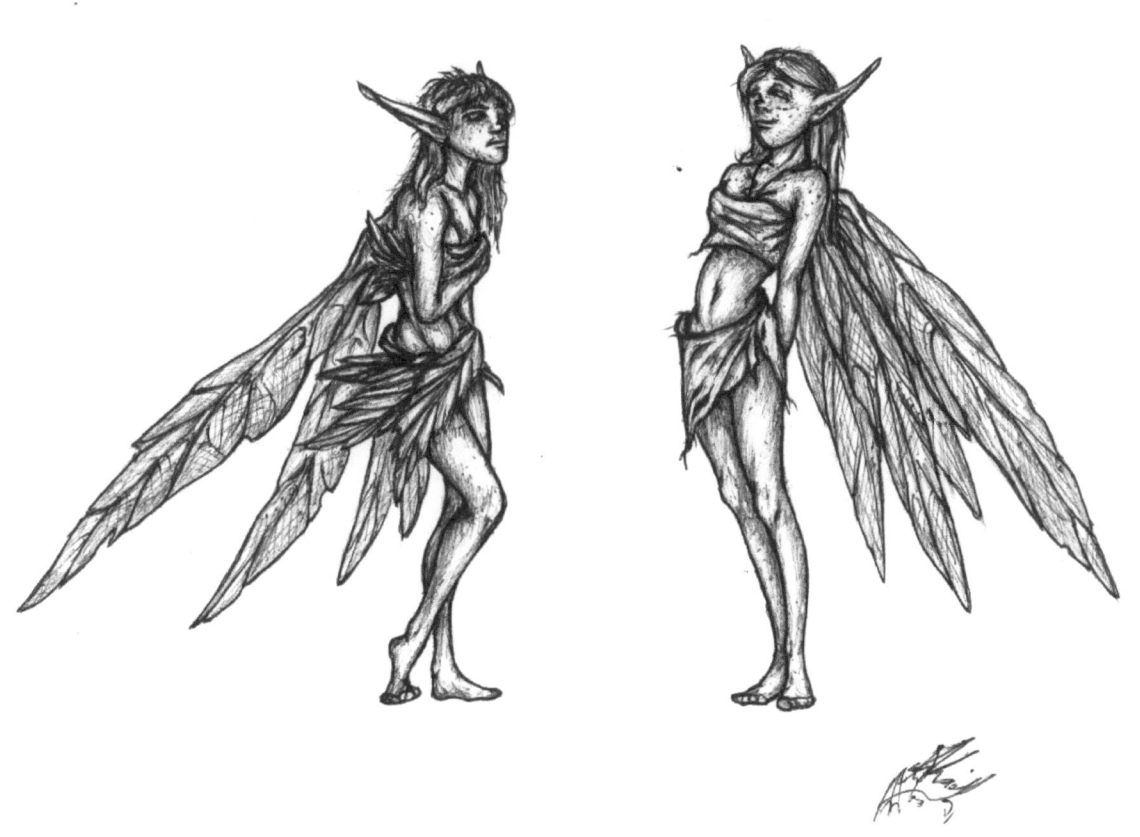

Turnip and Strawberry

Turnip scowled at the pixy in cloth garments of bright red, a rarity that matched her striking hair. In a community where it hardly mattered, Strawberry thought herself better than the rest…

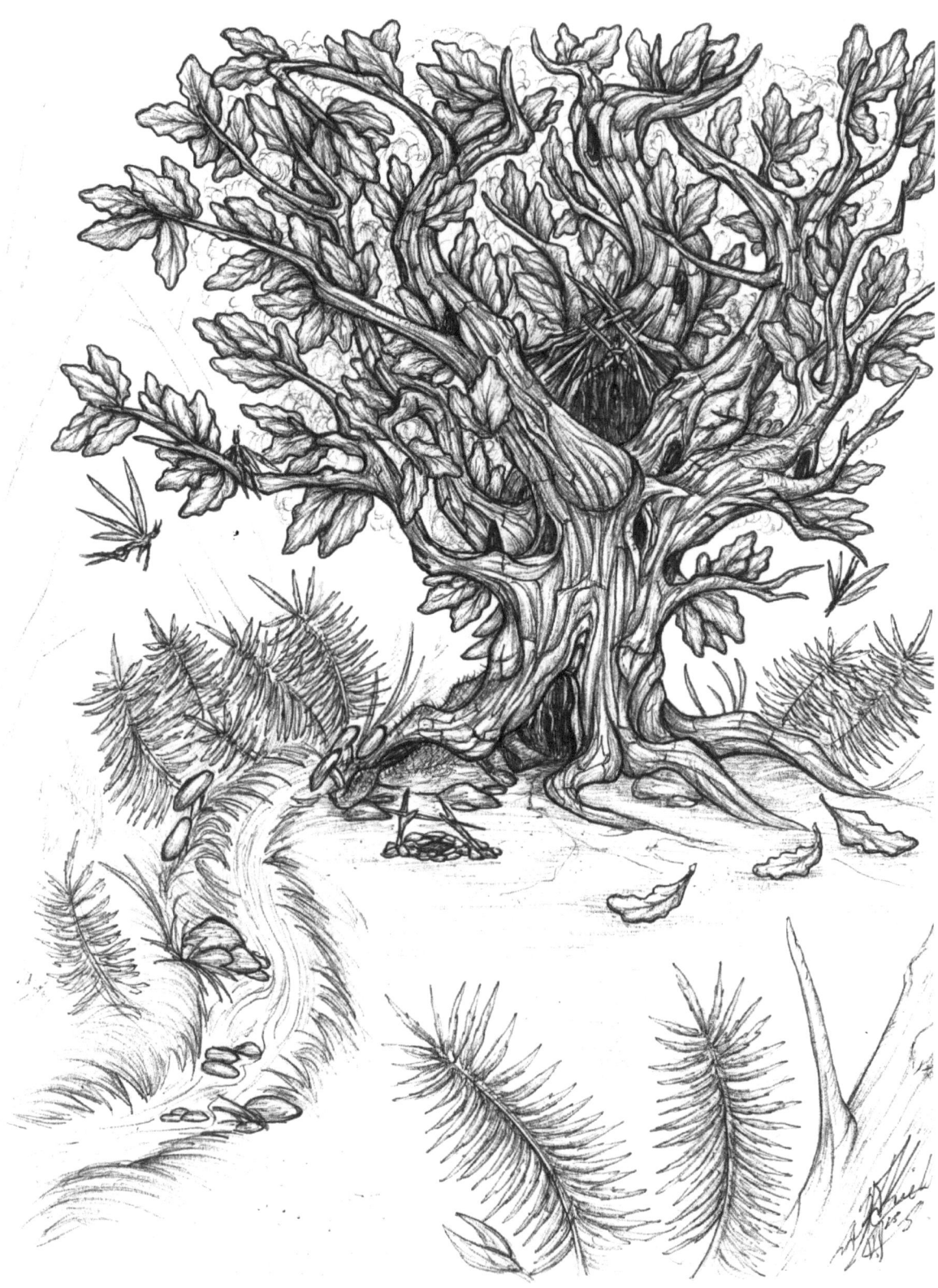

The Fairy Brake

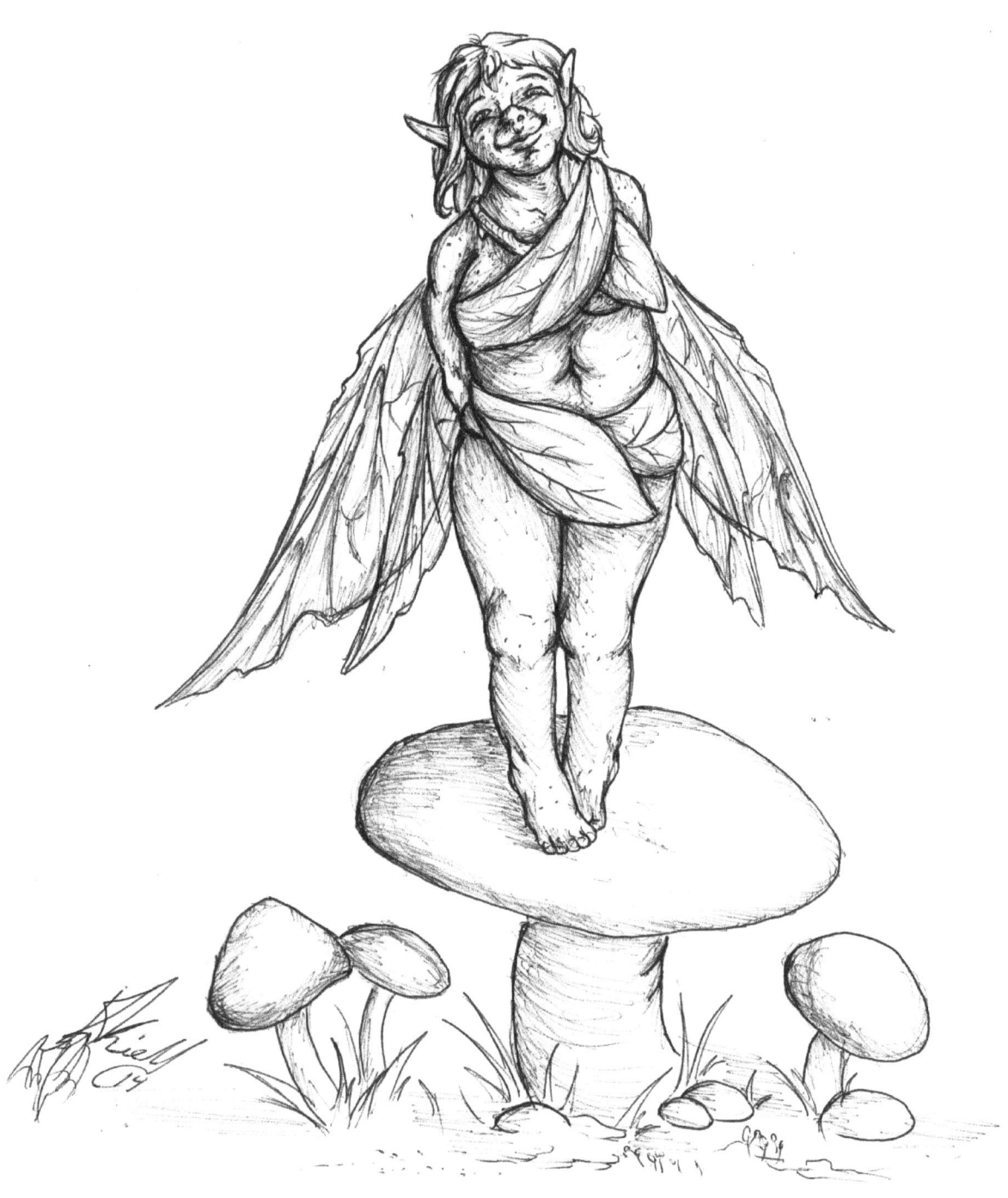

Kindly Fairy

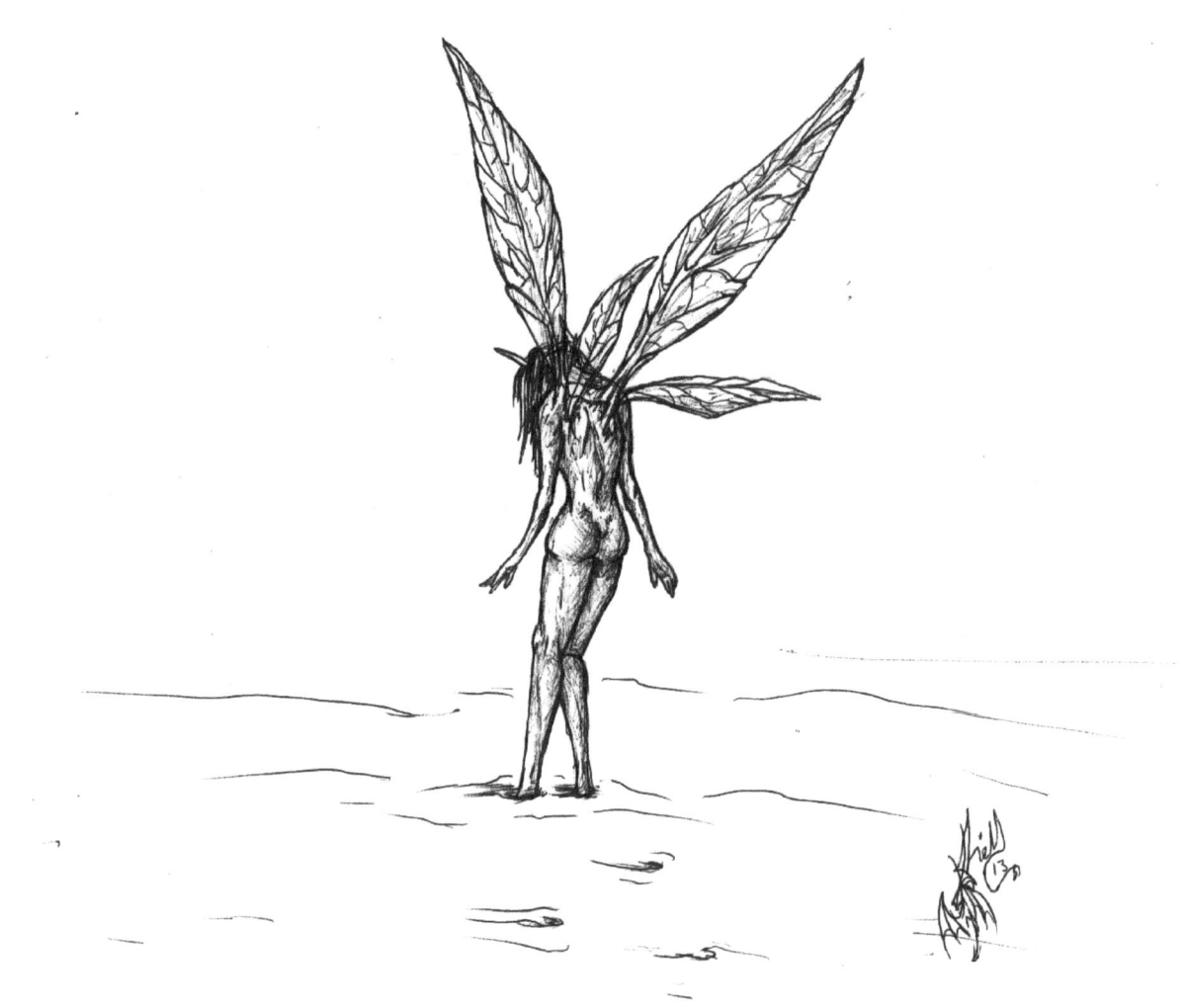

Fairy in the Snow

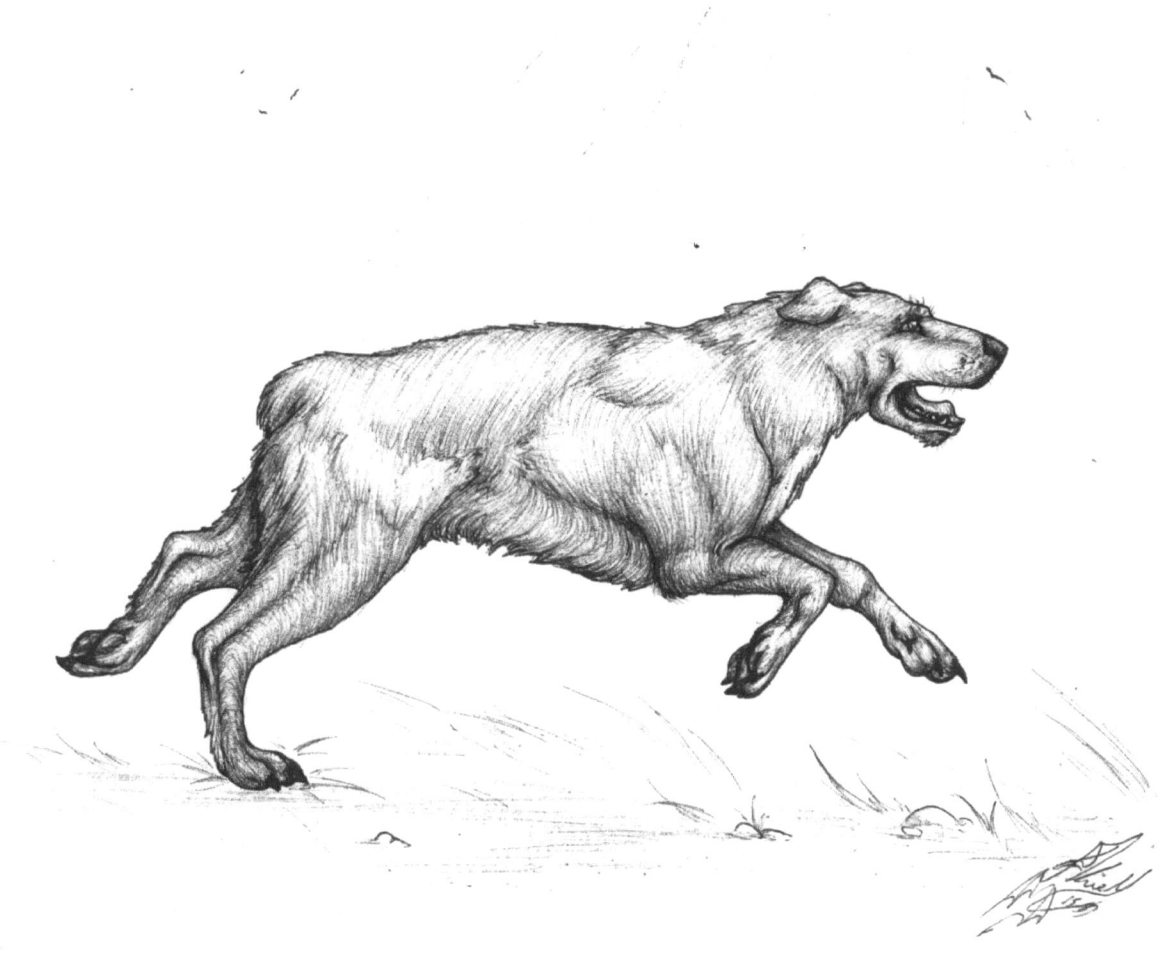

Shadow

A gentle touch, youth is a playful pup,

All the joy to bring, runs to chase the lives of spring.

Through summer falls, and friendly calls.

Black as night, and bright as day, patches soft of fading grey.

Lay warm hearts on cold, and leave footprints in the winter snows,

As light grows old and the north wind blows.

In memoriam to you my love,

In changing fields,

In growth bent with good natures will.

Run in spirit still.

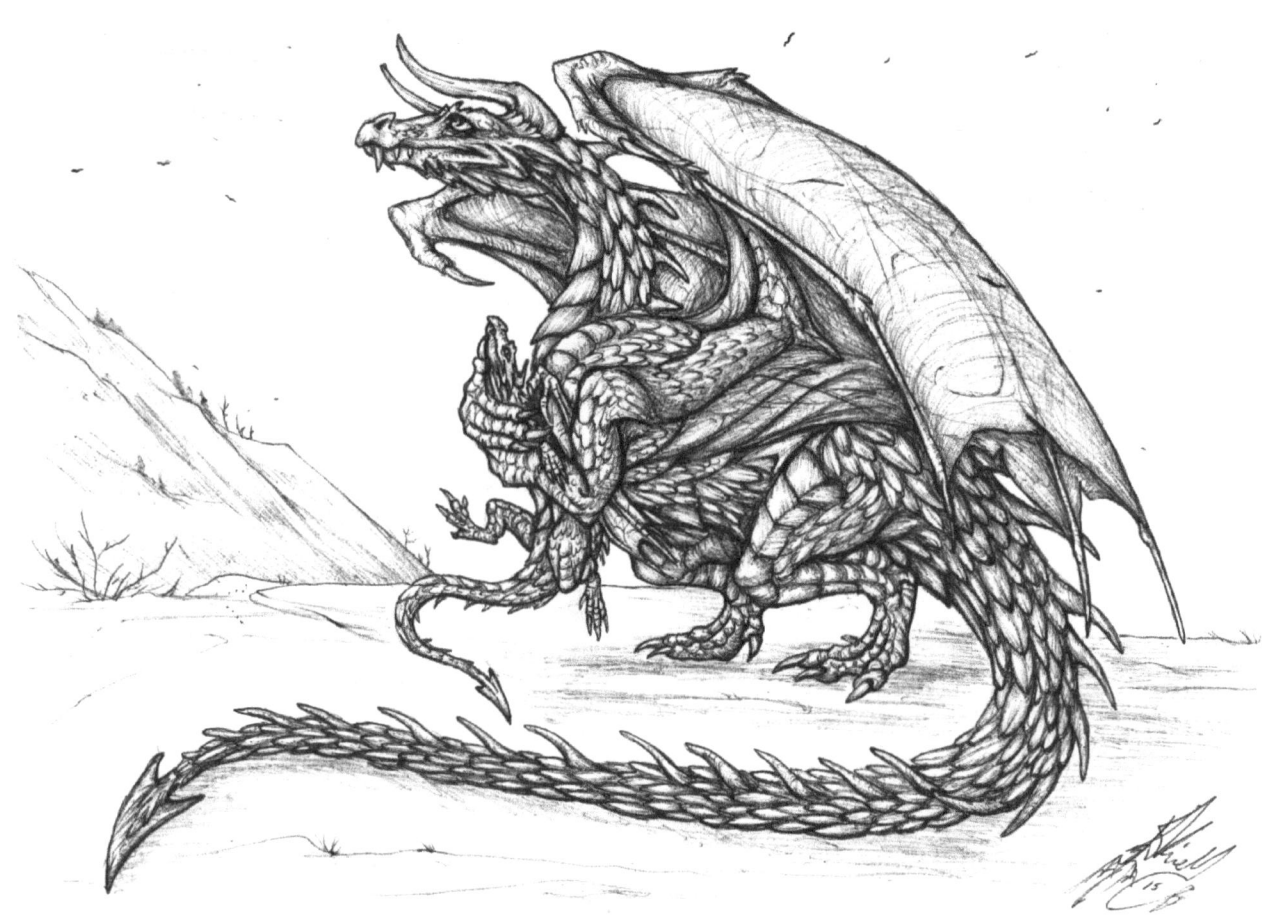

Youngling Dragon

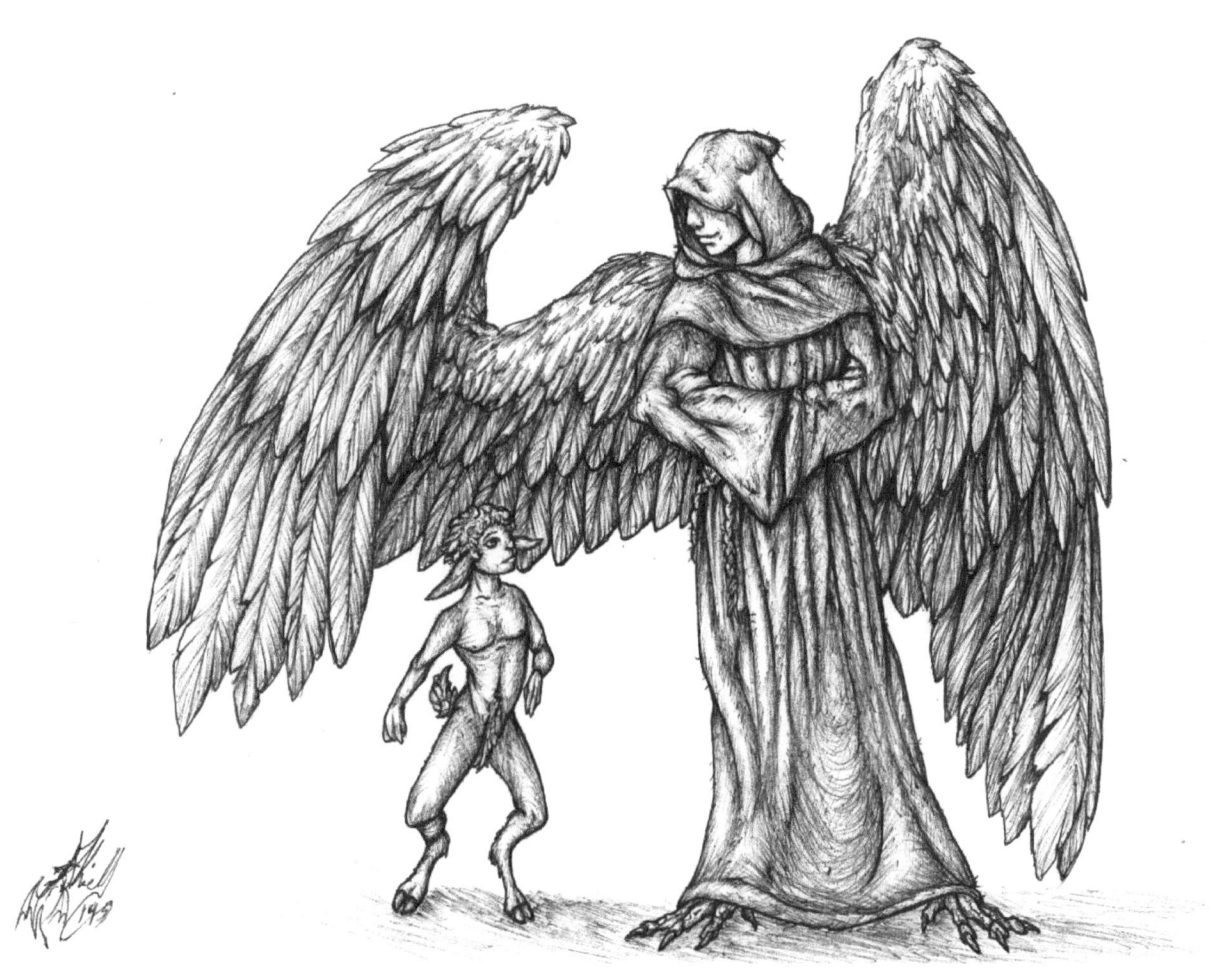

Shield the Lamb

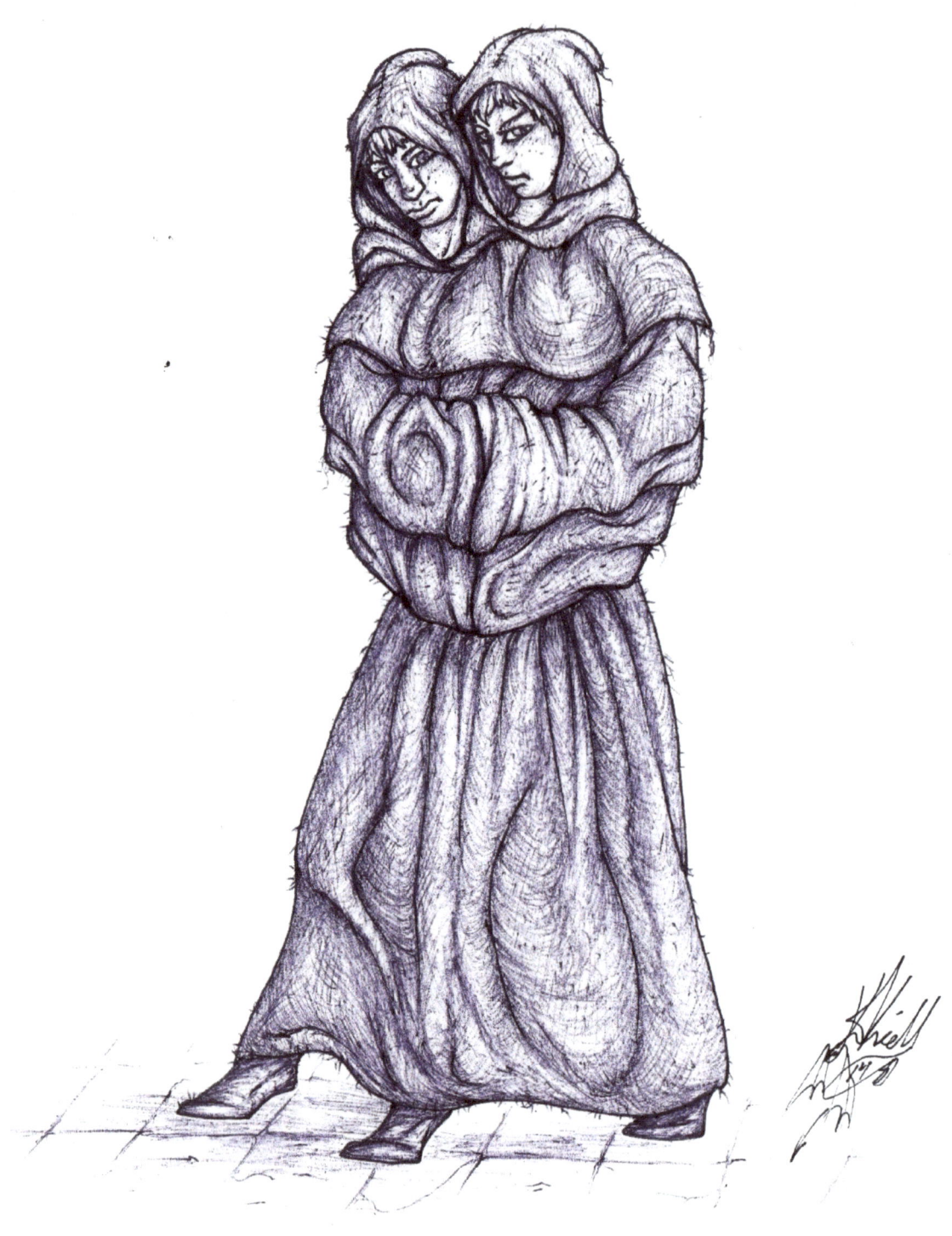

Twins

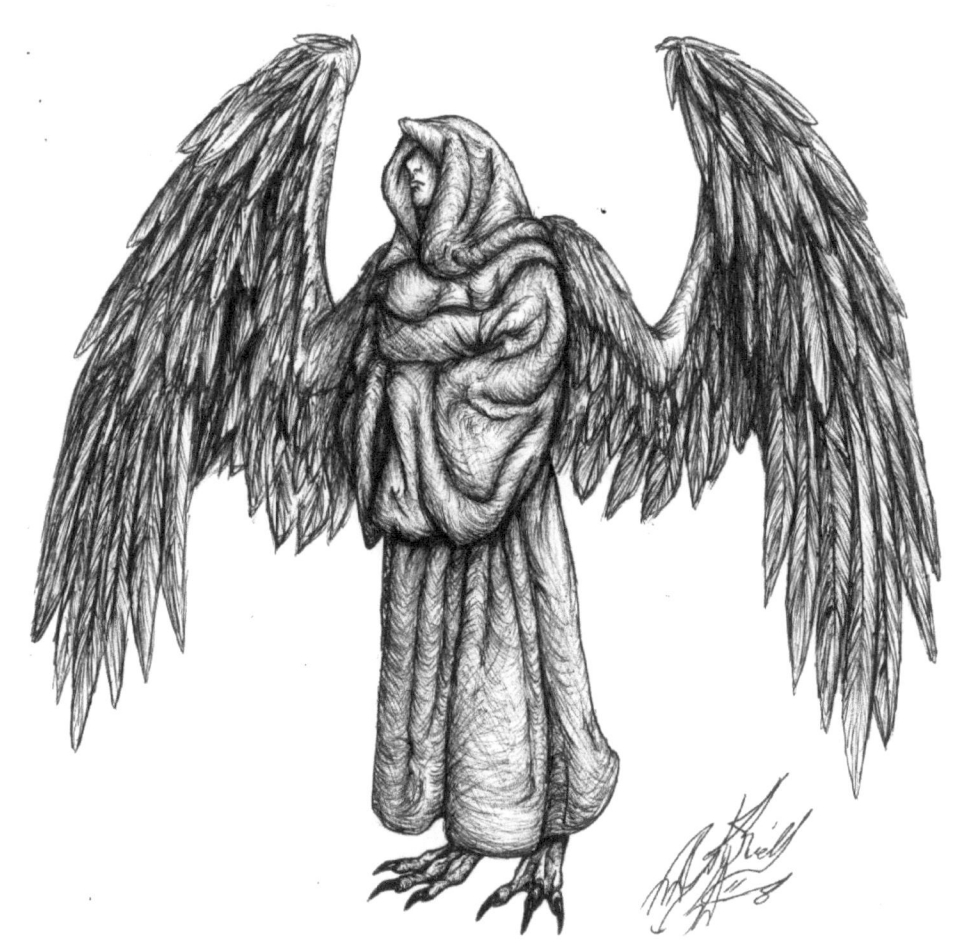

Winged Monk

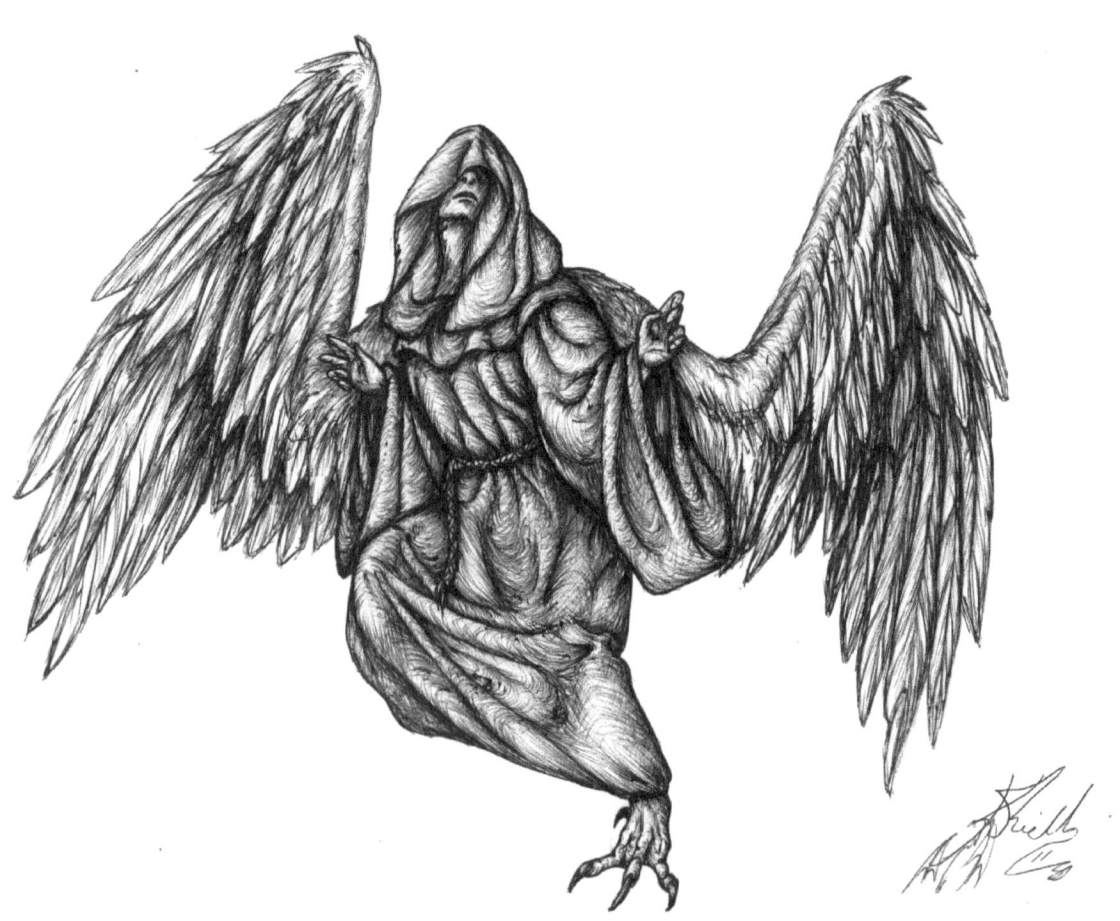

Flying Monk

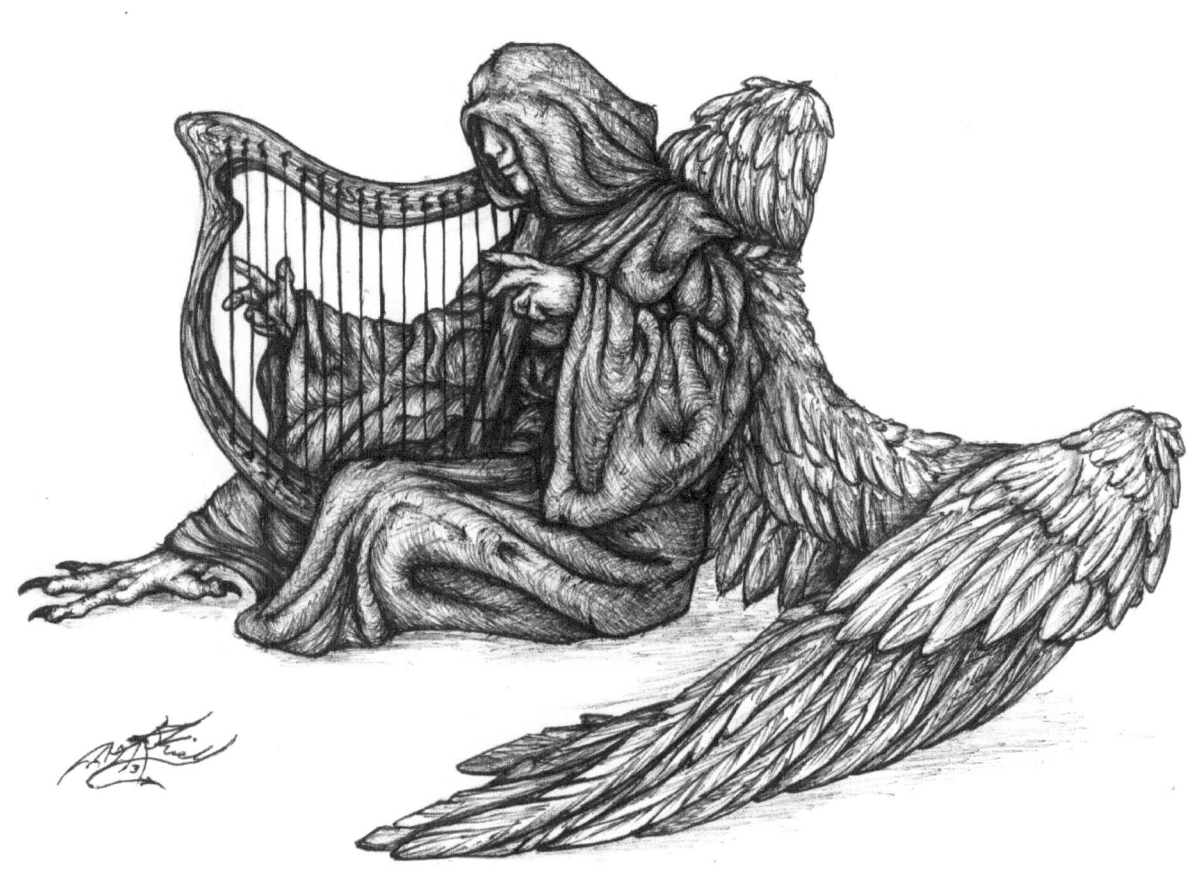

Brother Harpist

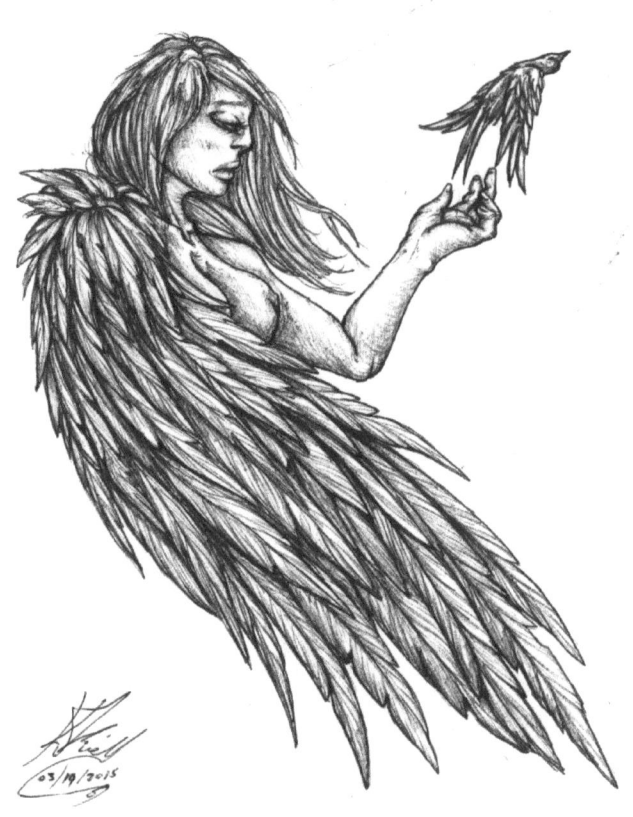

Goodbye

Lay still these old bones,

Upon cold and dark stone,

Light fades above,

Beyond these walls flies a pure white dove,

The soul, who's wings cast a pale glow over the land,

Take thy hand in mine and know,

I am with you always as you live and grow.

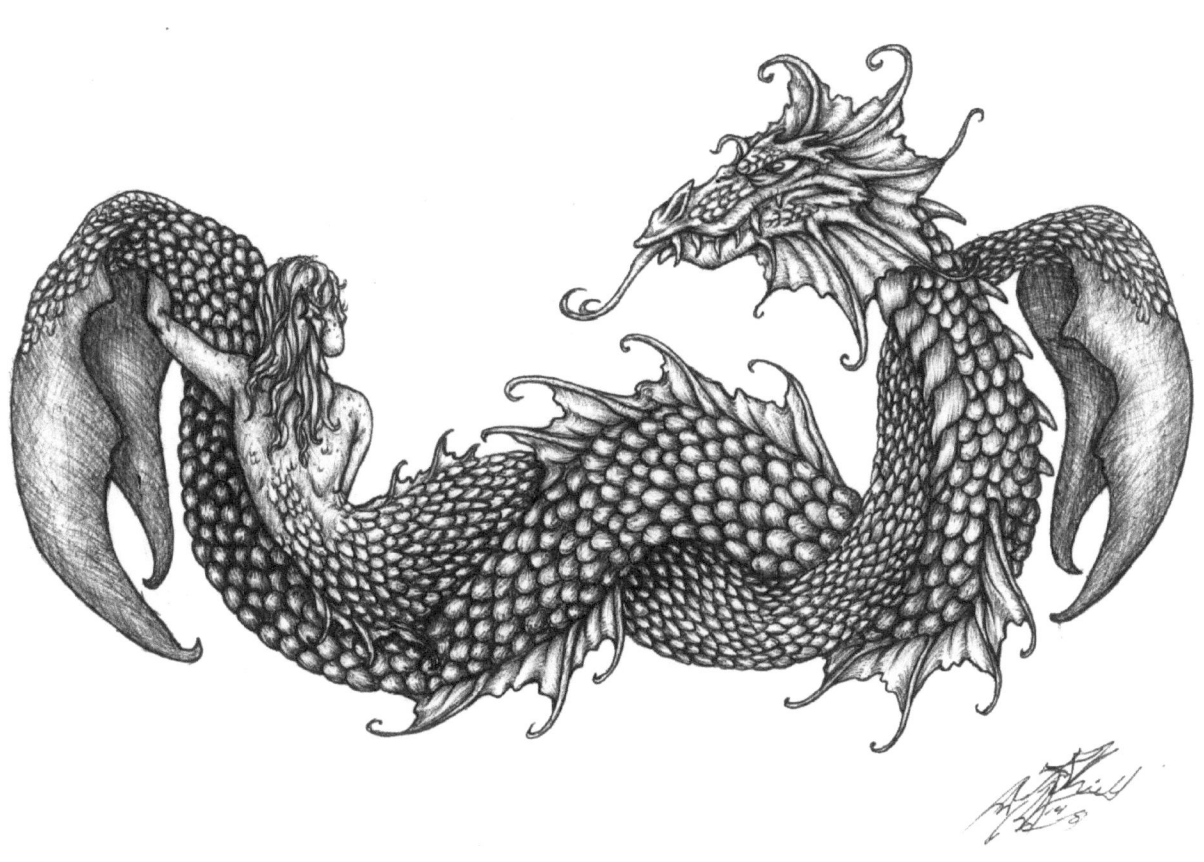

Unda

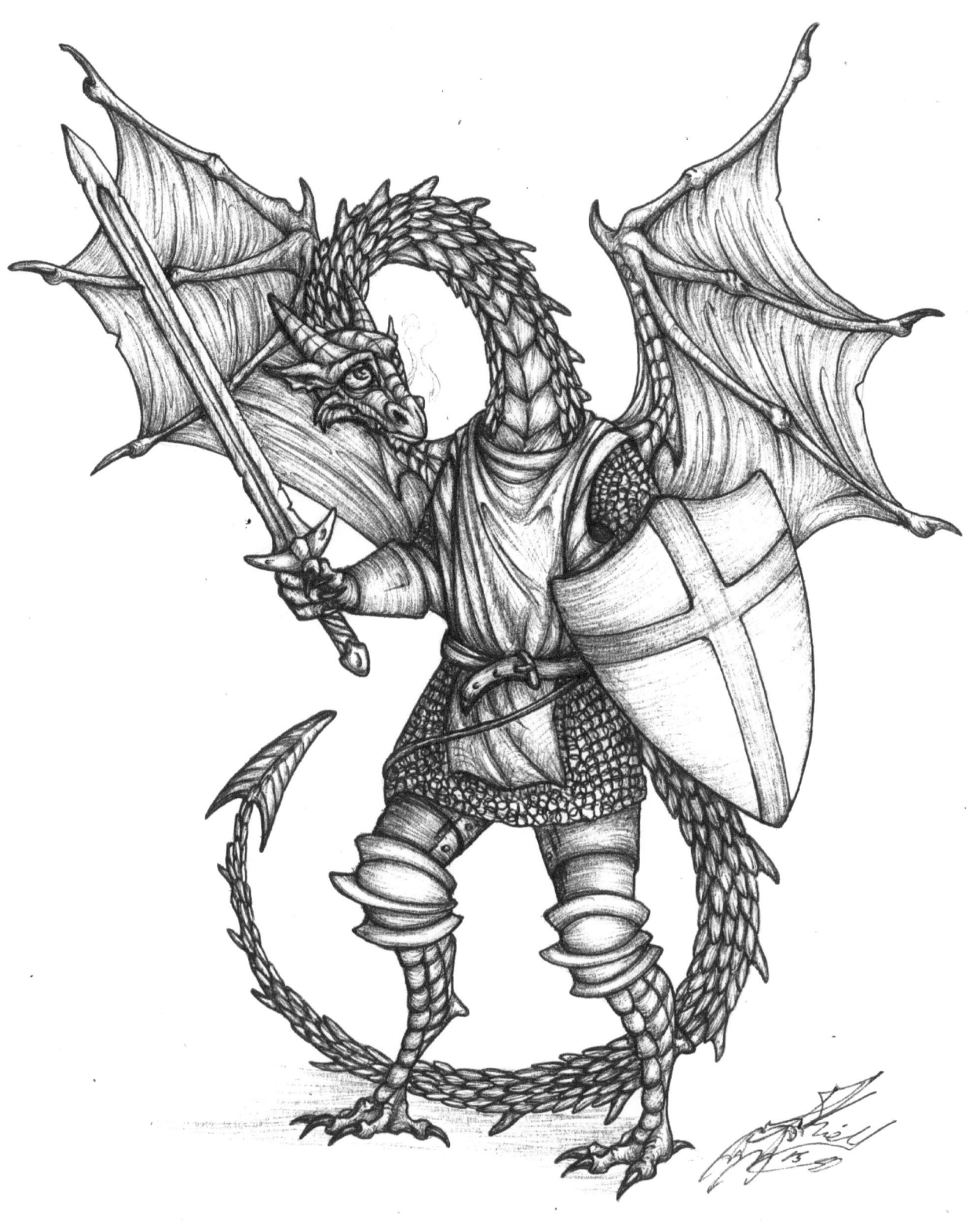

Draconic Knight

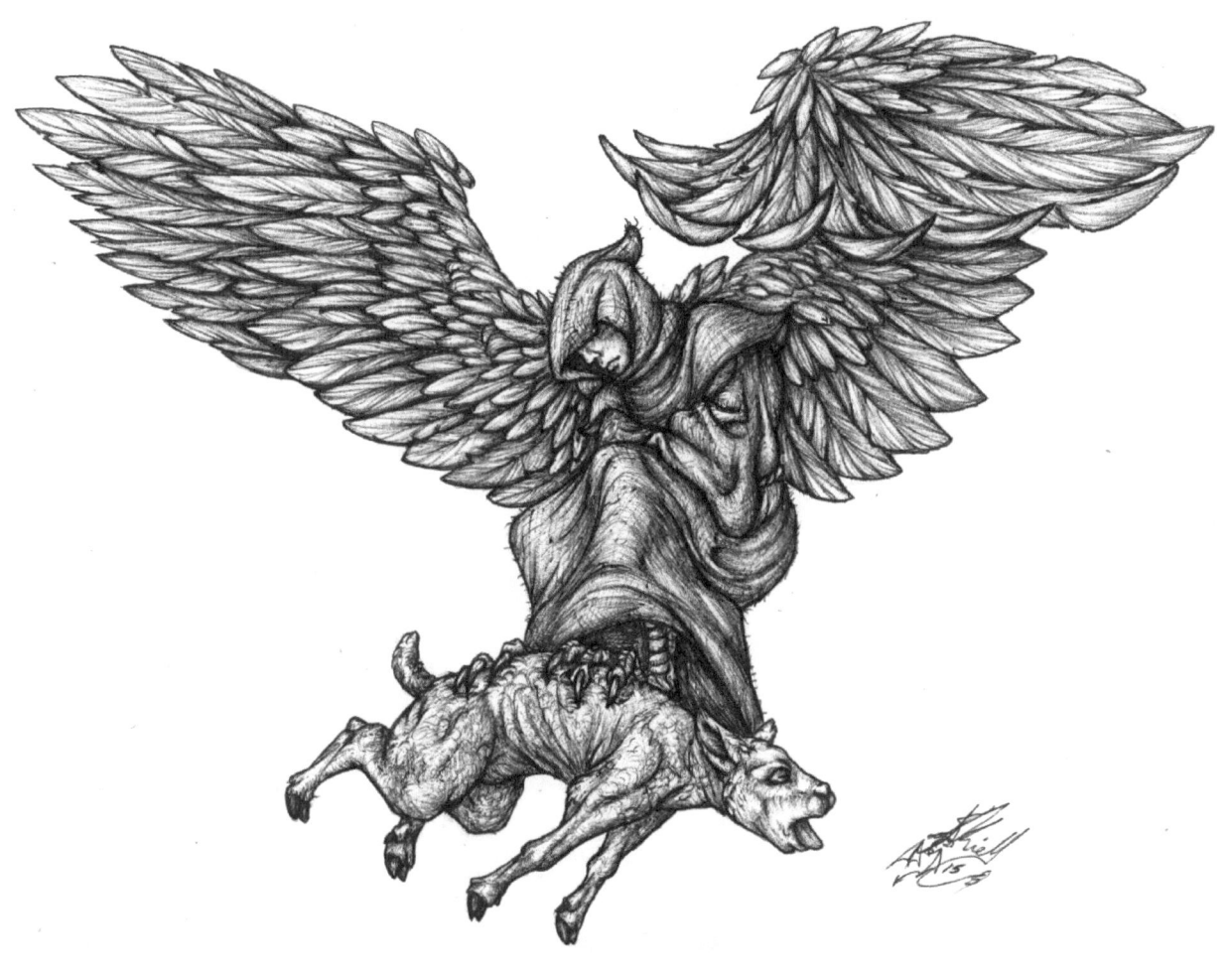

Sacrificial Lamb

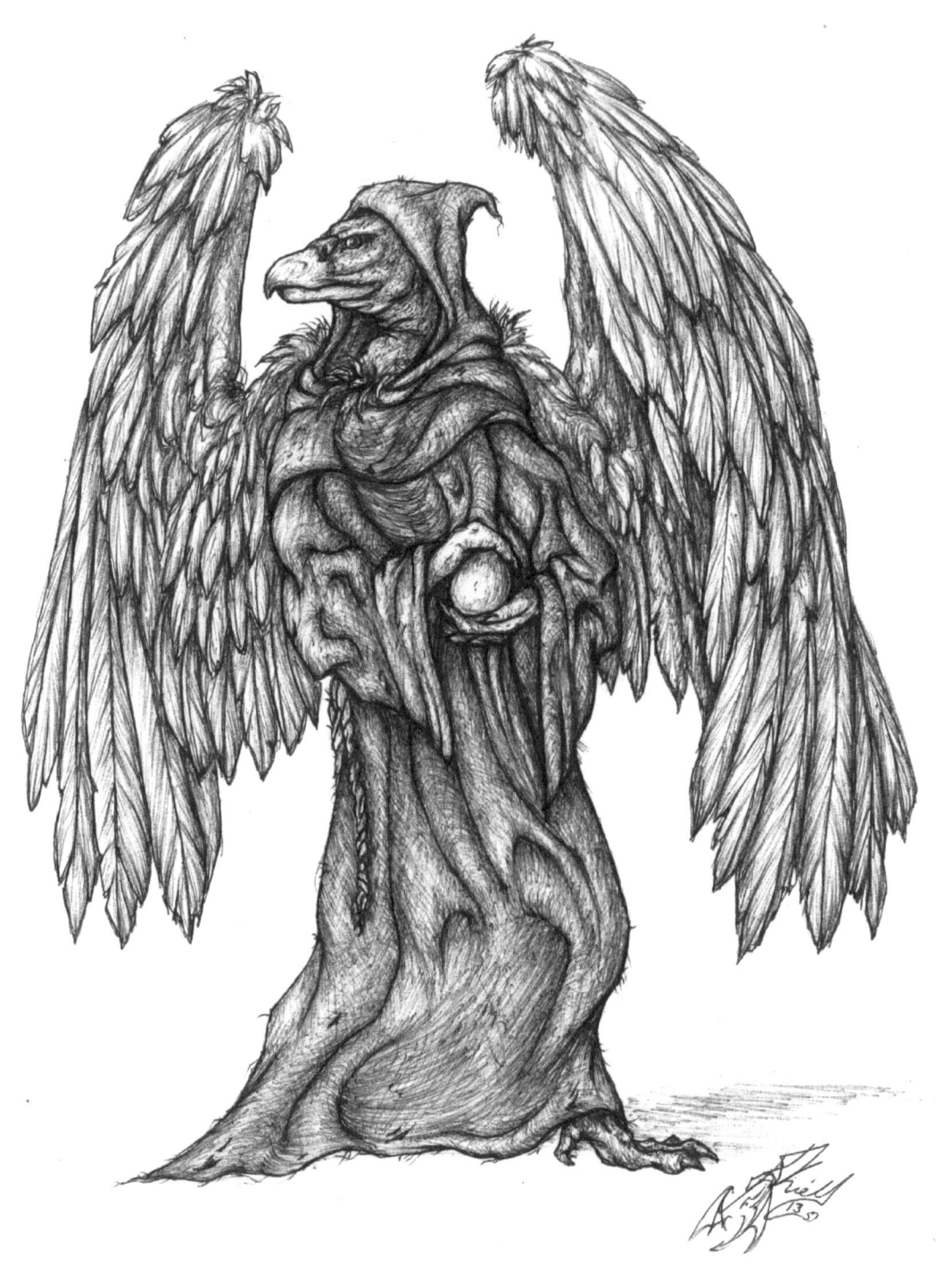

Monk Vulture

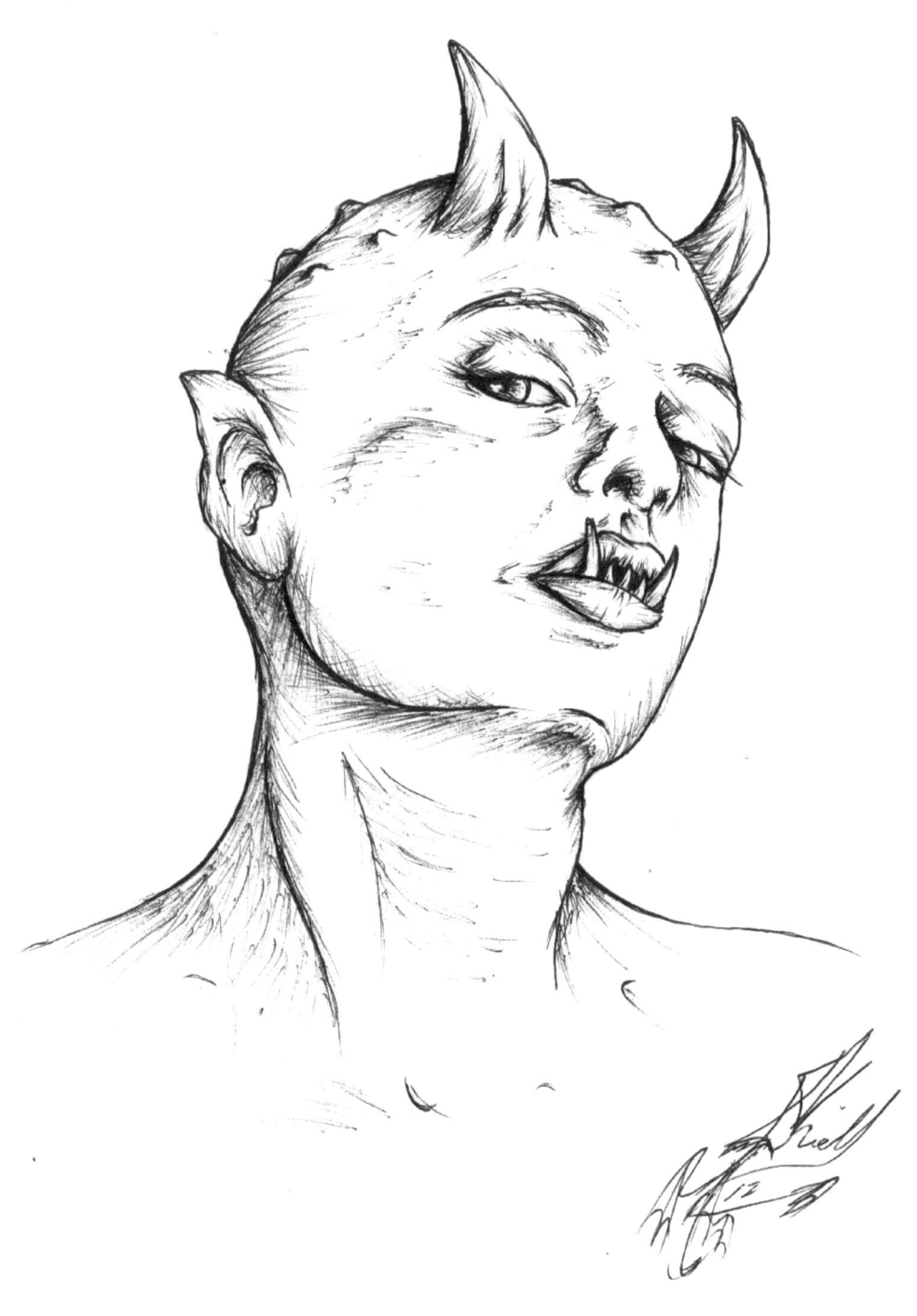

Orcish

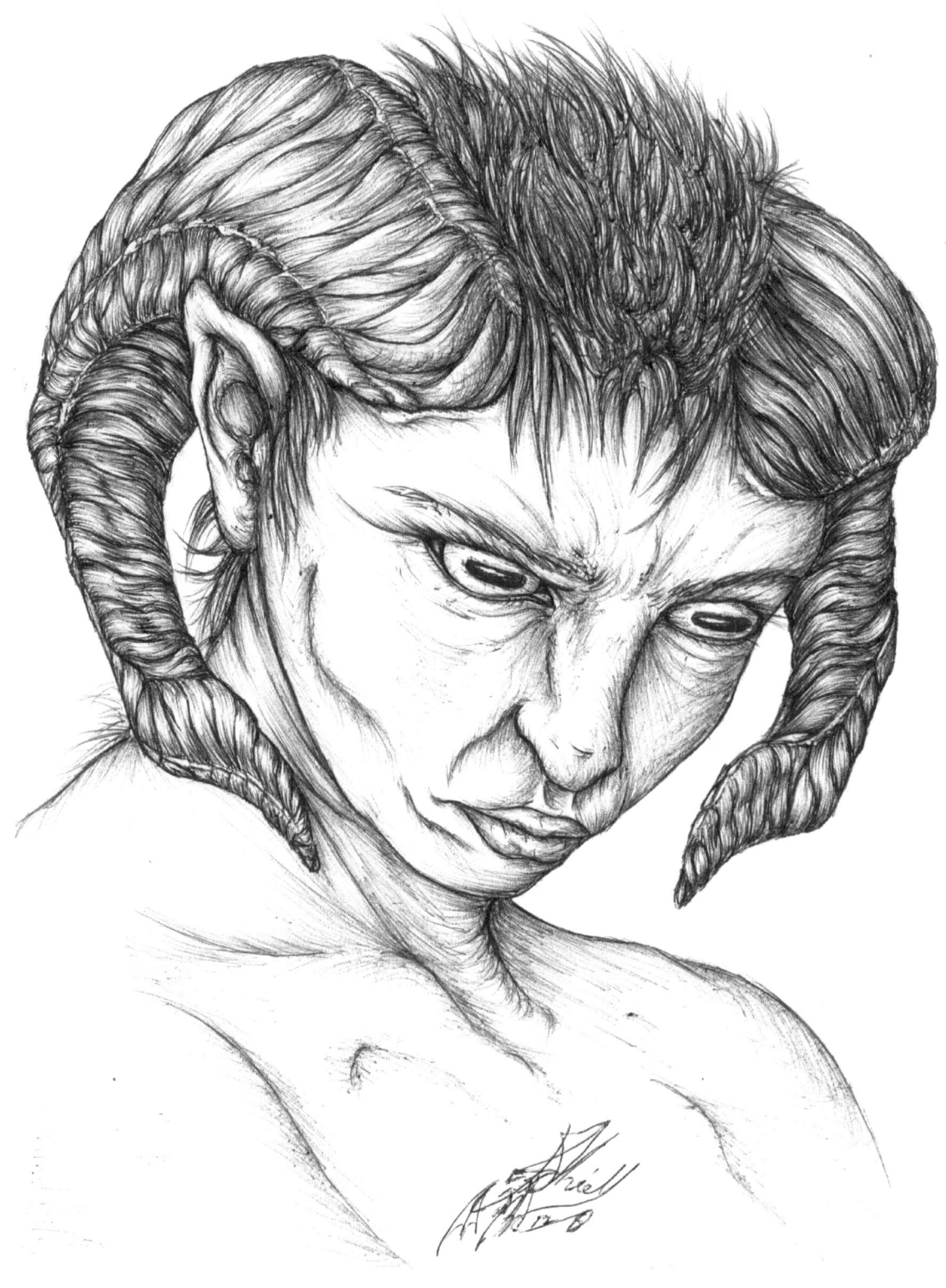

The Ram

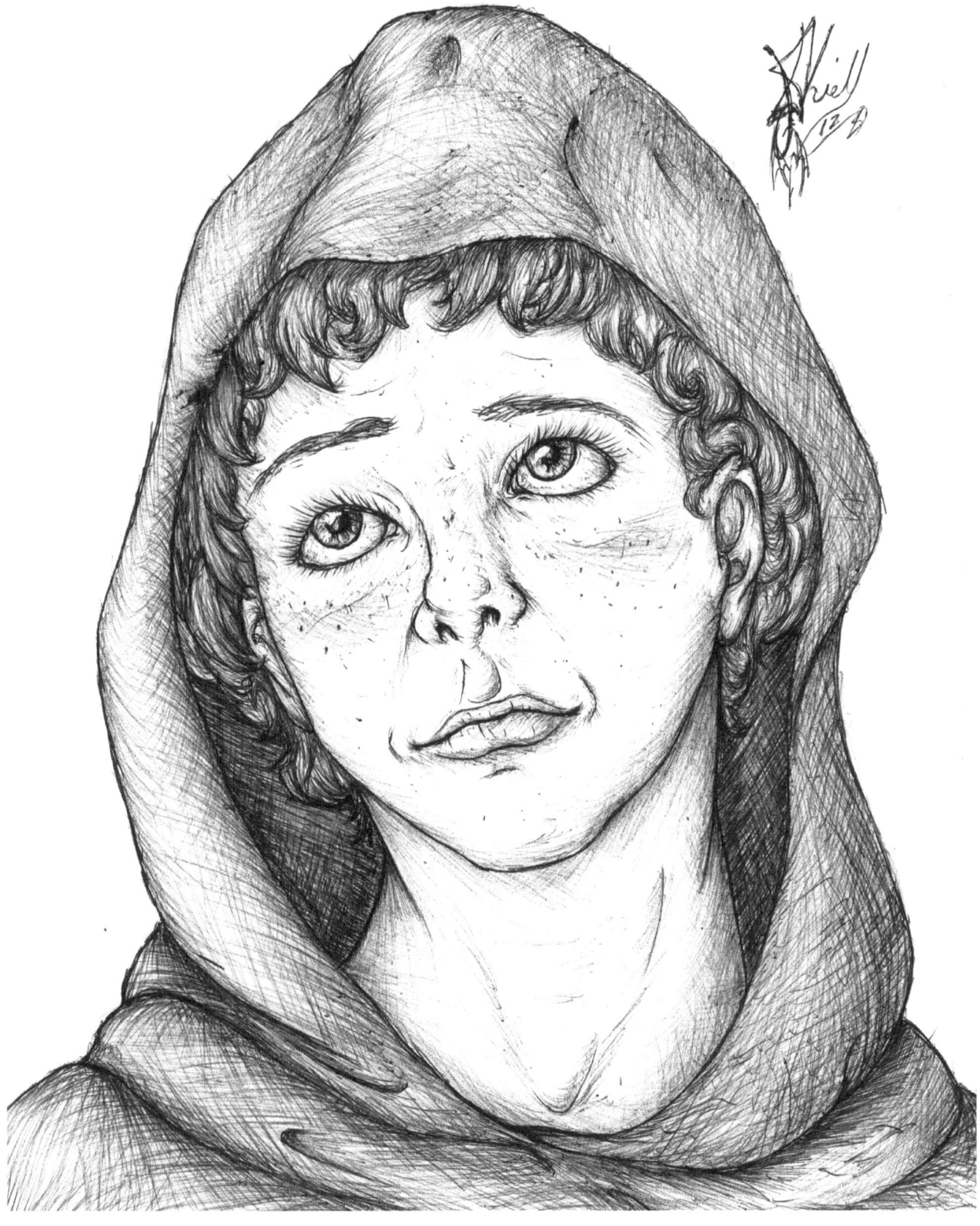

Novice

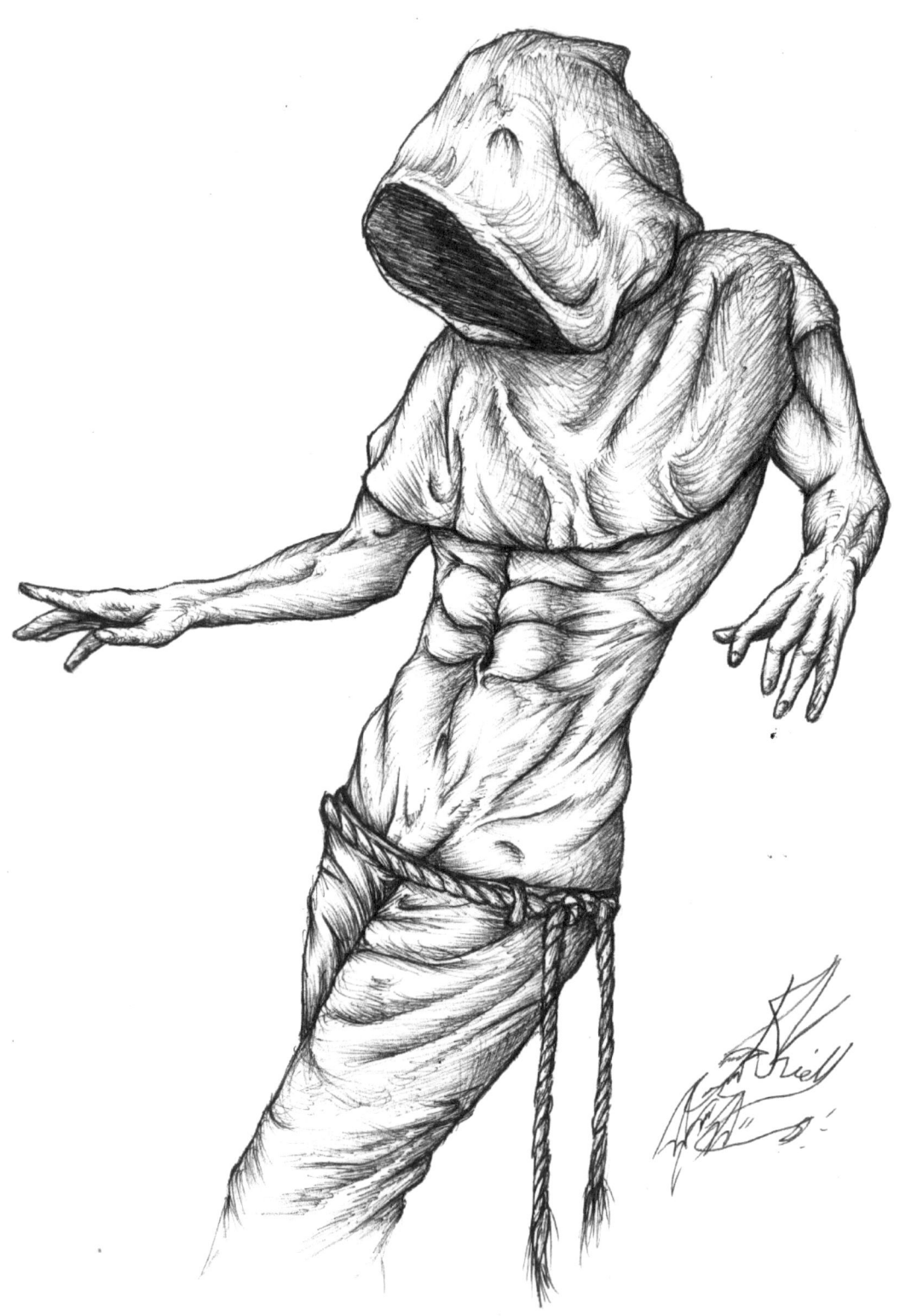

Holy Dancer

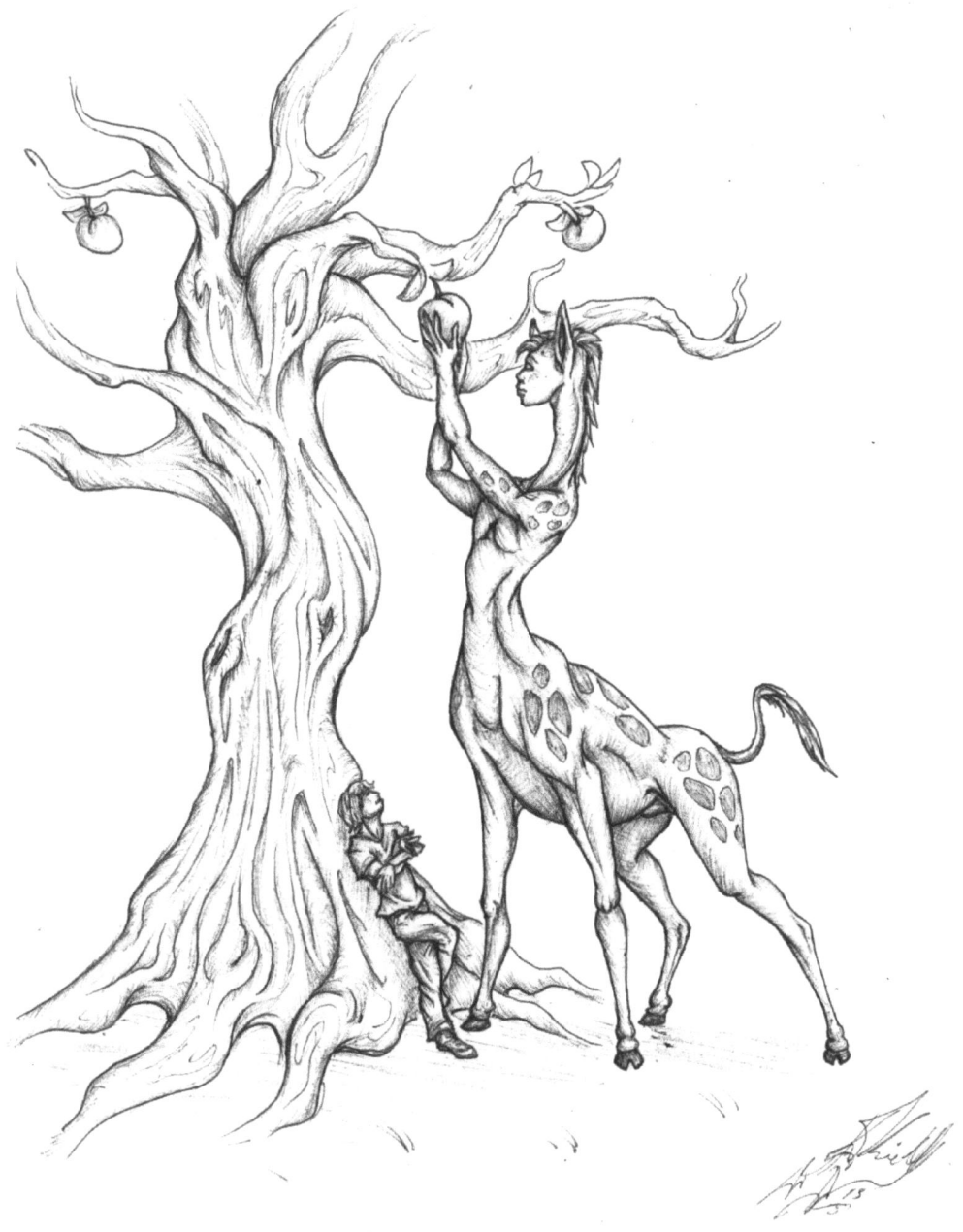

Plains Peach Tree

Here's an odd and unlikely pair, wanderers of some far away grasslands. There is a strong relationship between the tall and the small, it is useful to have one to watch the skies while the other watches your feet.

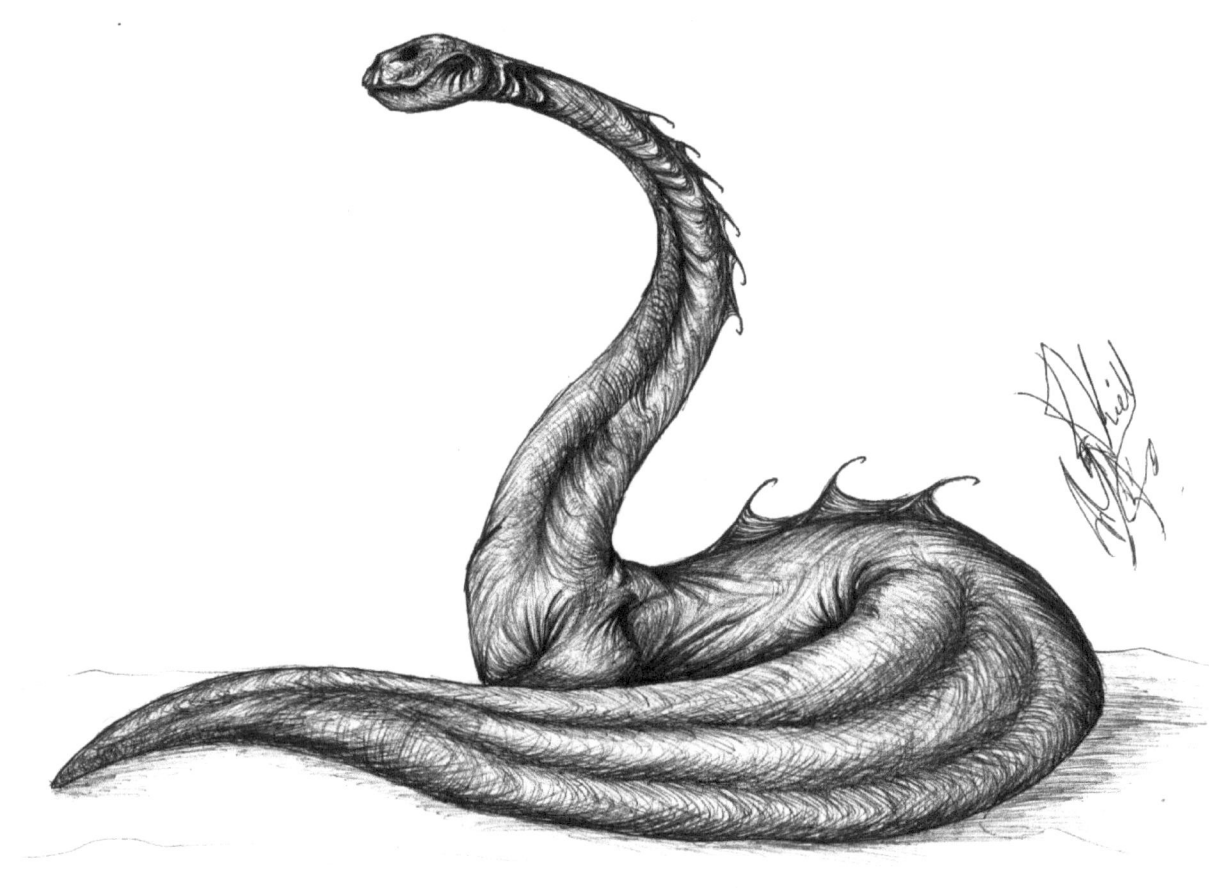

Nesse

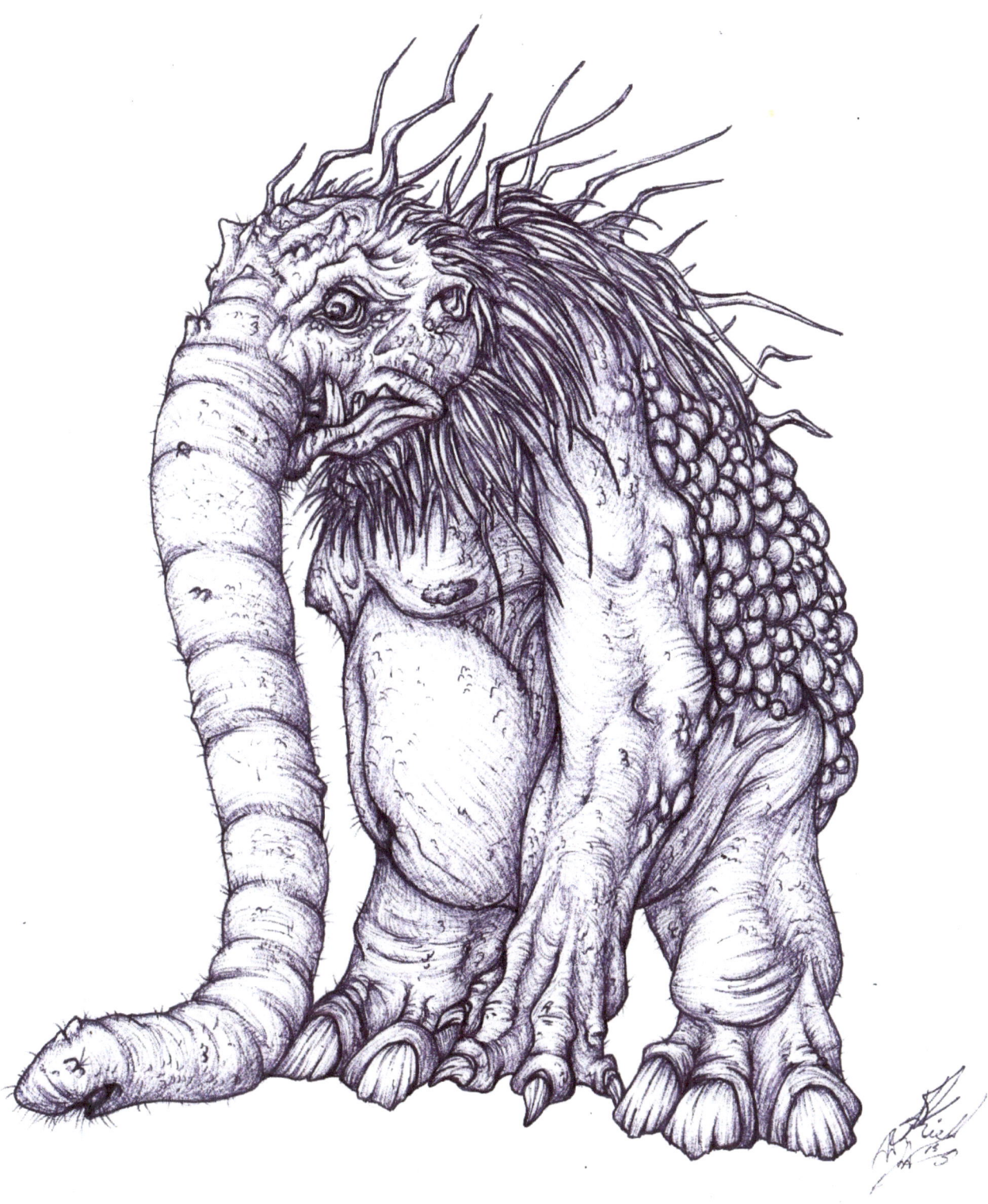

Snoz Troll

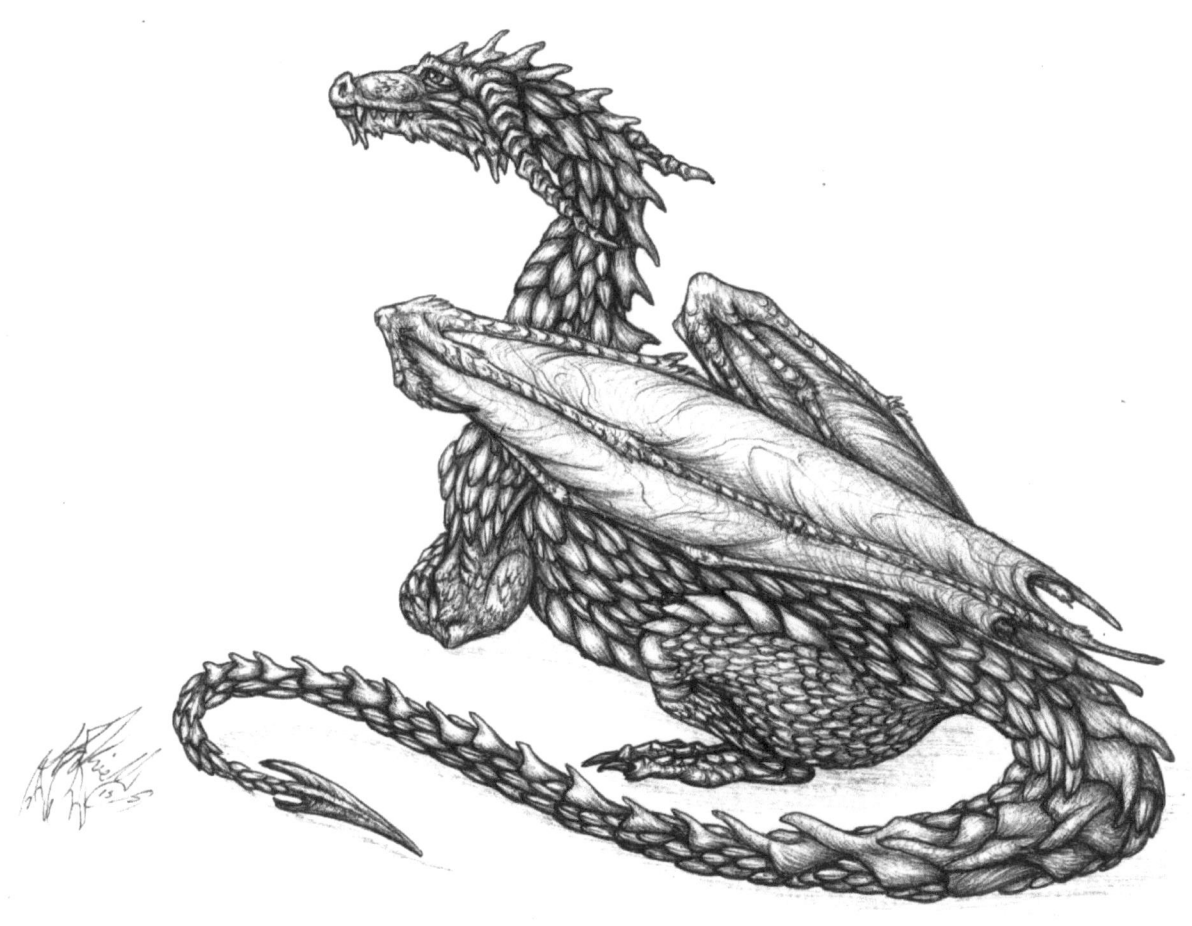

Droopy Horns

Poetry

Poetry is like a rose,

Layers upon Layers,

Rows upon rows.

Flint and Desire

Love is like fire struck from flint and desire,

Emotions like sparks rise higher and higher,

With sanity balanced on the thinnest of wire.

You and I

Why should I forsake the sky,

Unless my wings refuse to fly,

Pound the ground with weary feet,

Your doom a day you walk to meet,

There is little difference between you and I,

We all lay upon the dirt to die.

The Eye

Come fall with me,

Beneath the trees,

To the lark and buzz of birds and bees,

There lies an eye that ever sees,

In the secret love beneath the trees,

On moss cradled knees,

Hidden by the budding leaves,

There lies a secret need,

Beneath the trees,

Where only the eye of love ever sees.

Alight on me

Sing in the sun,

Feather in the air,

Whistling beauty so small and fair,

Alight on me and shelter from the breeze,

Raise a tune high and sweet,

Lift the spirits from winter, mourning for the spring,

Come home from the seas, nestle softly in the trees,

Warm in the sweet life and joyful as you sing.

Part 3
Coloured Work

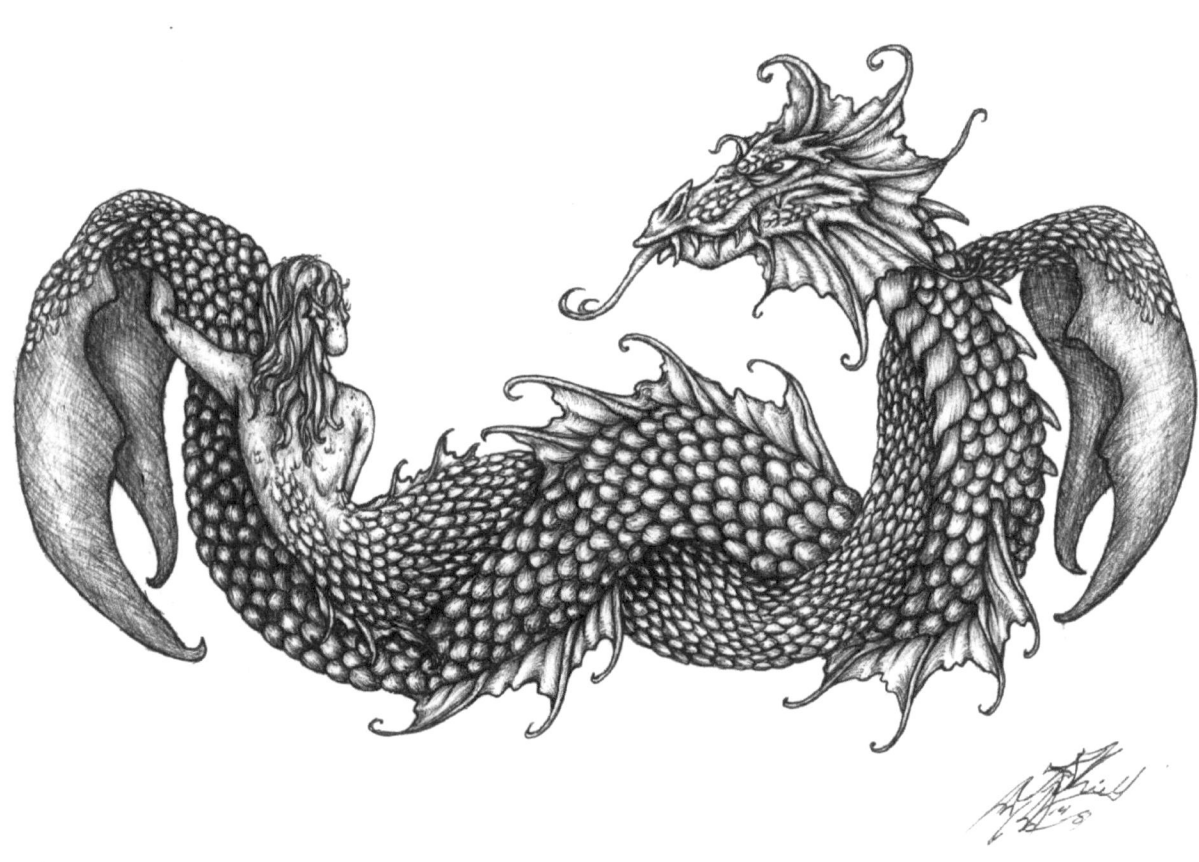

Unda

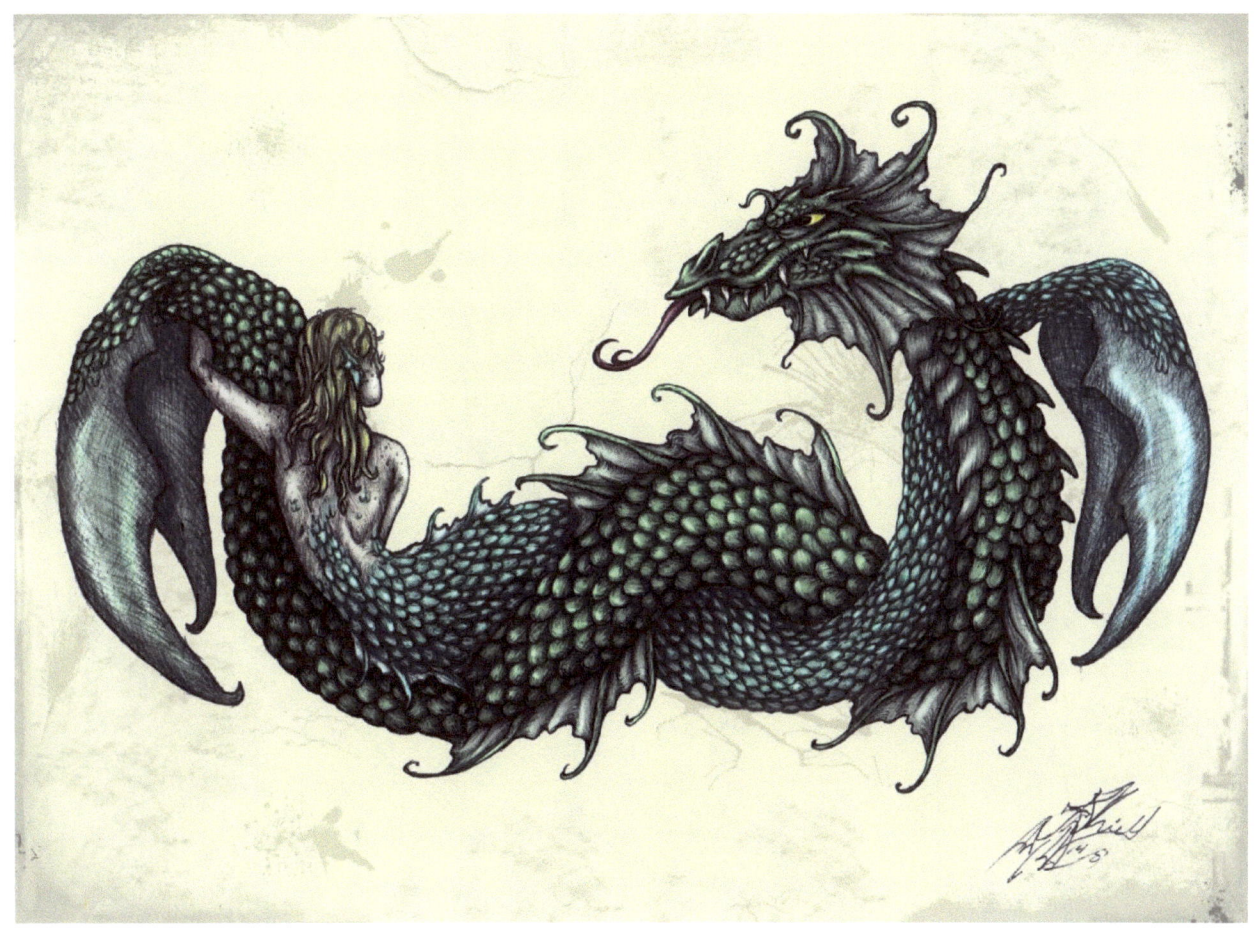

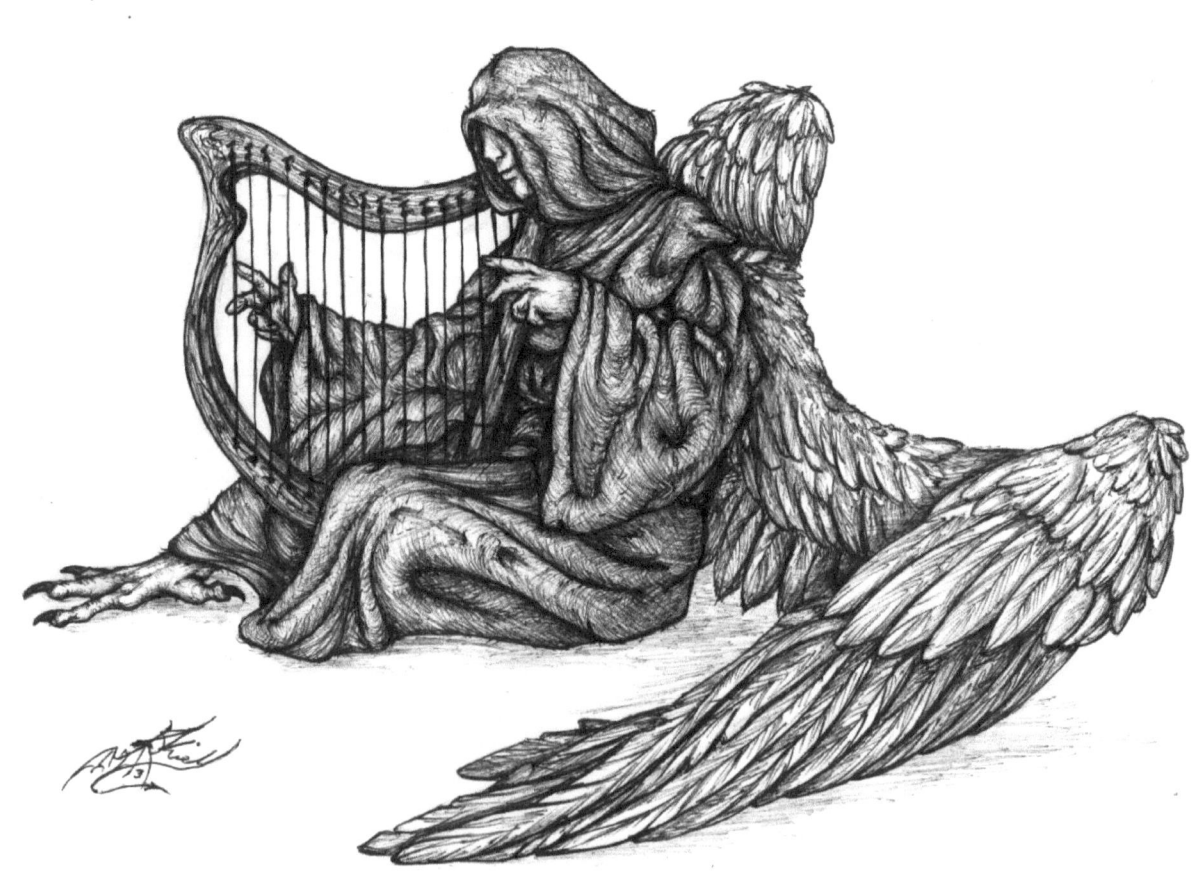

Brother Harpist

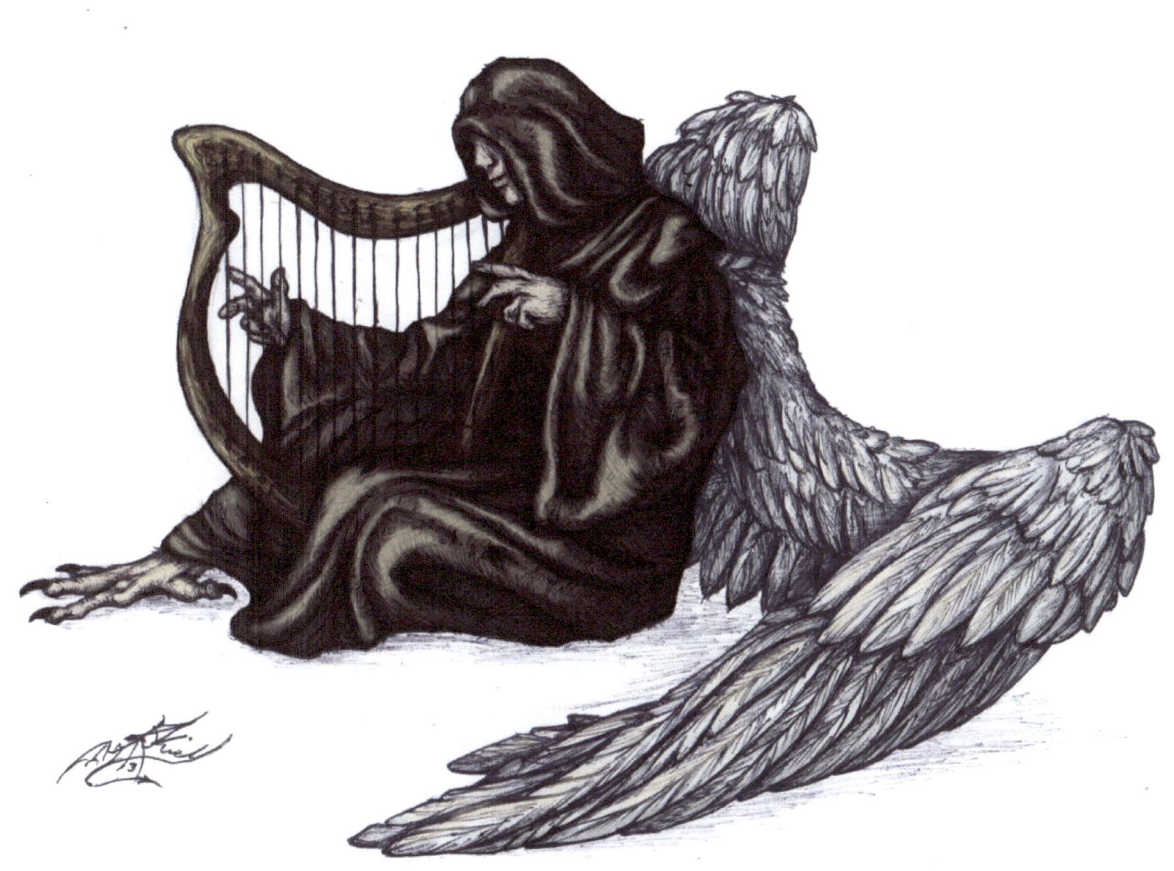

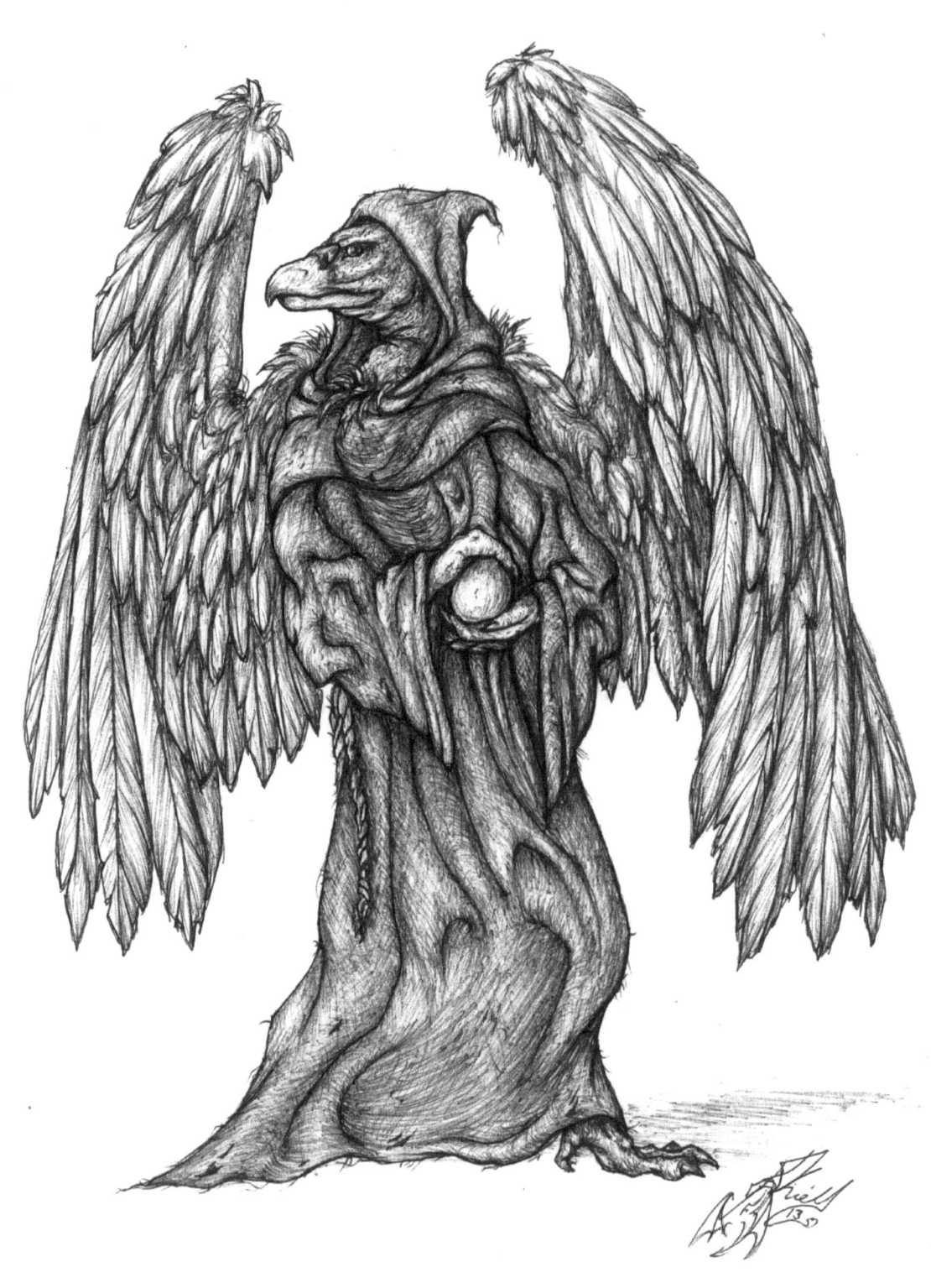

Monk Vulture

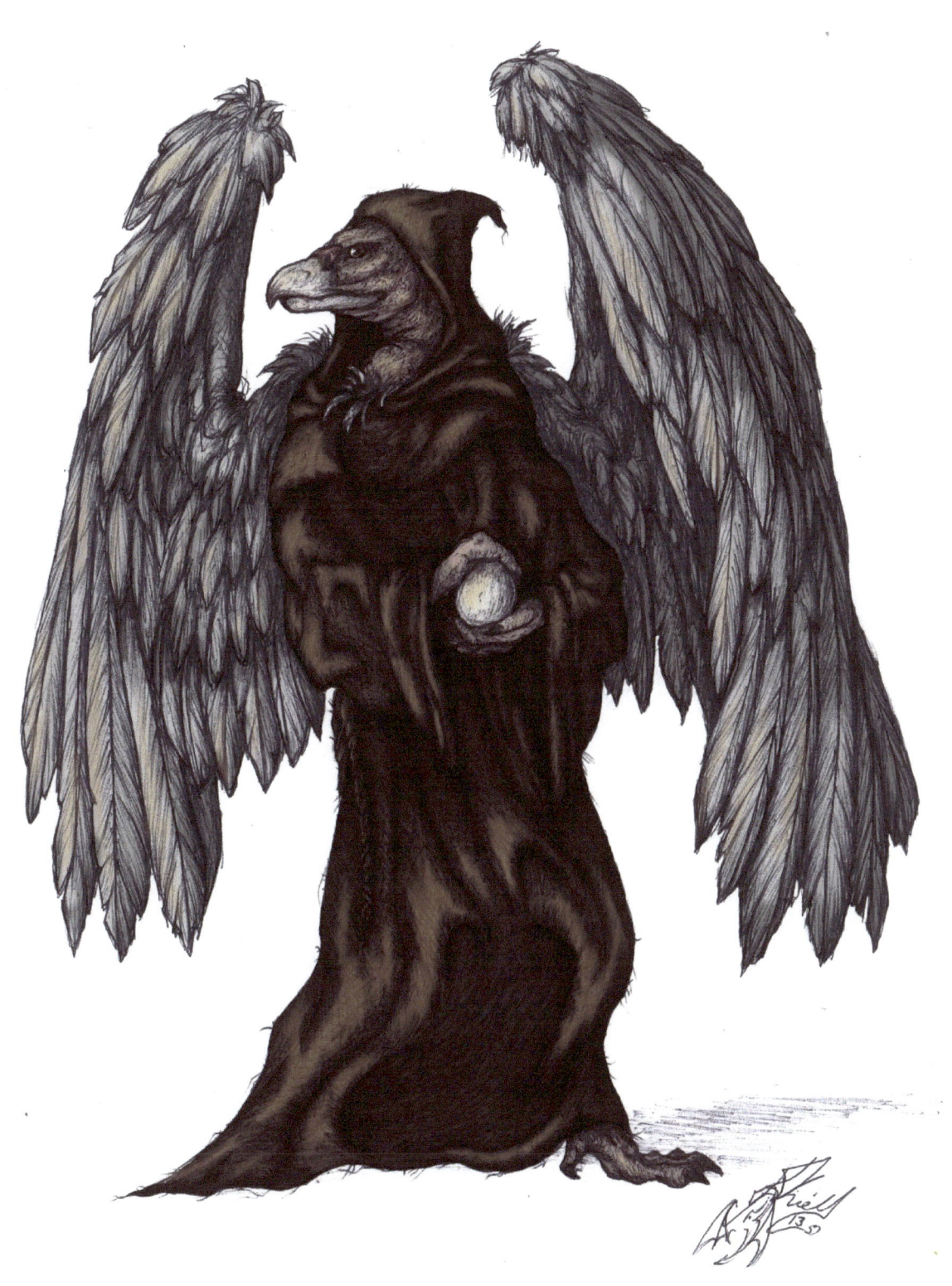

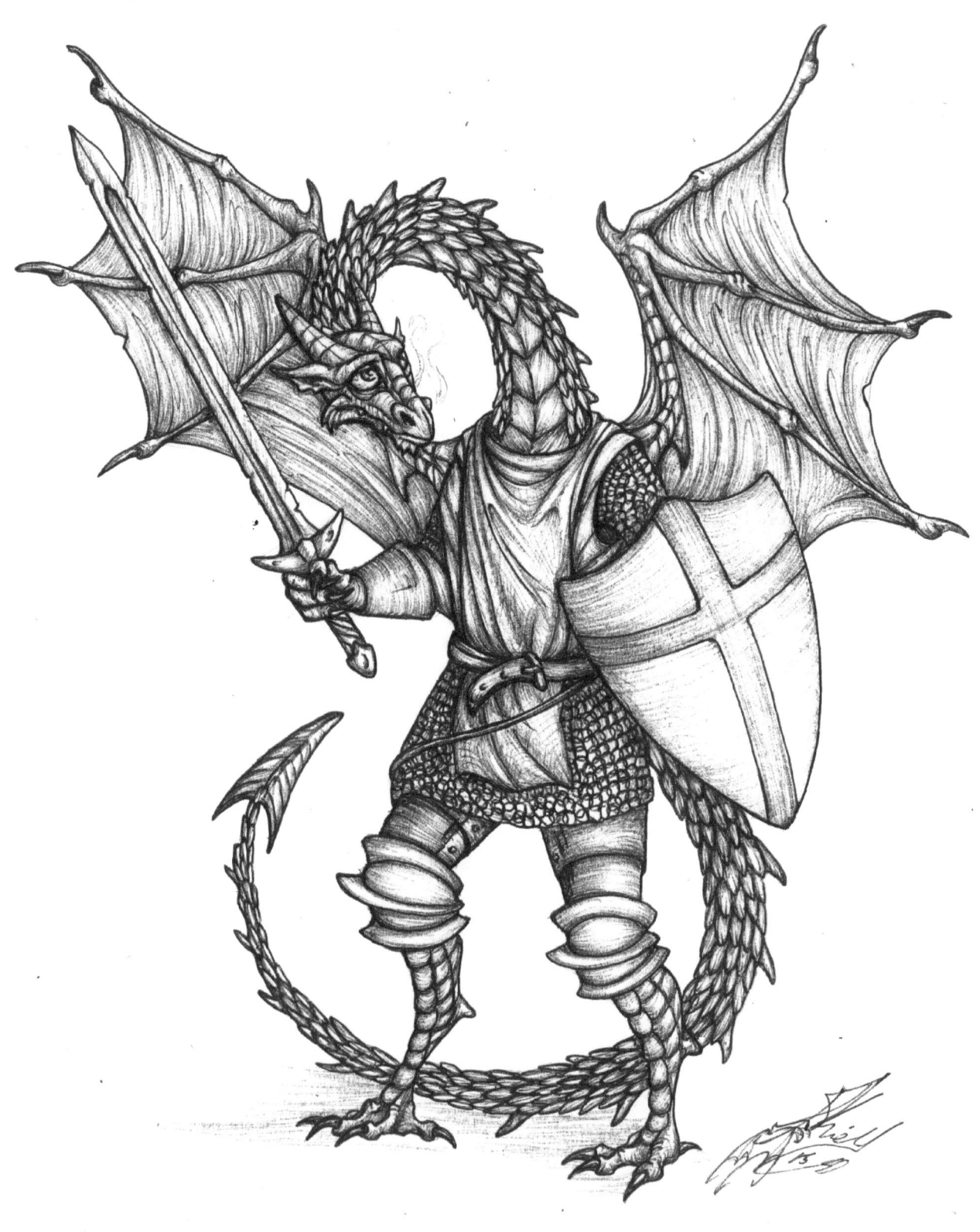

Draconic Knight

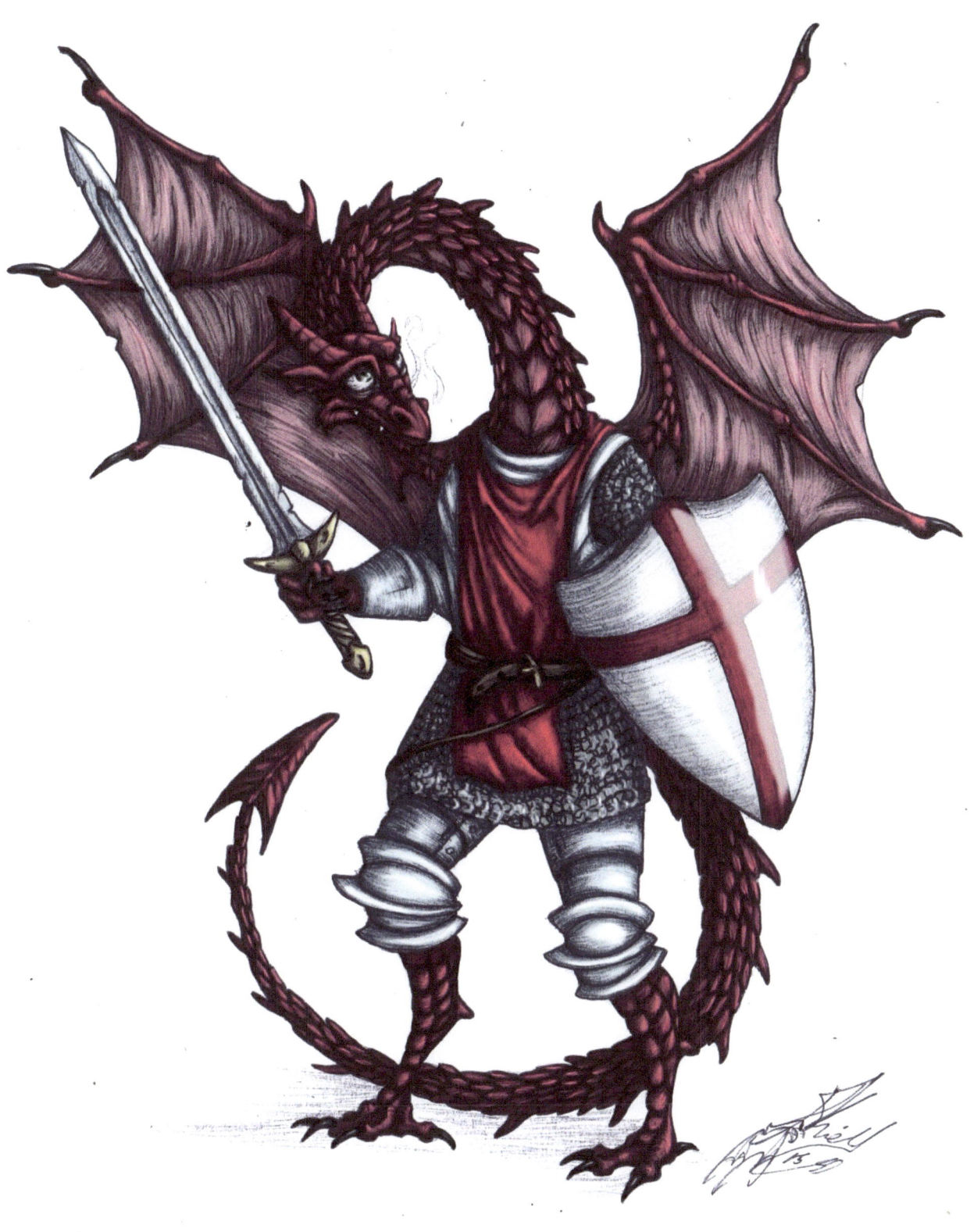

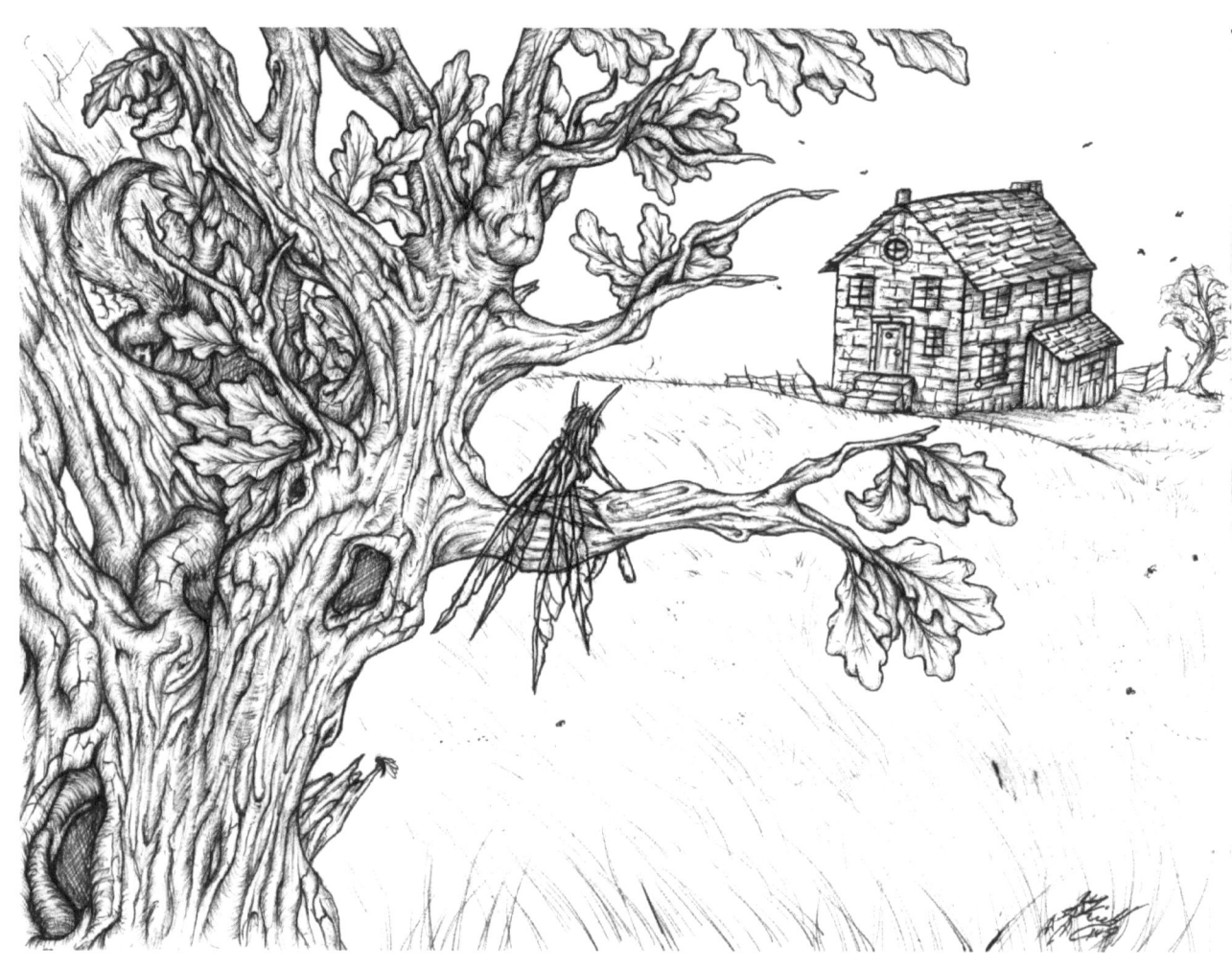

Turnip's Tale

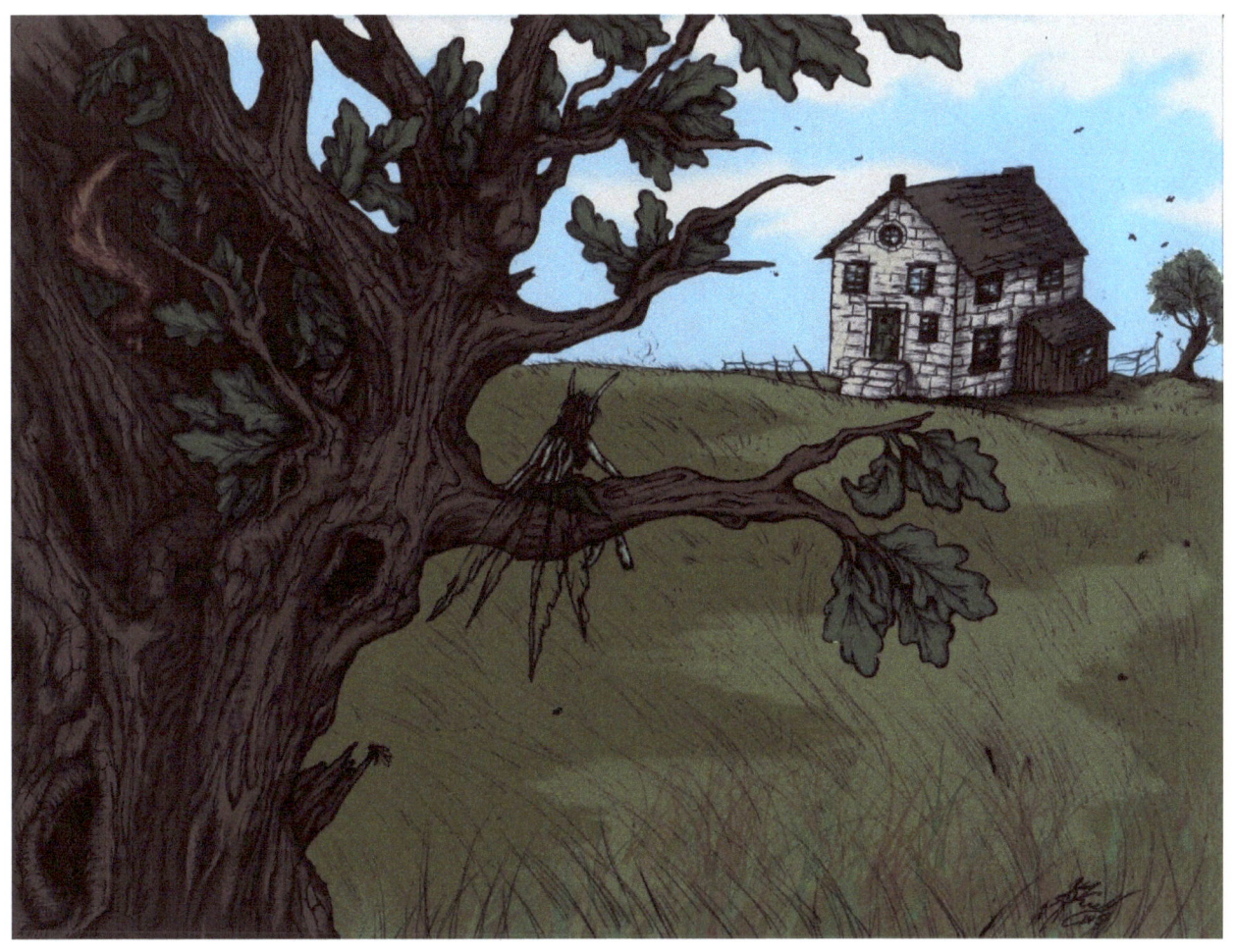

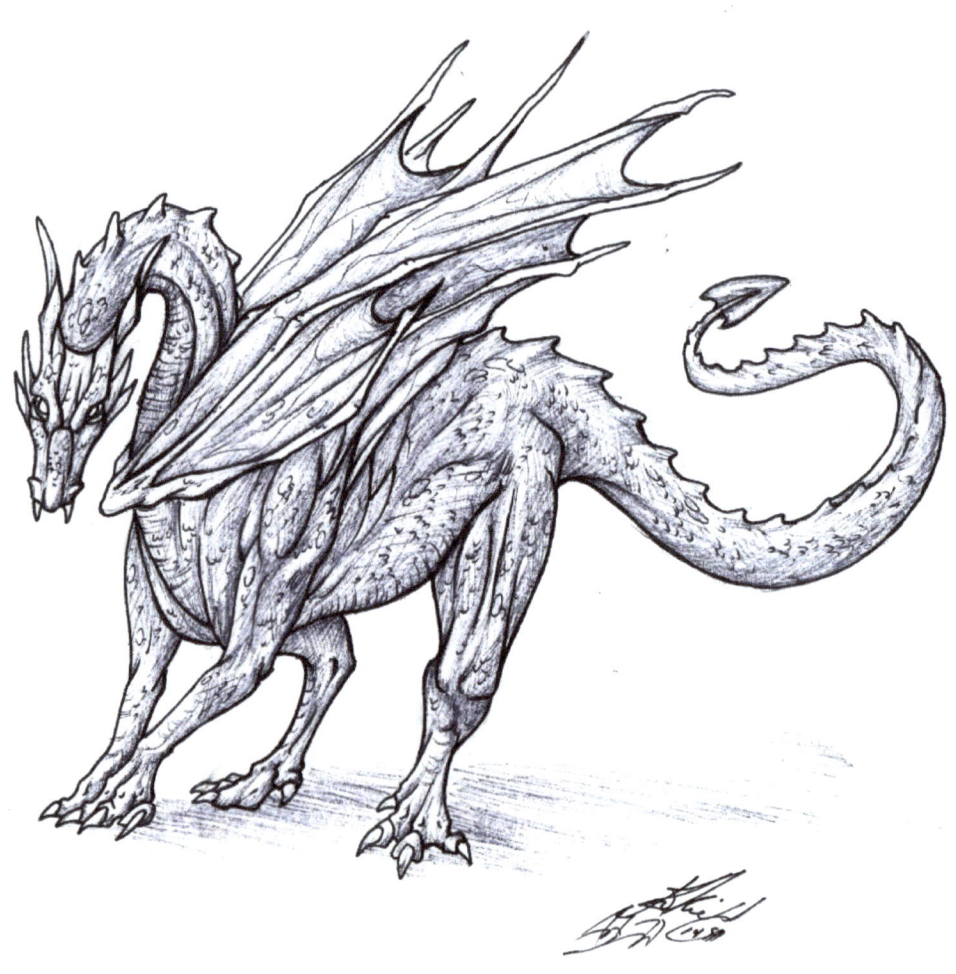

Golden Dragon

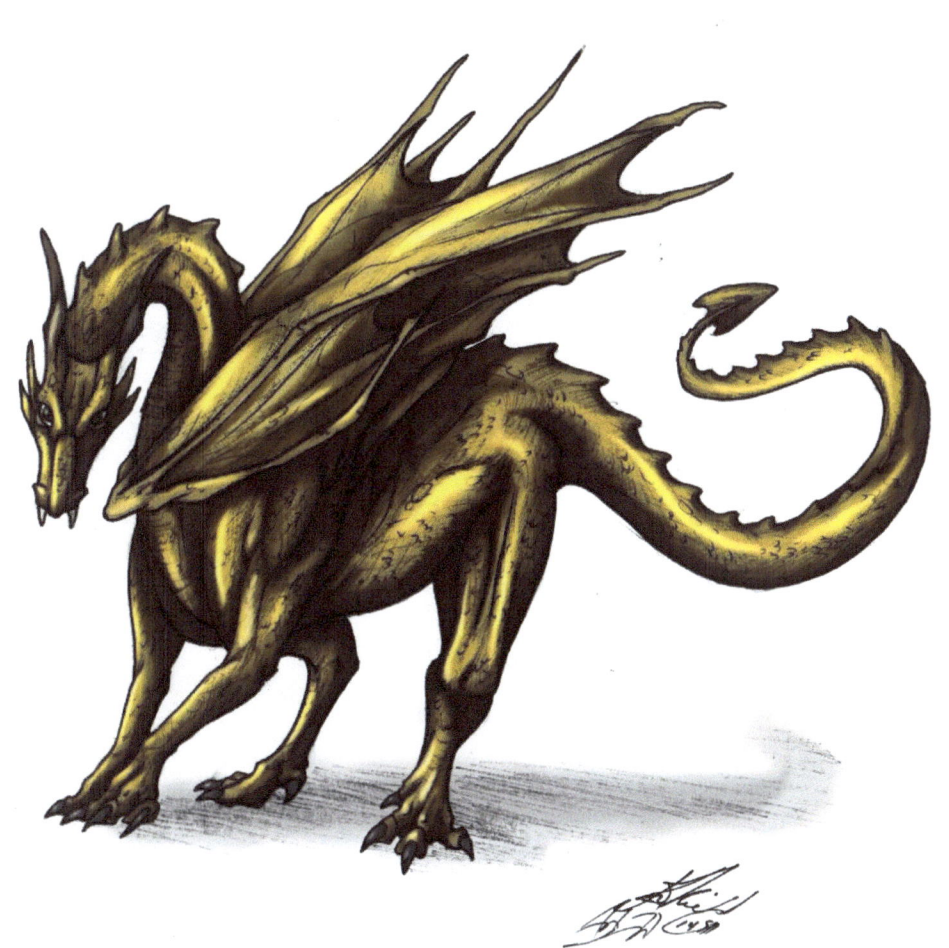

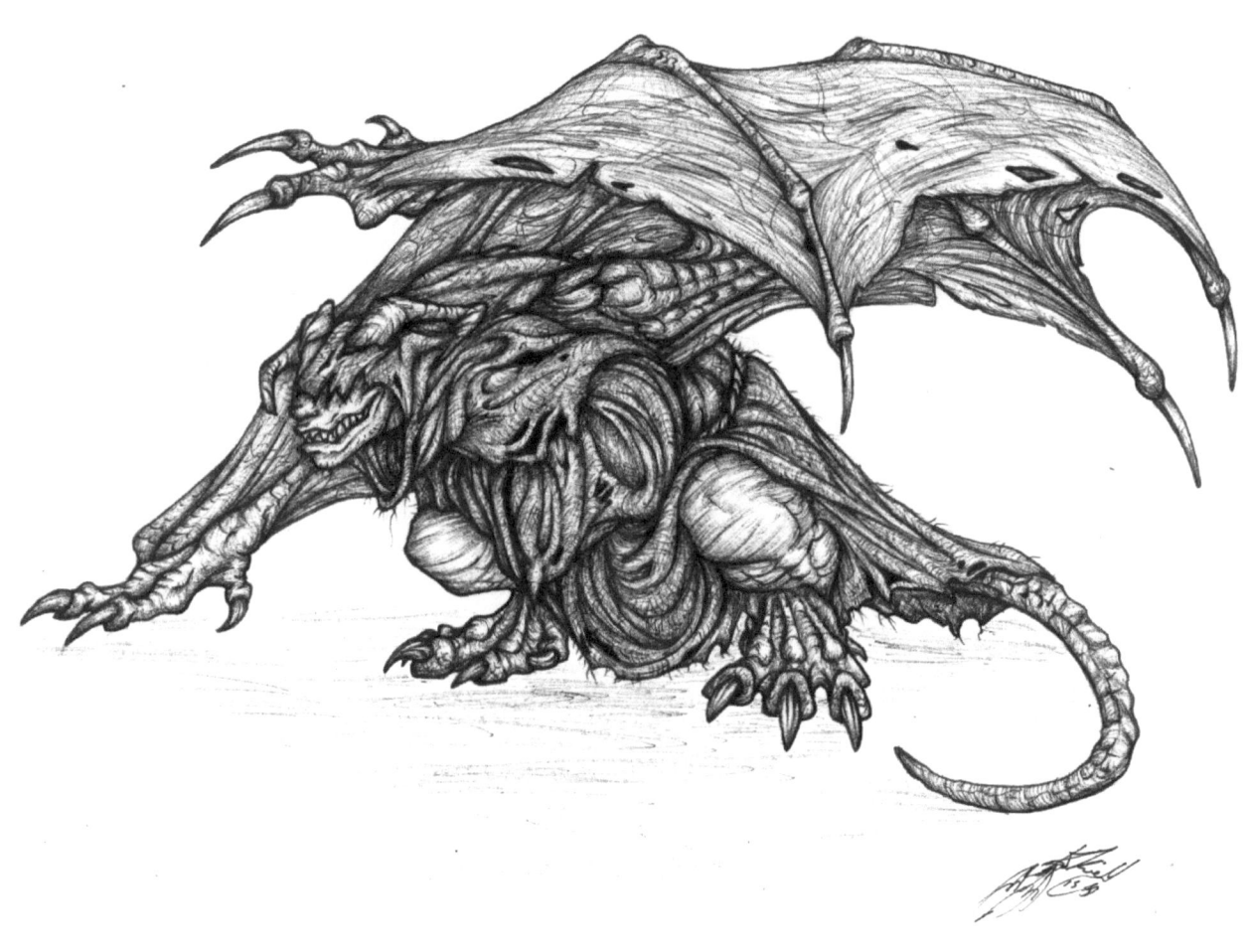

Ascended Dragon Cultist

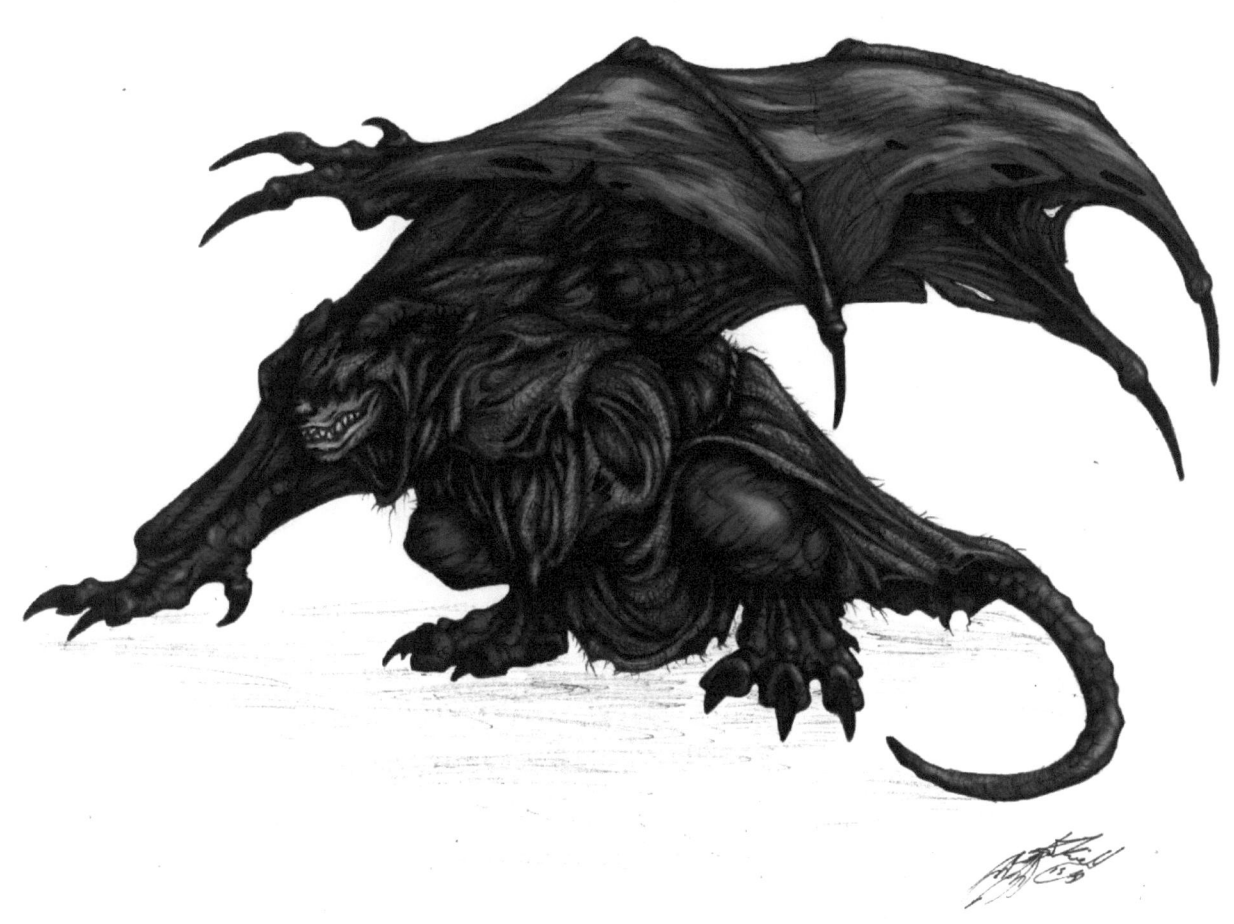

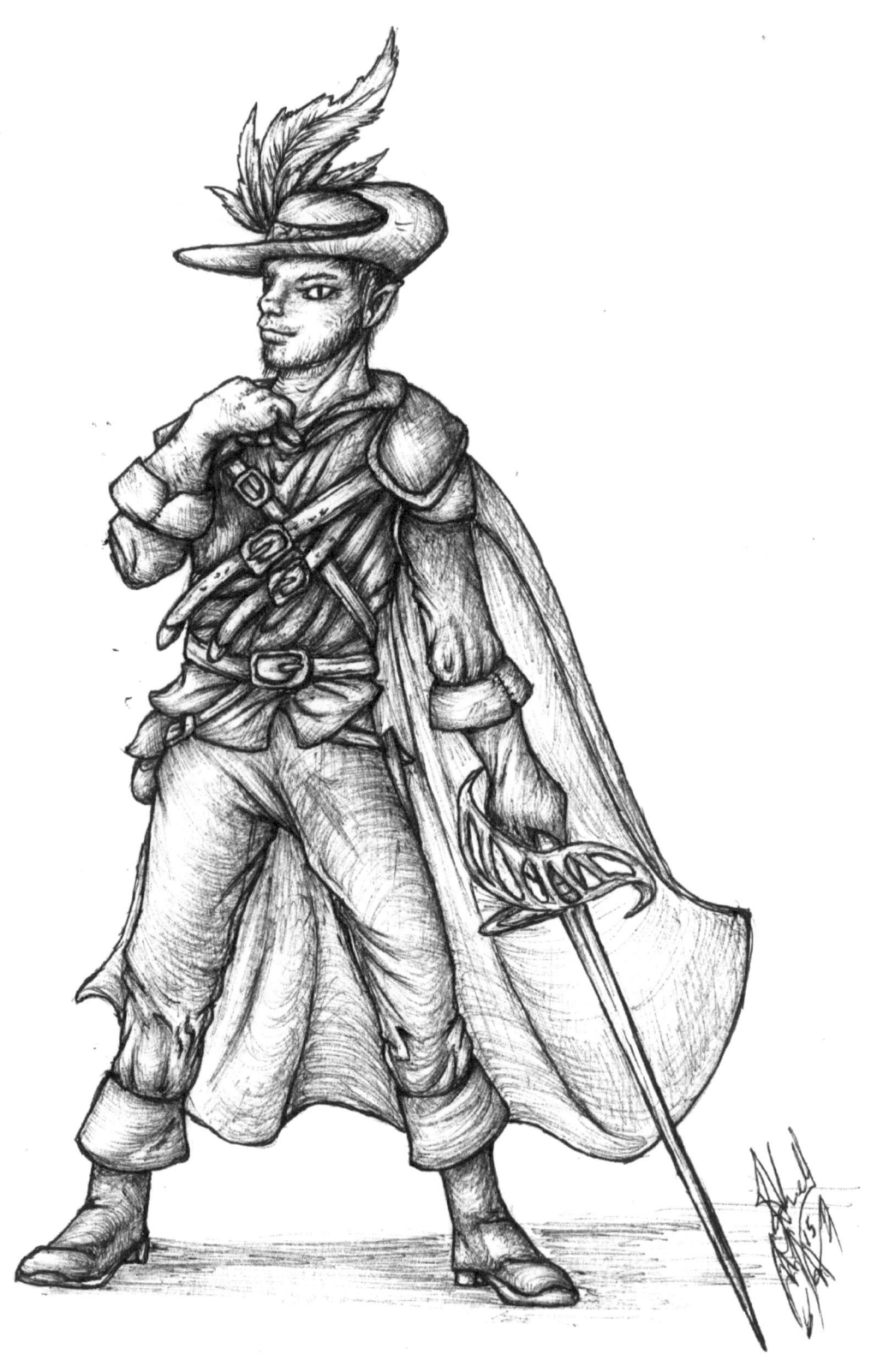

Lanethill

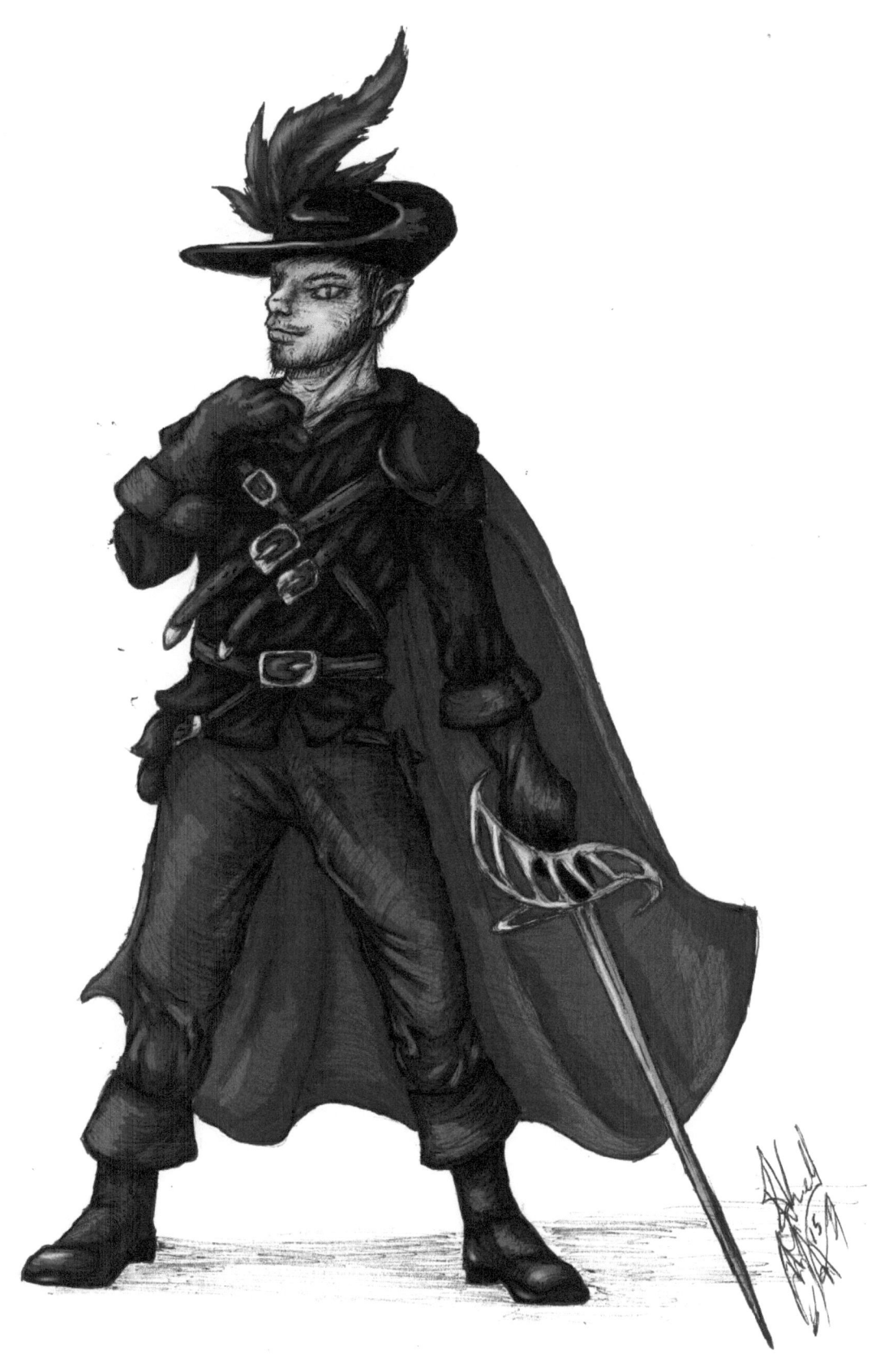

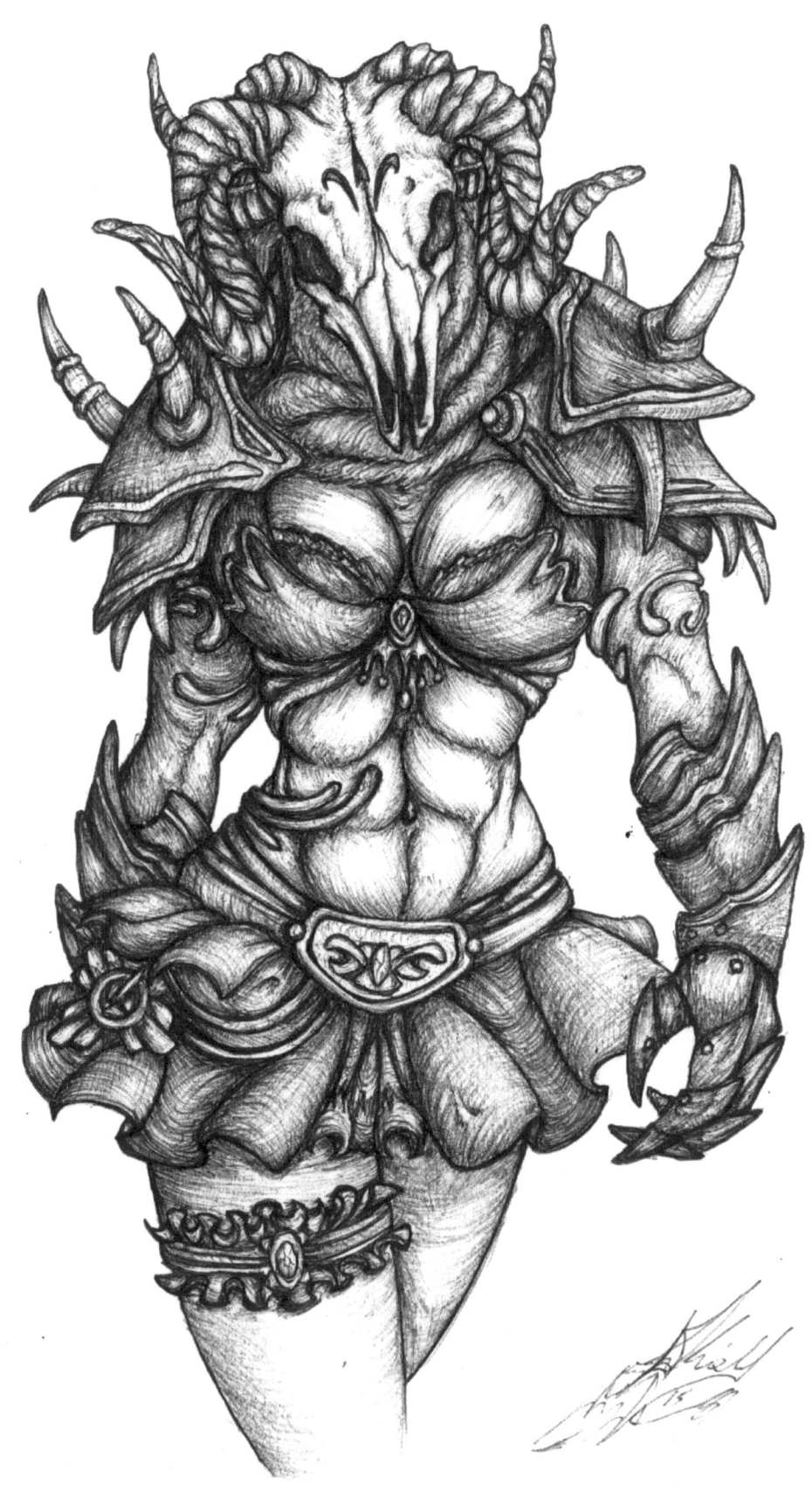

Deleese

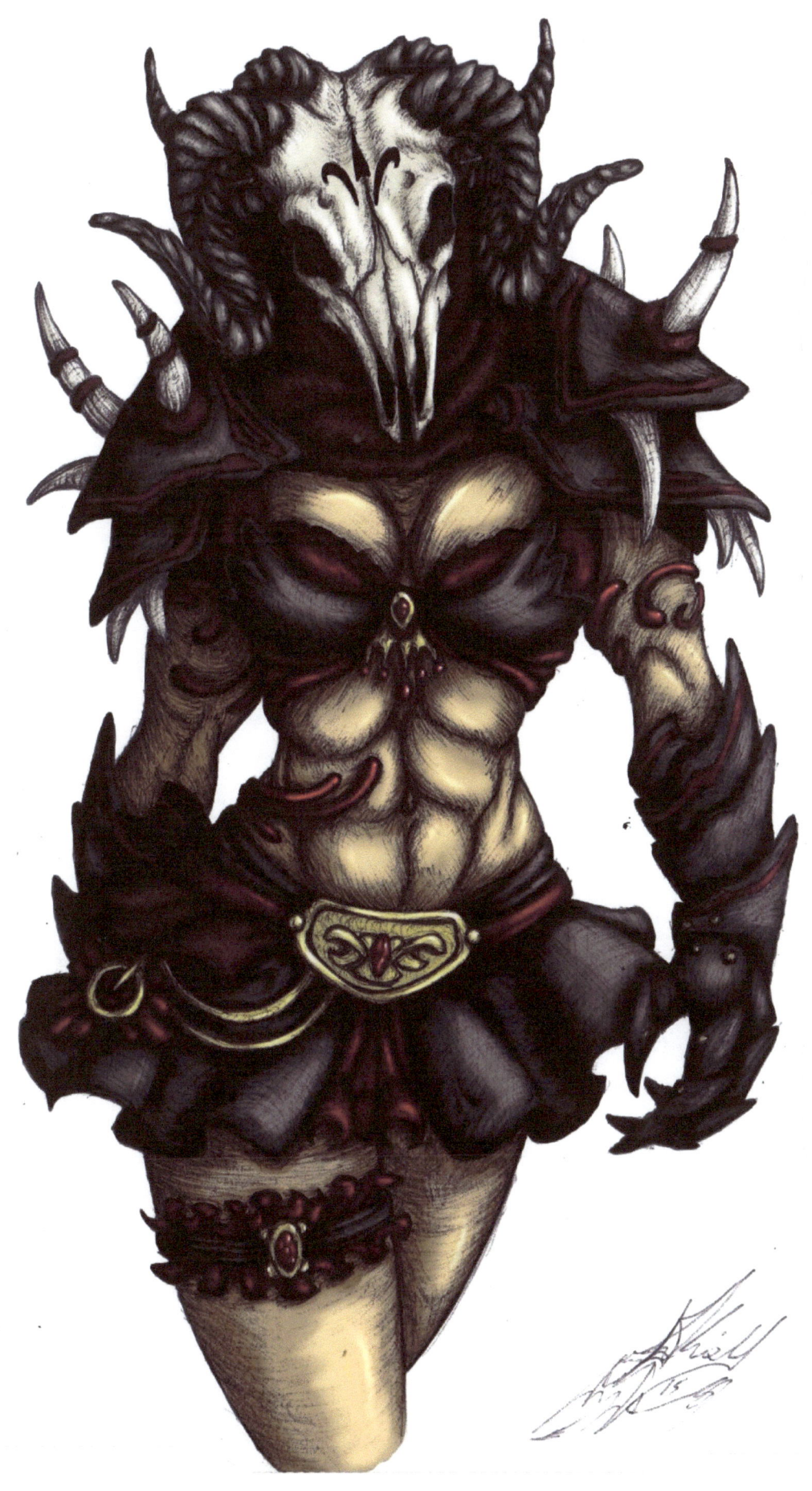

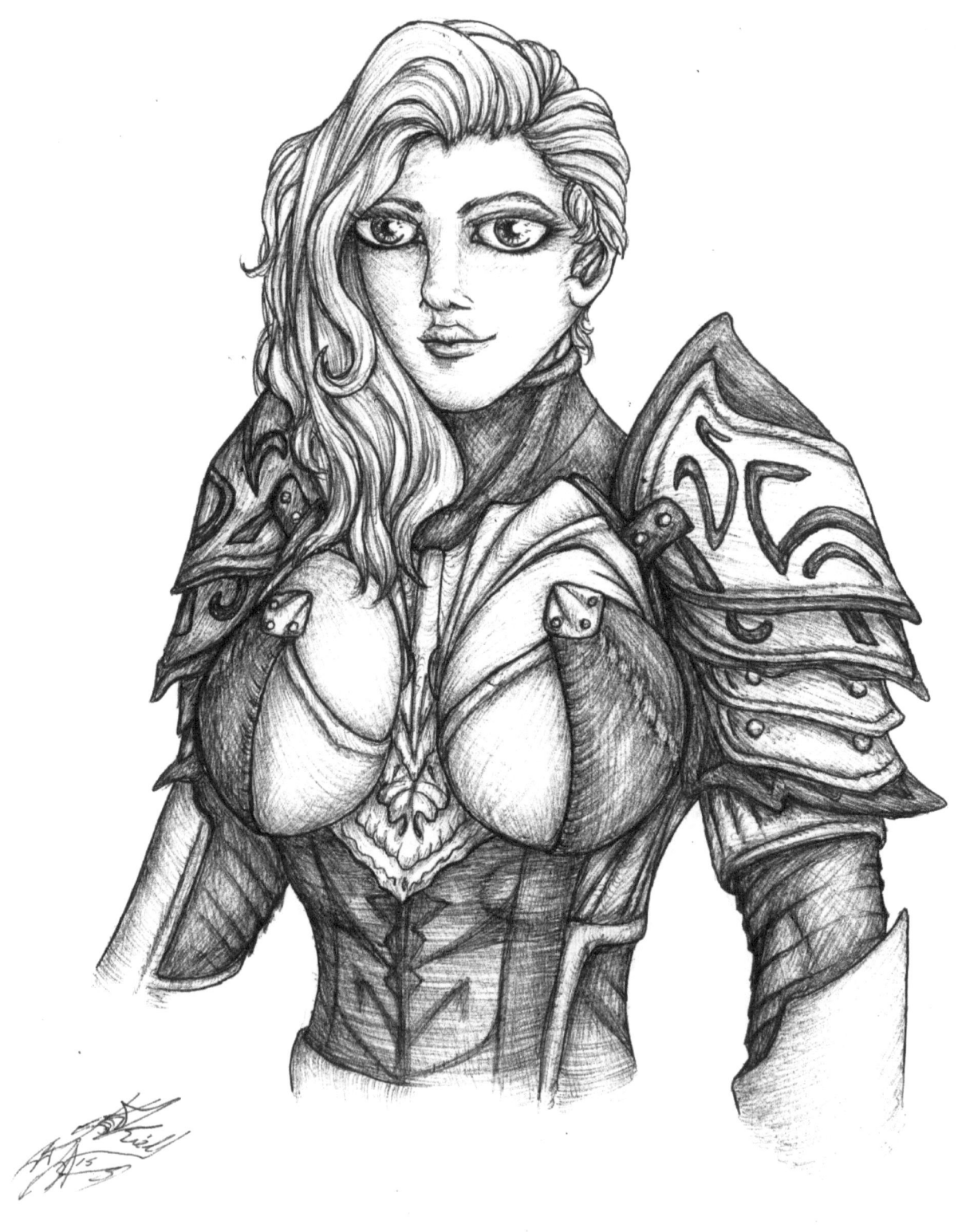

Bella

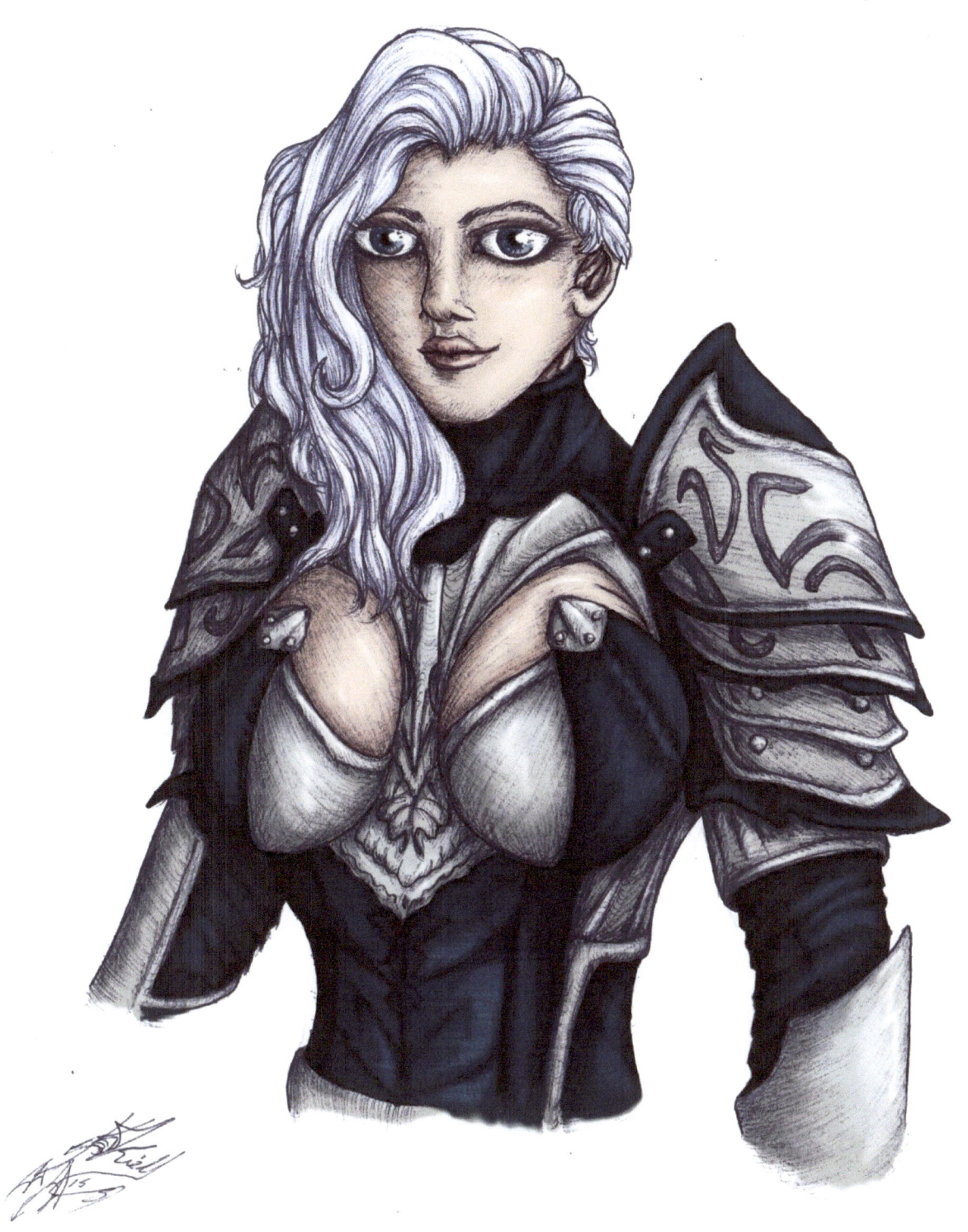

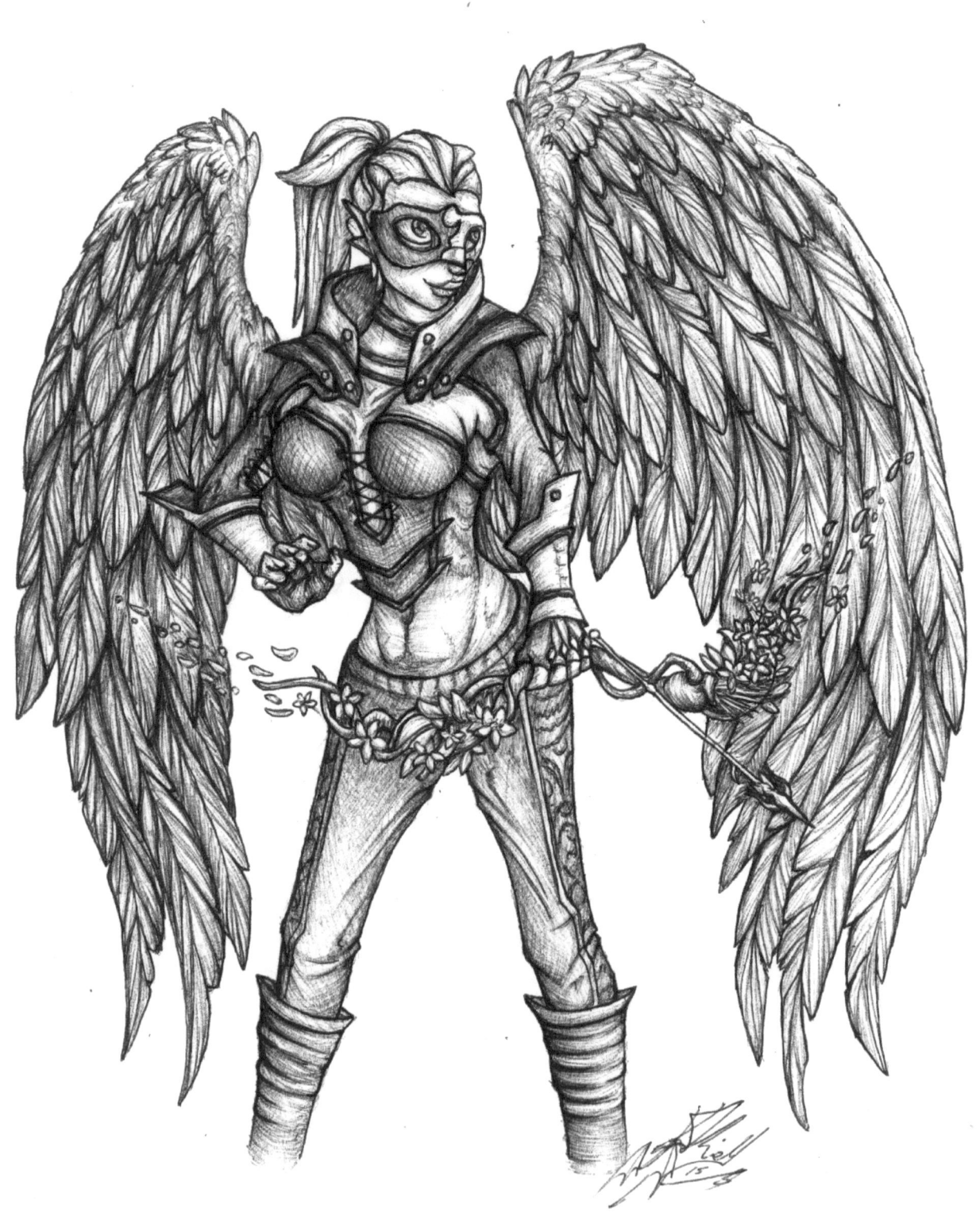

Sass

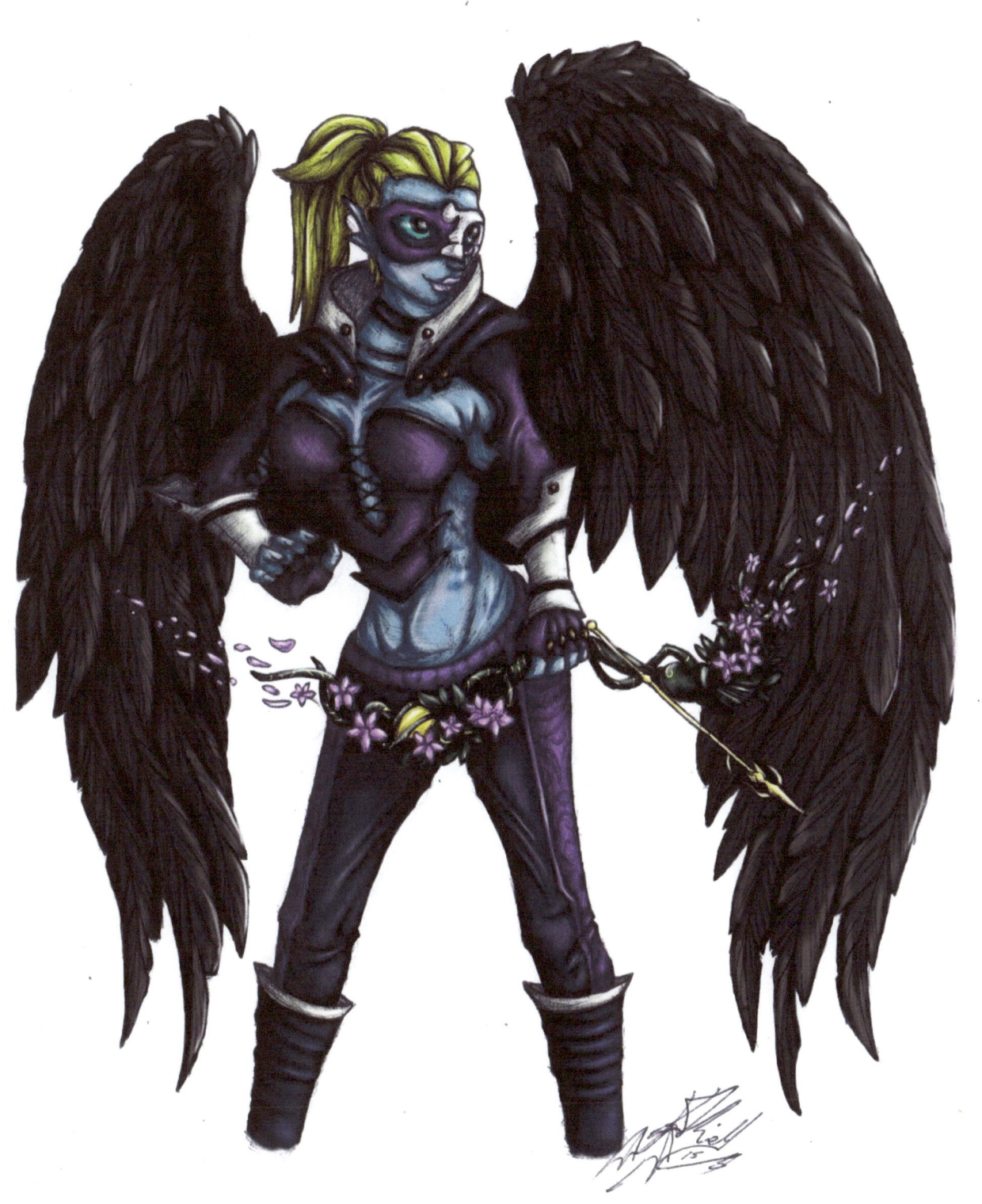

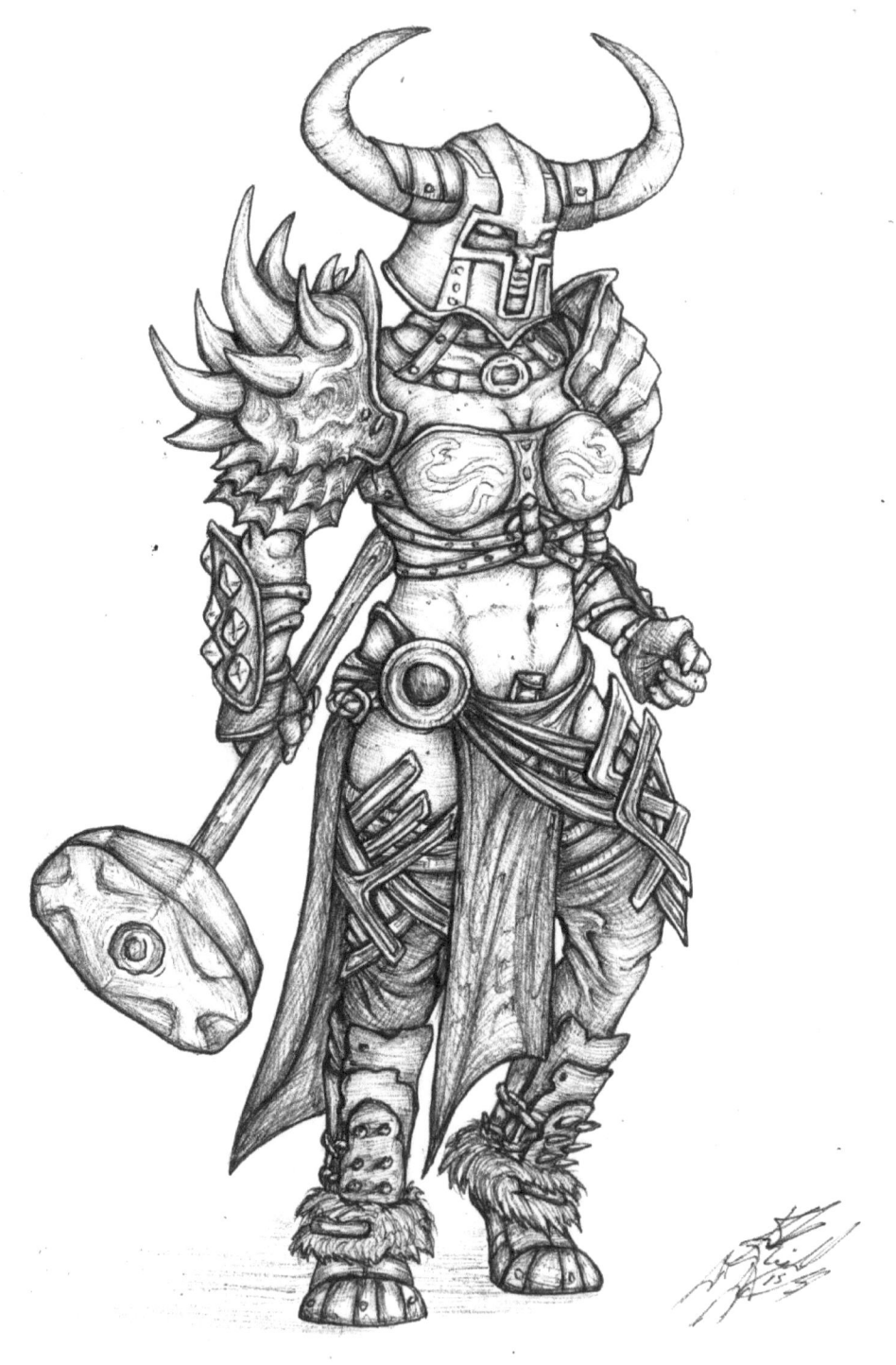

Ogress Natlout

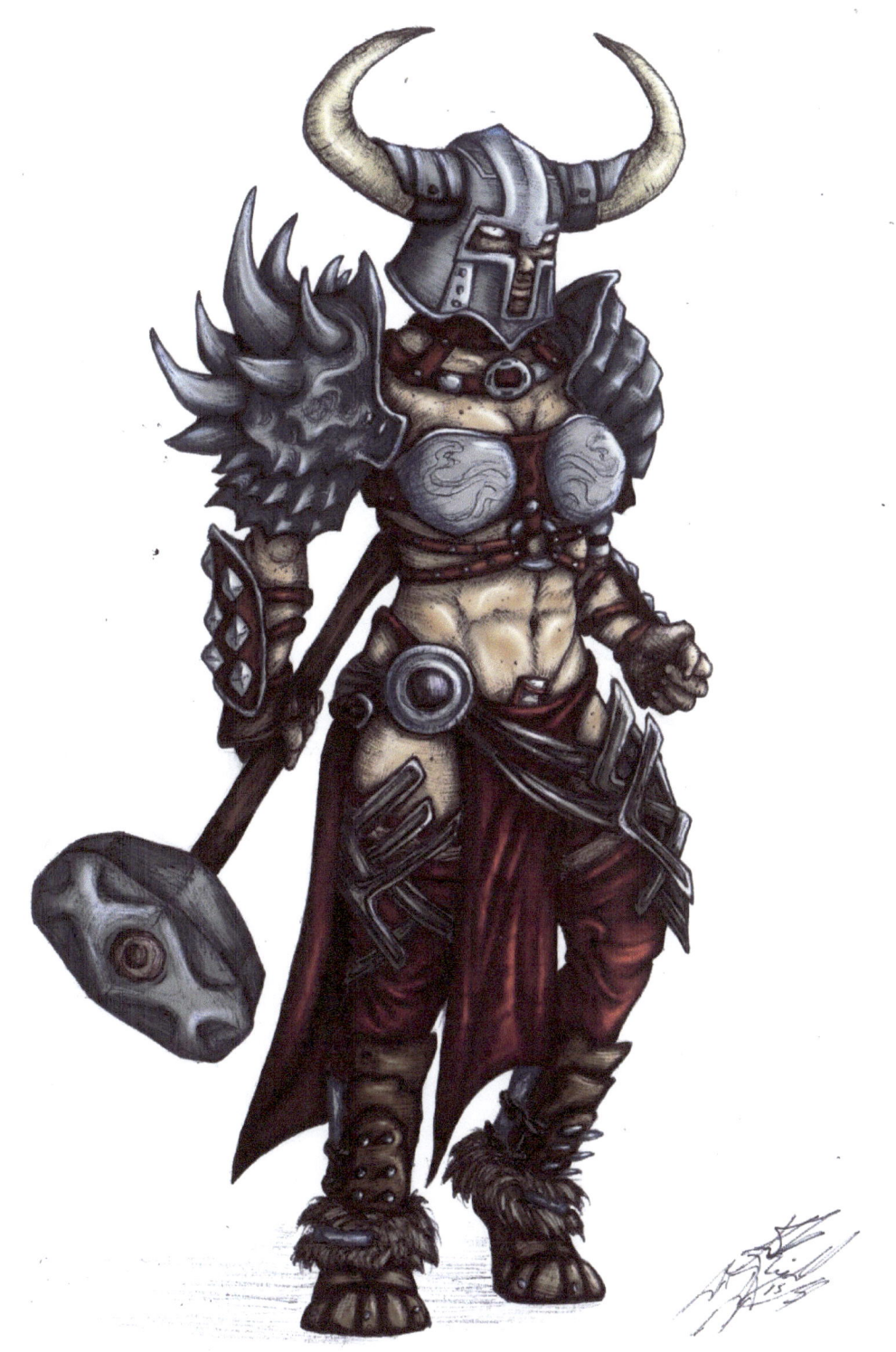

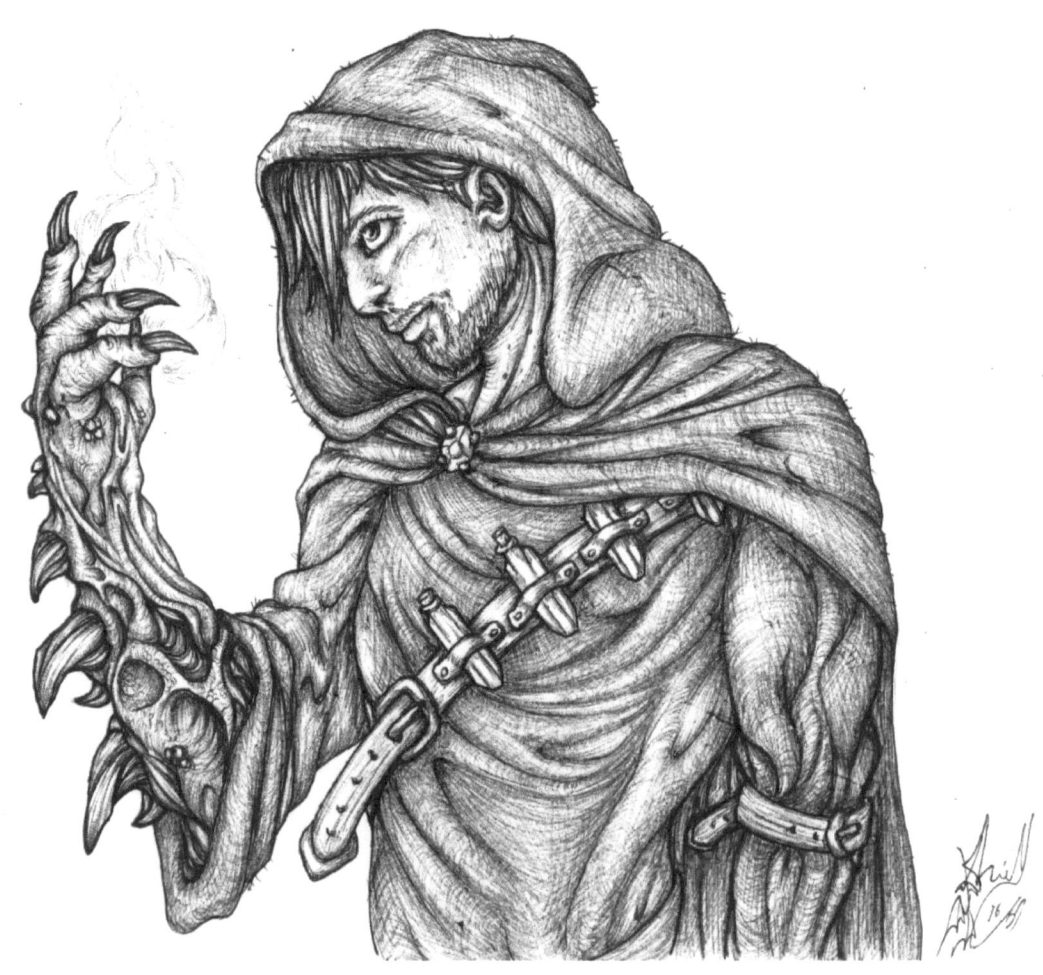

Necromancer Ossoono

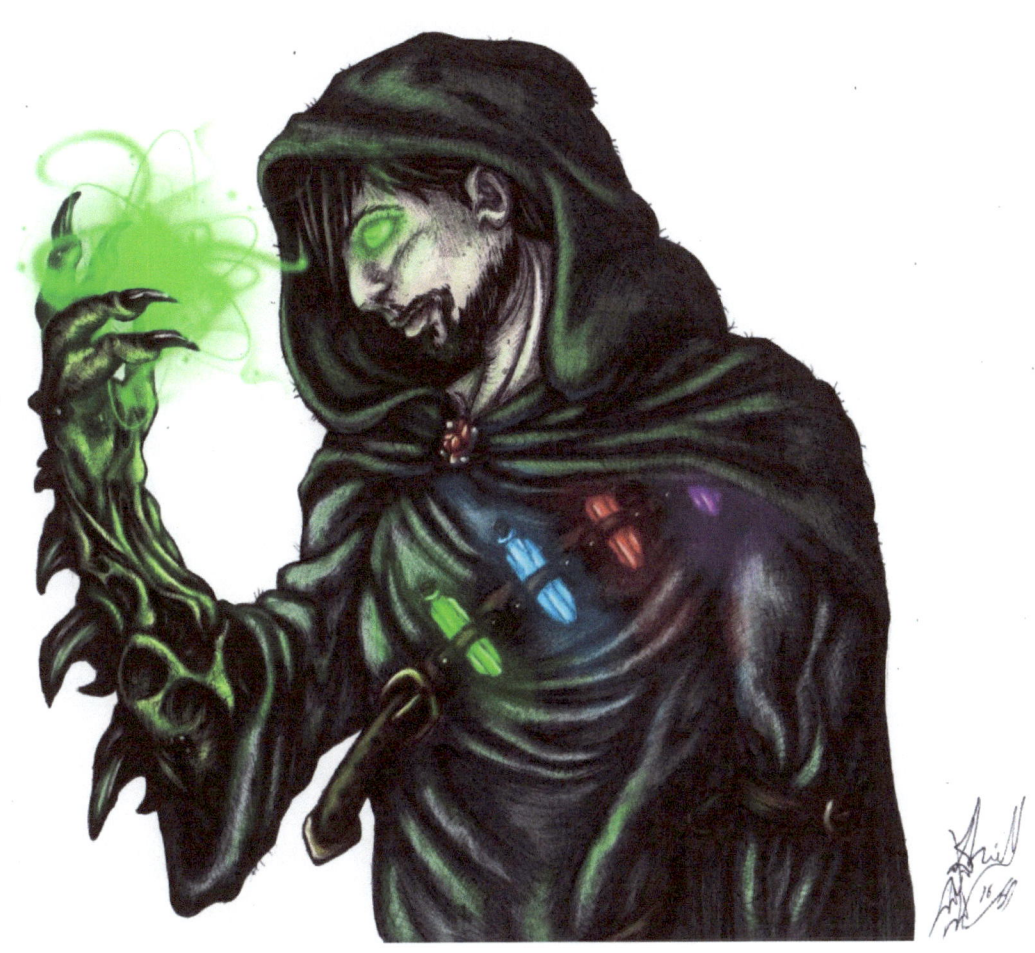

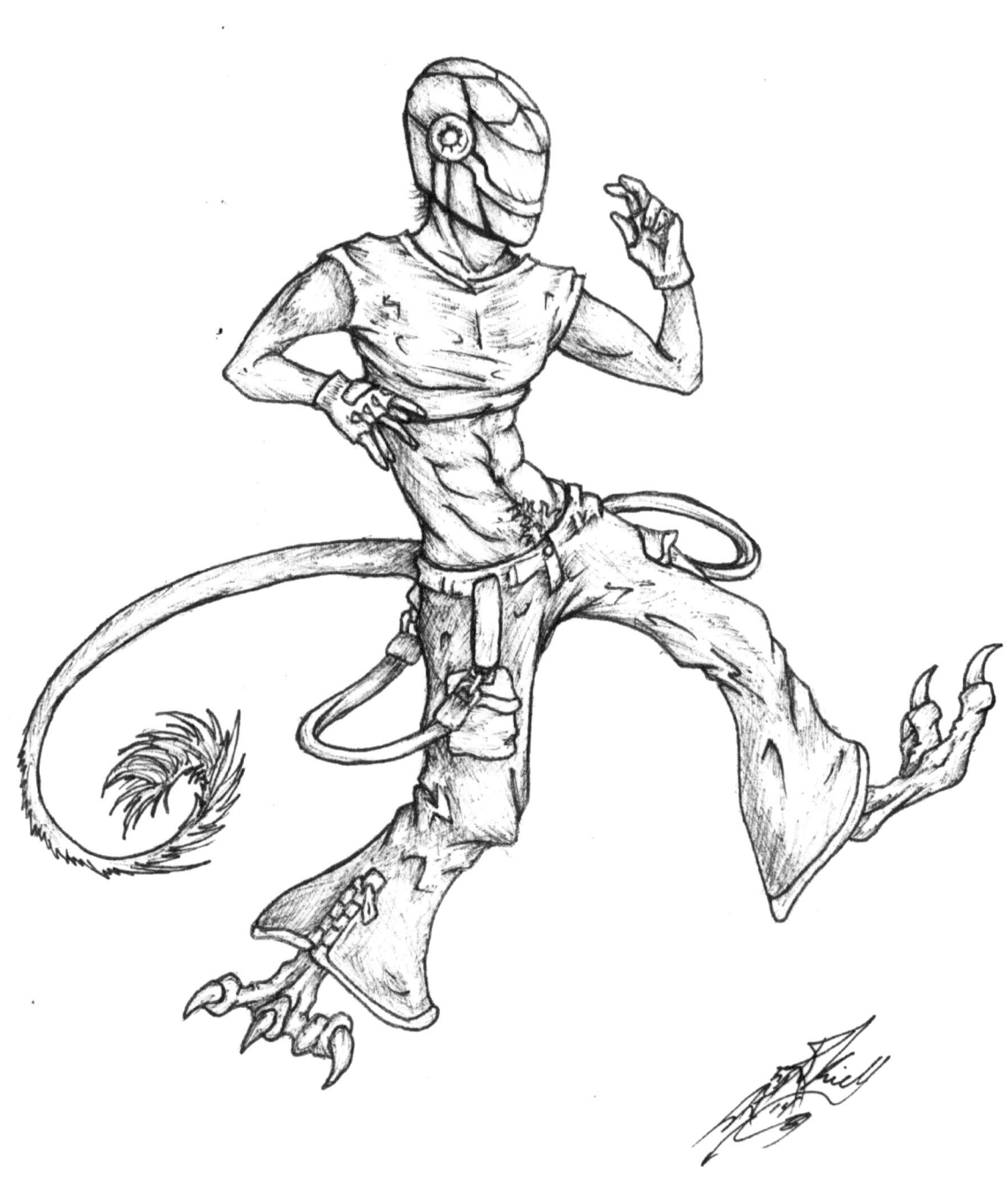

Jumpstyle

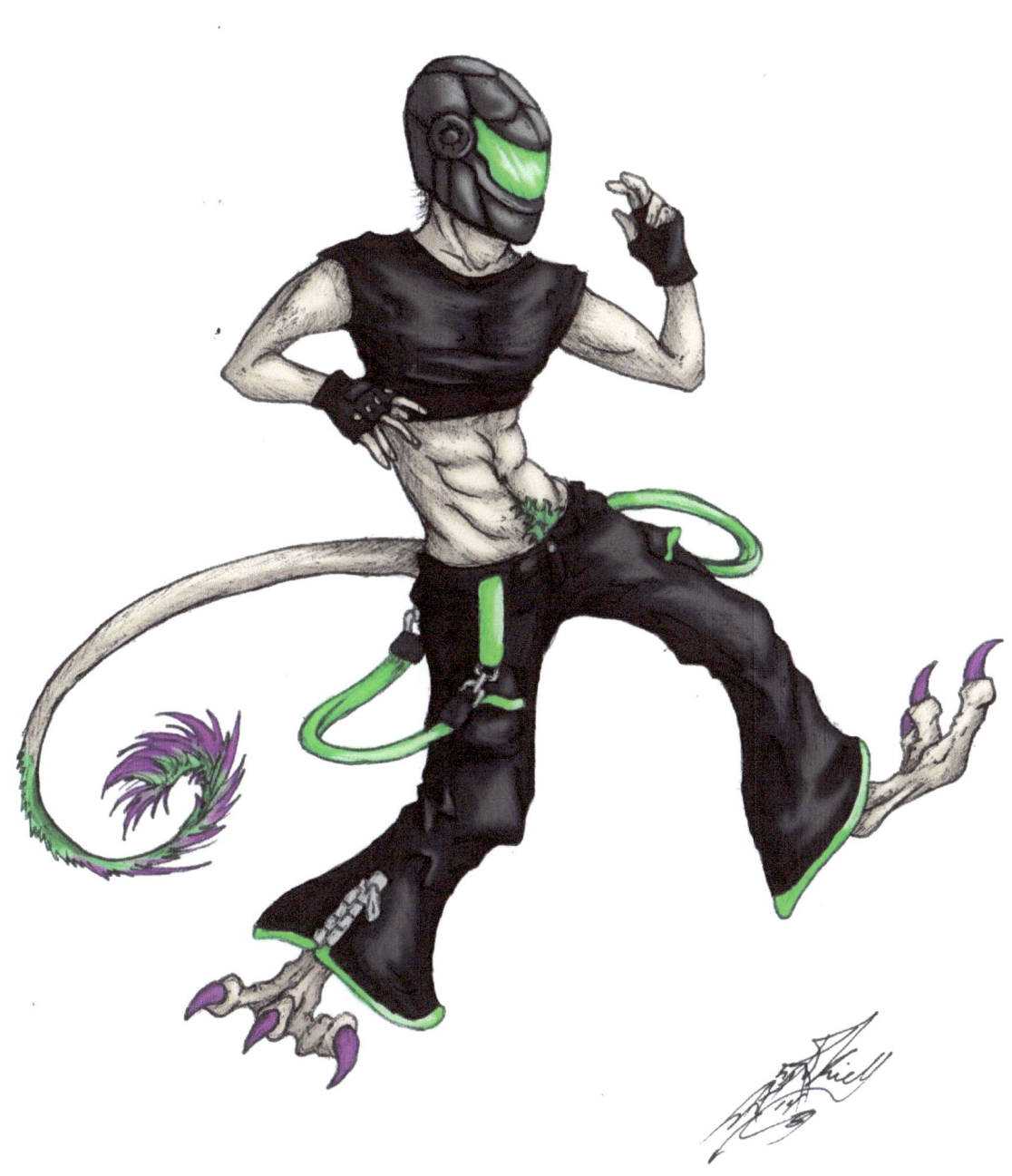

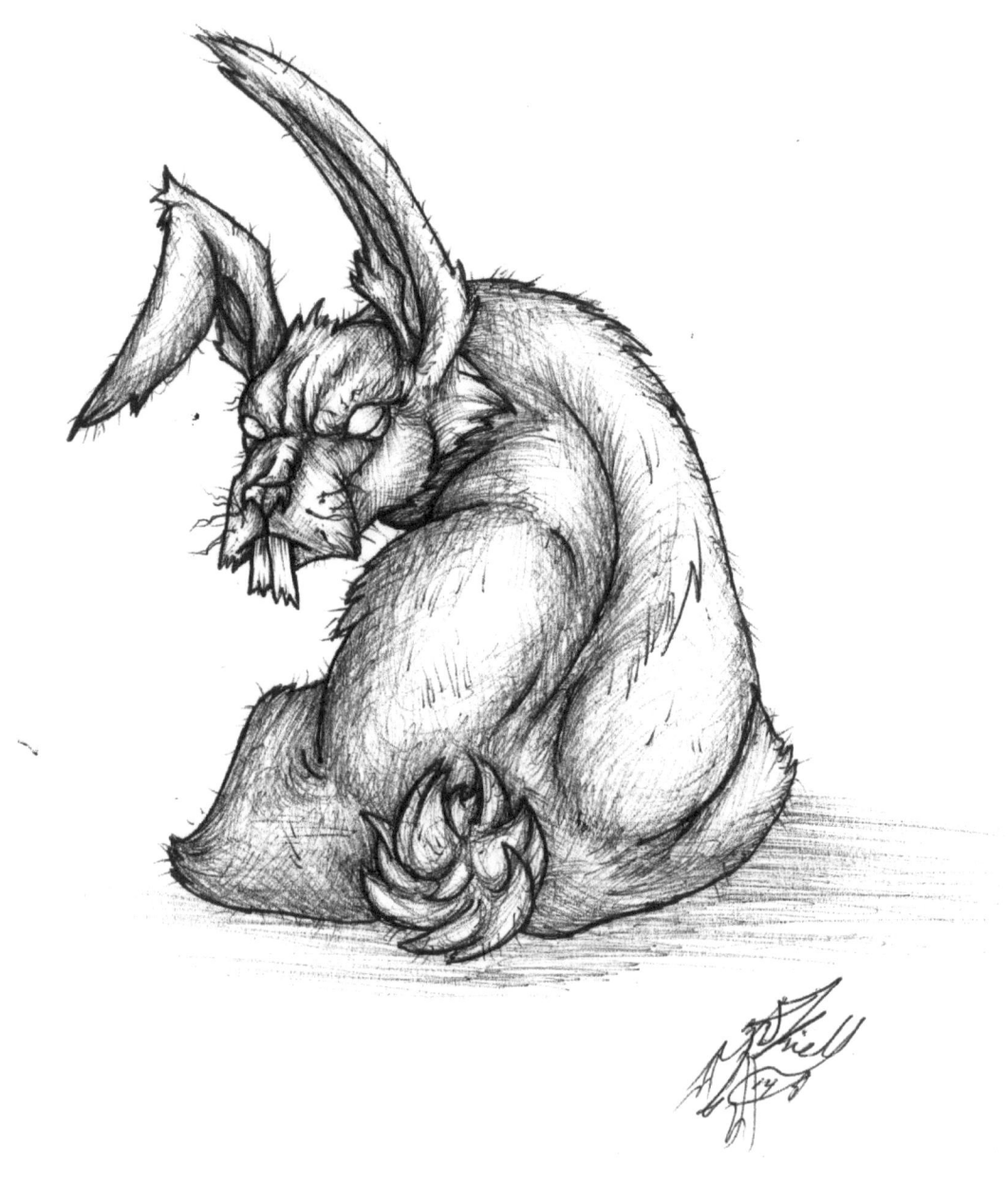

Bun

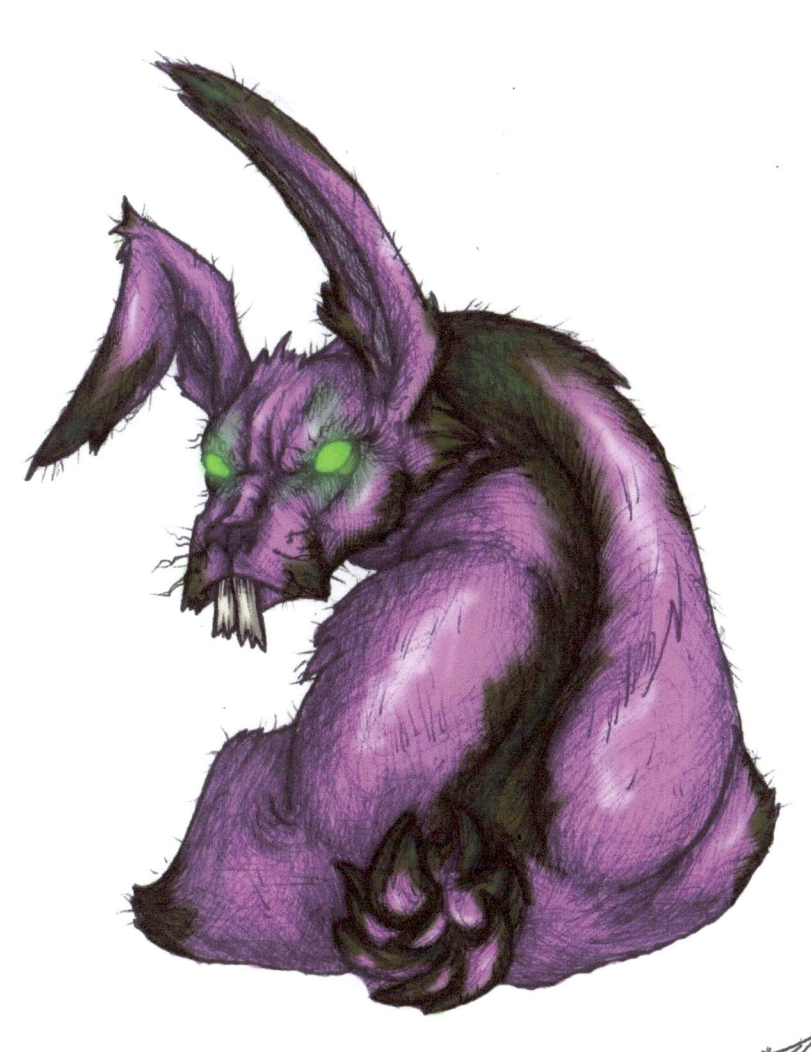

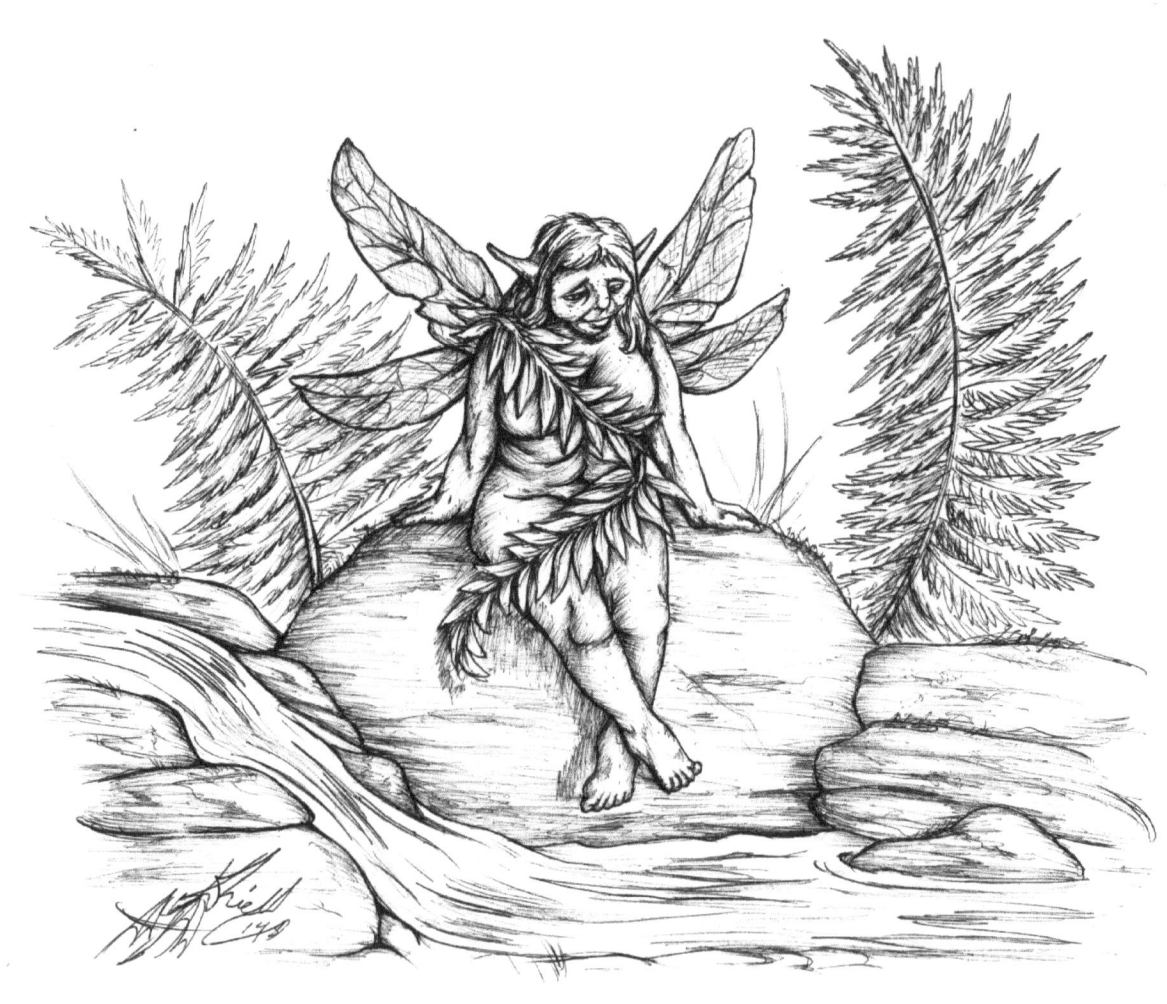

Fern

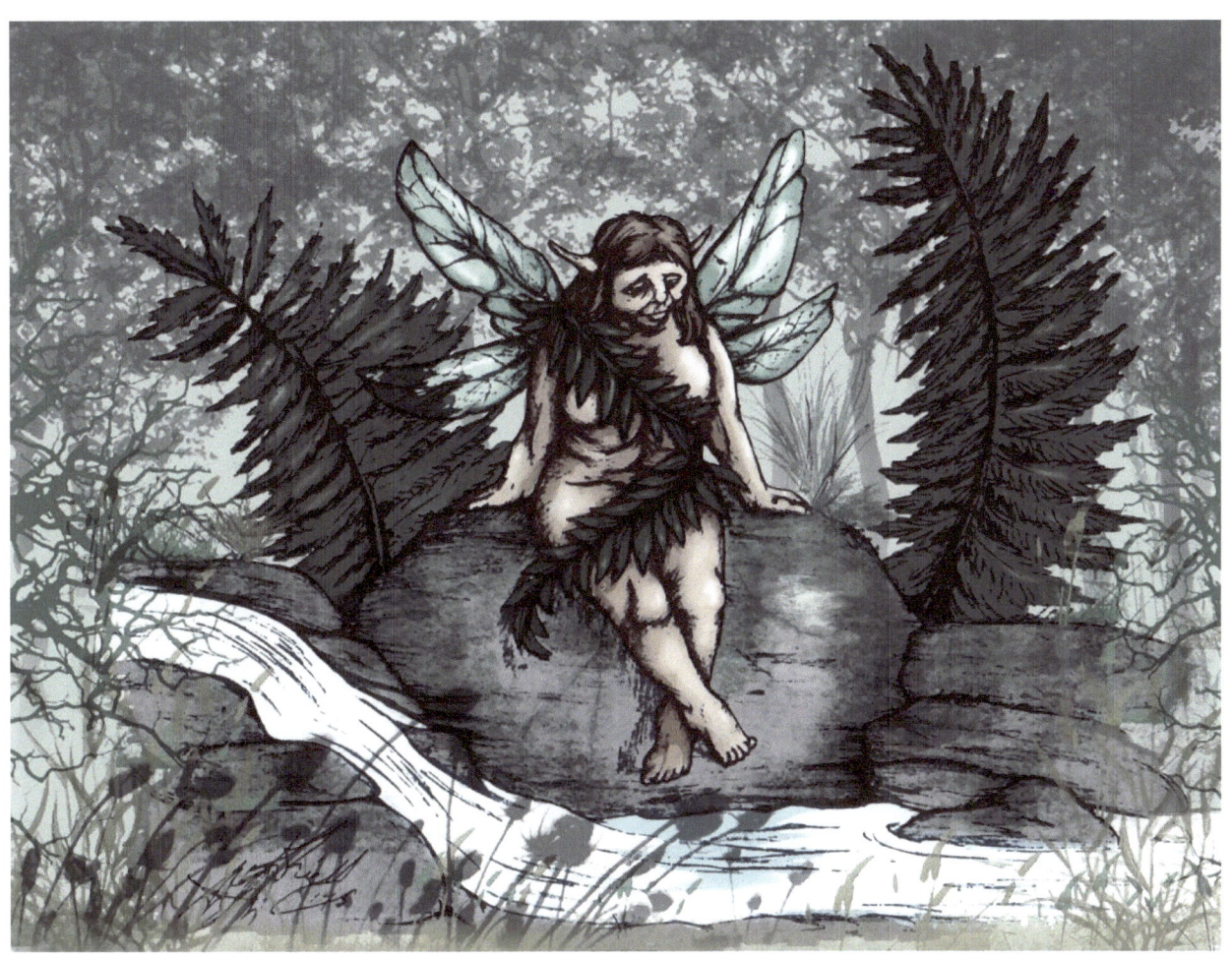

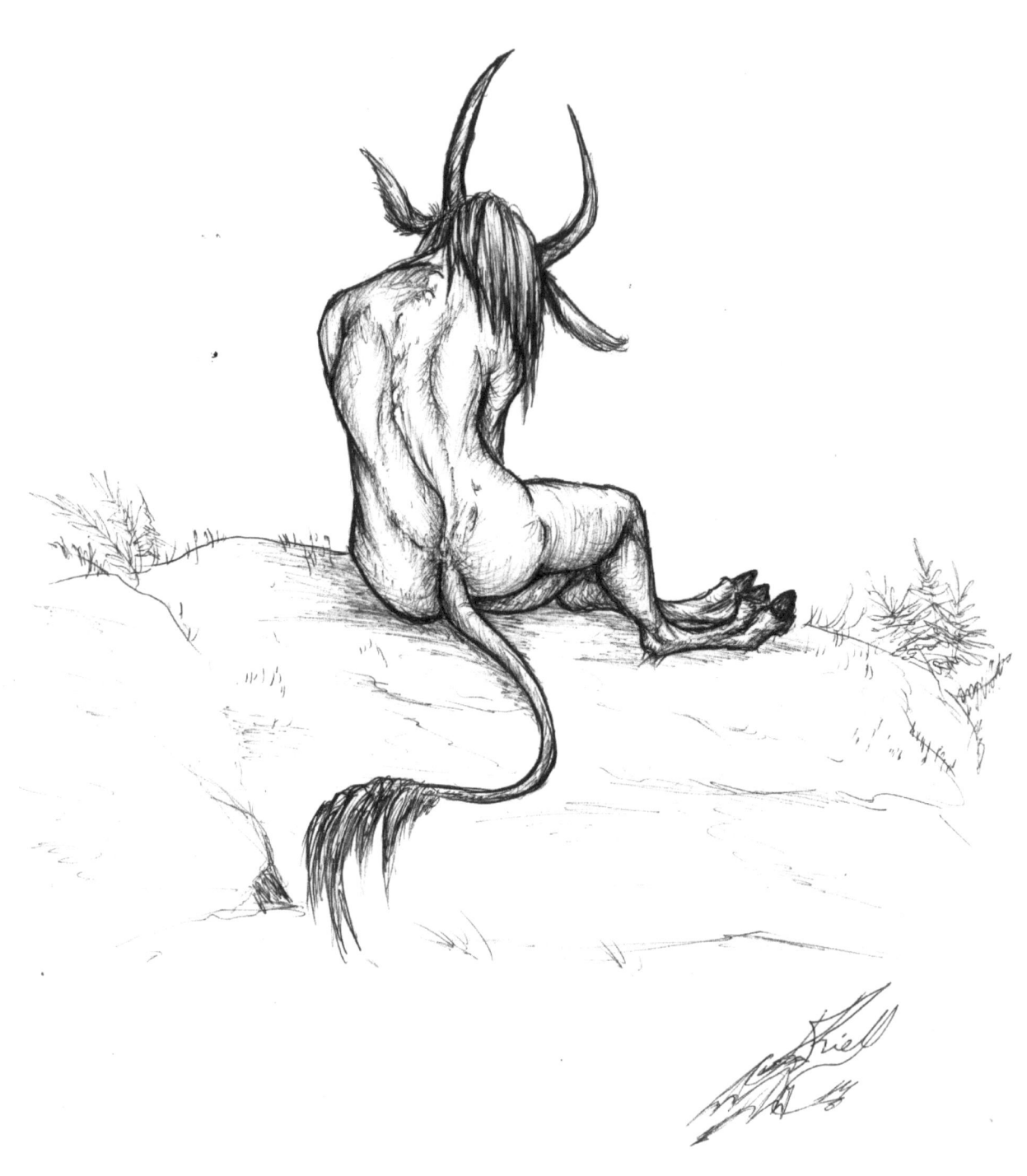

Faun

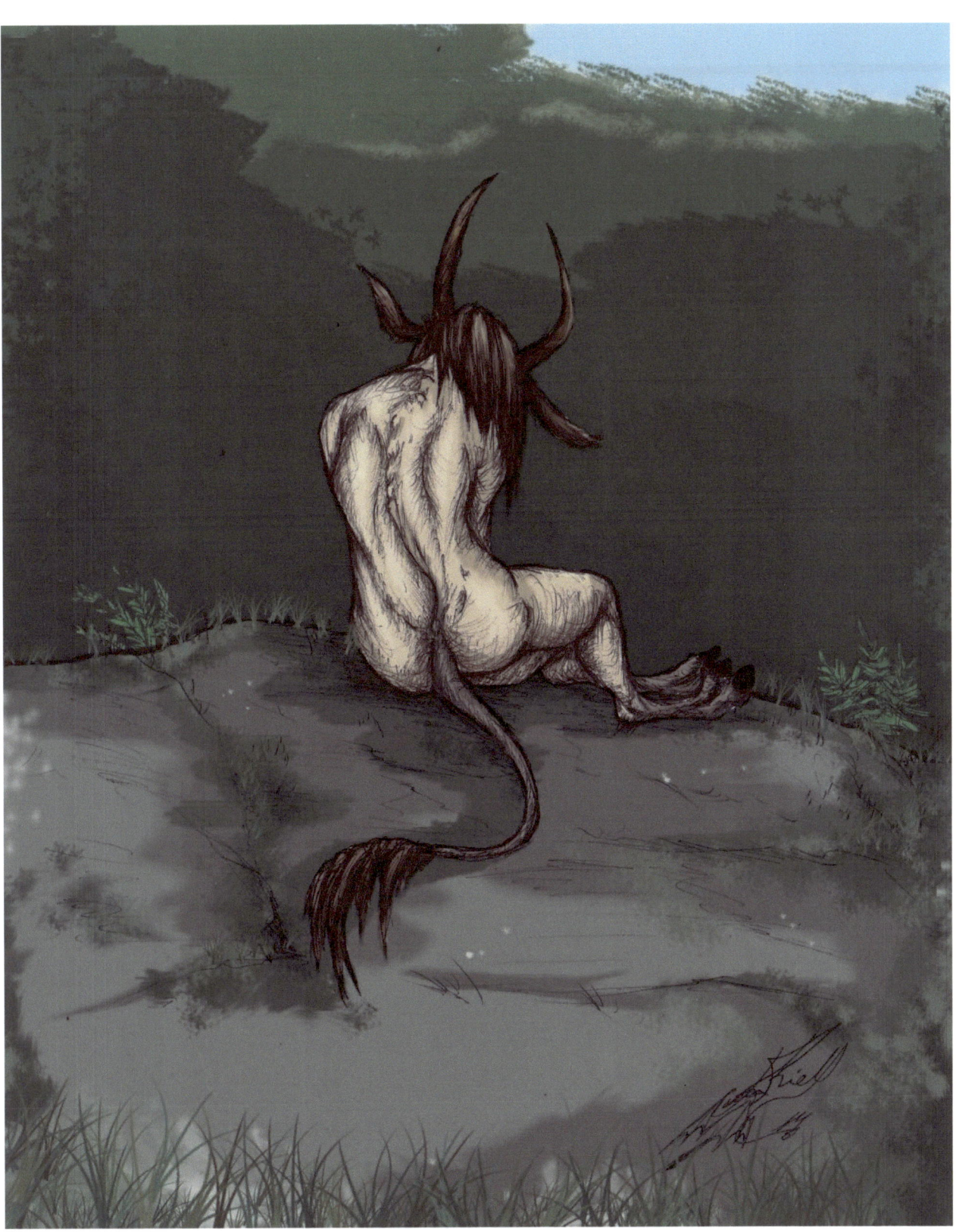

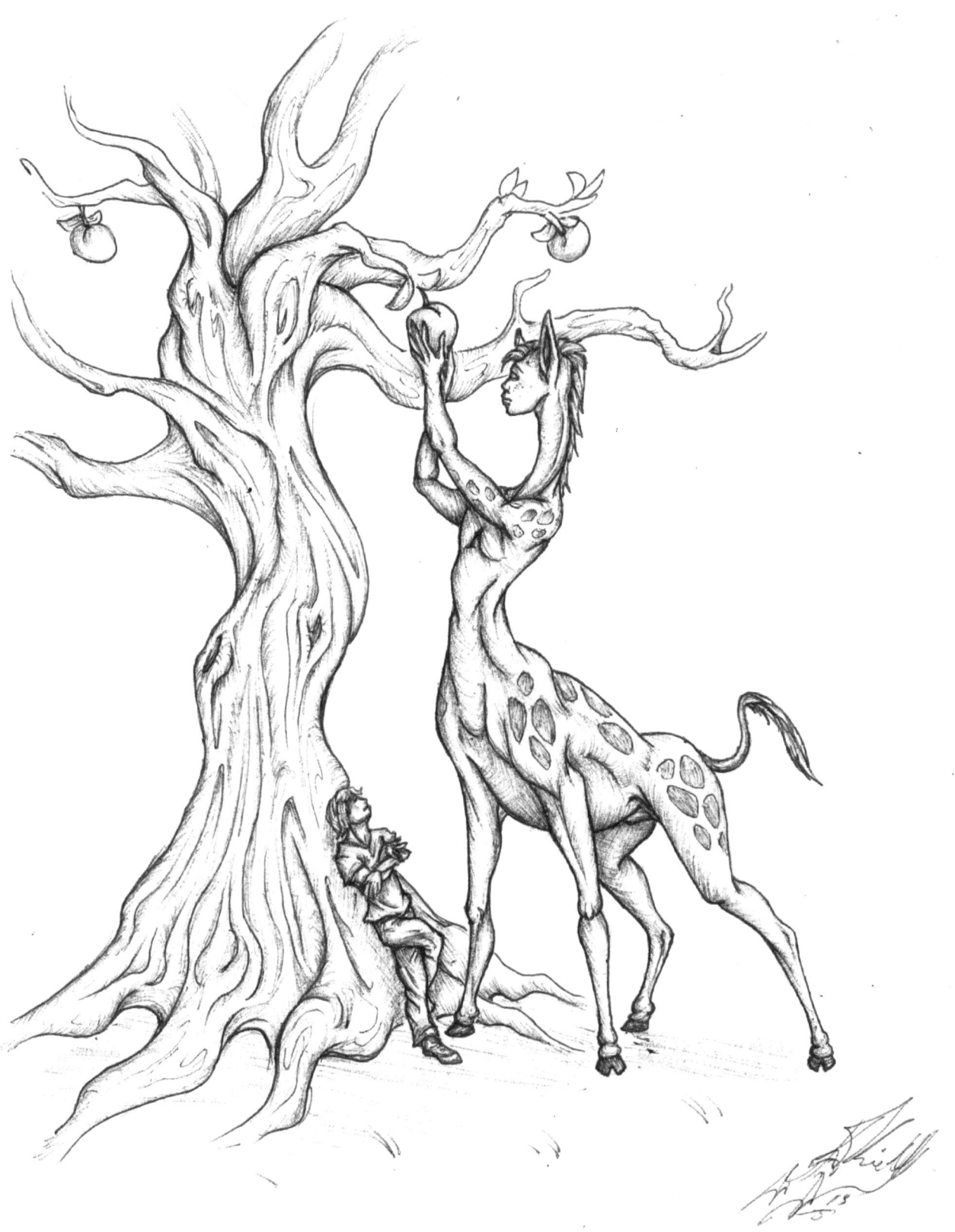

Plains Peach Tree

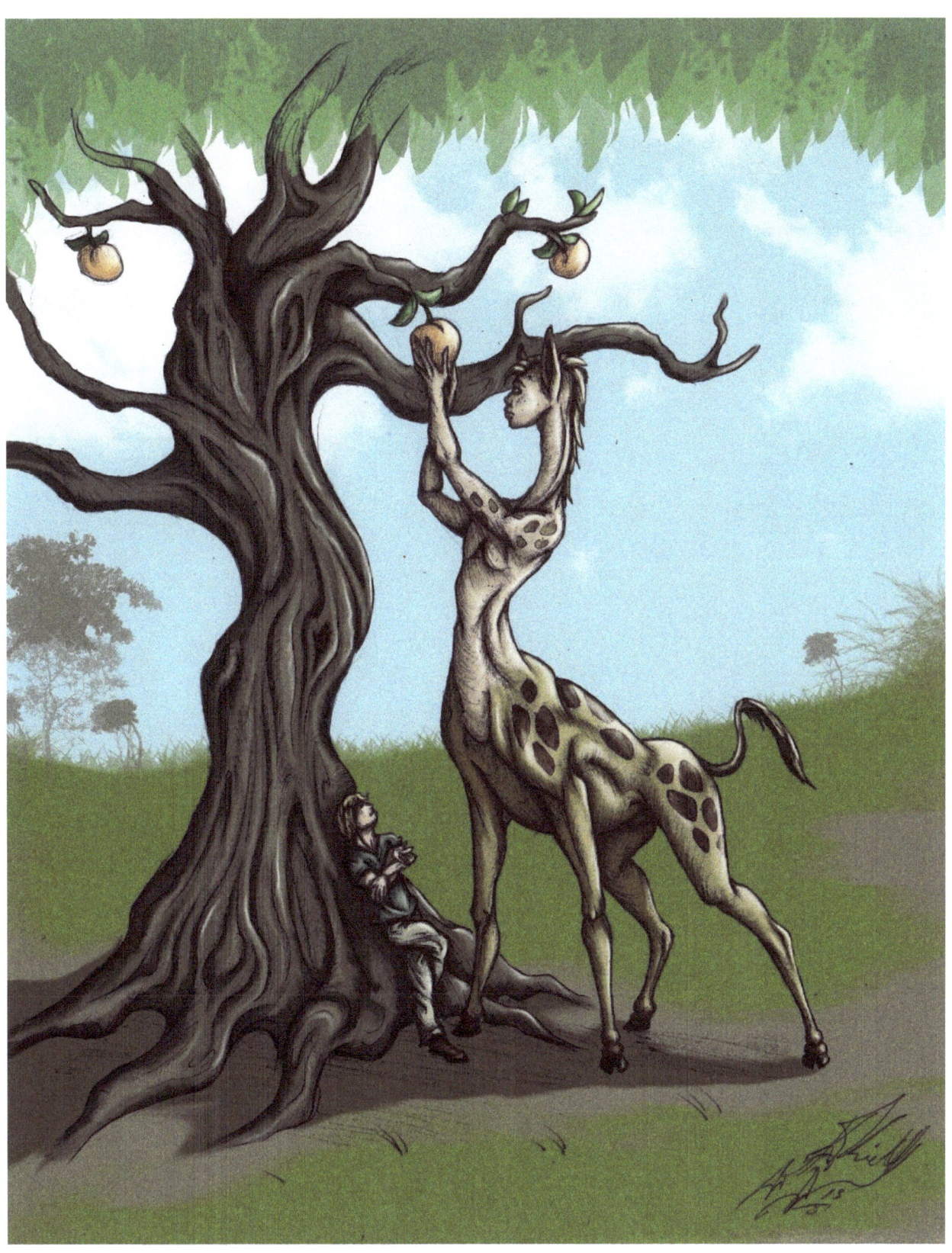

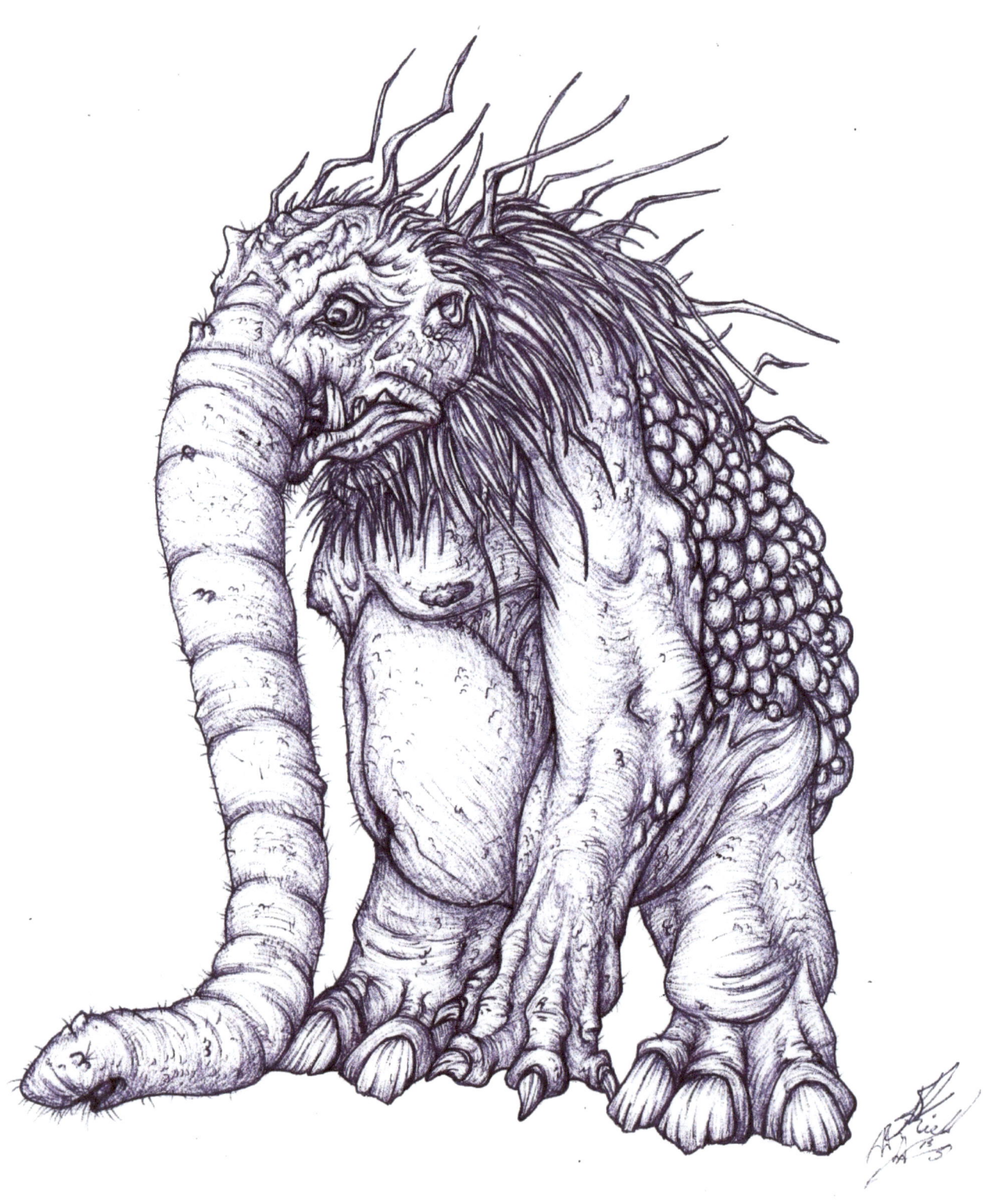

Snoz Troll

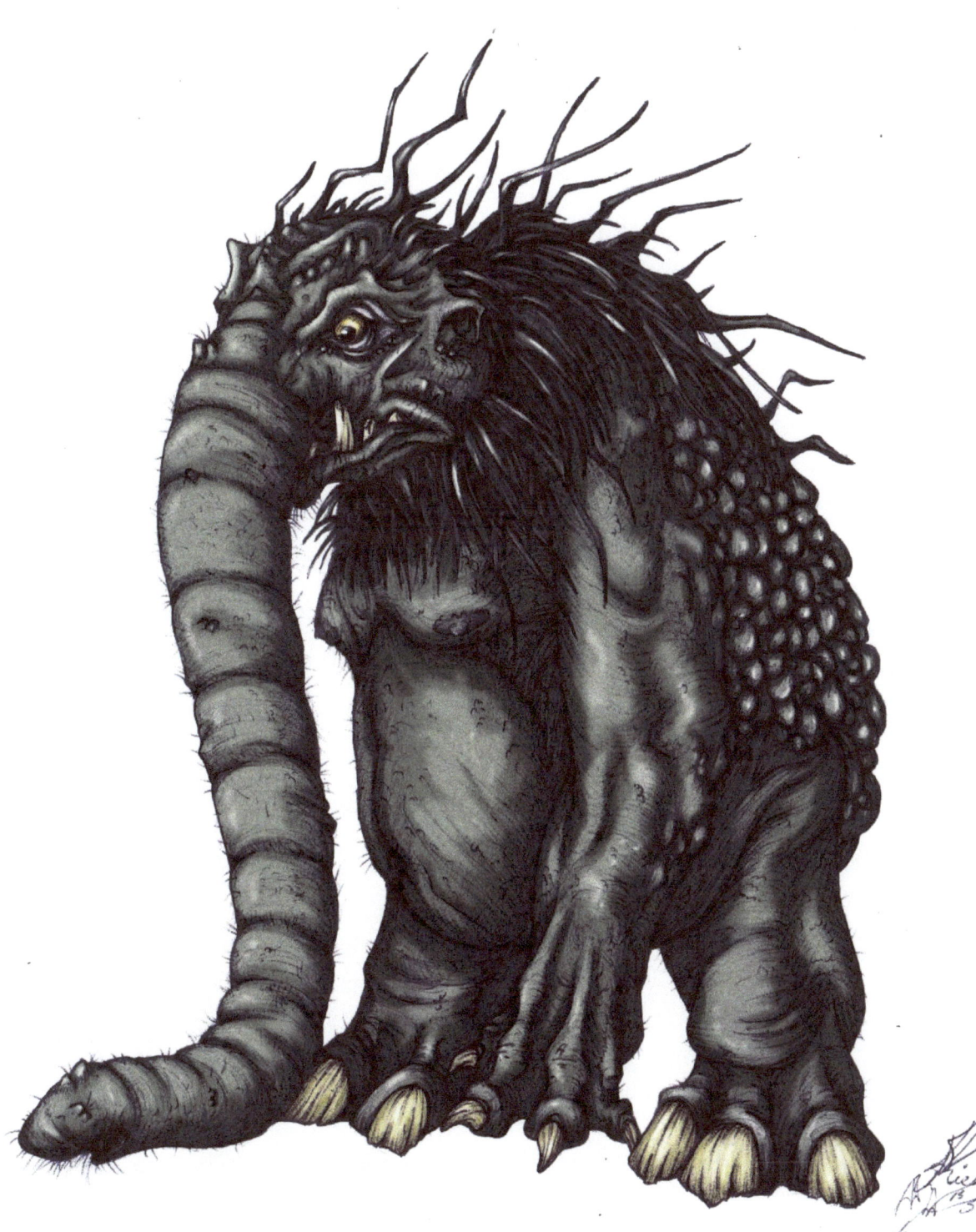

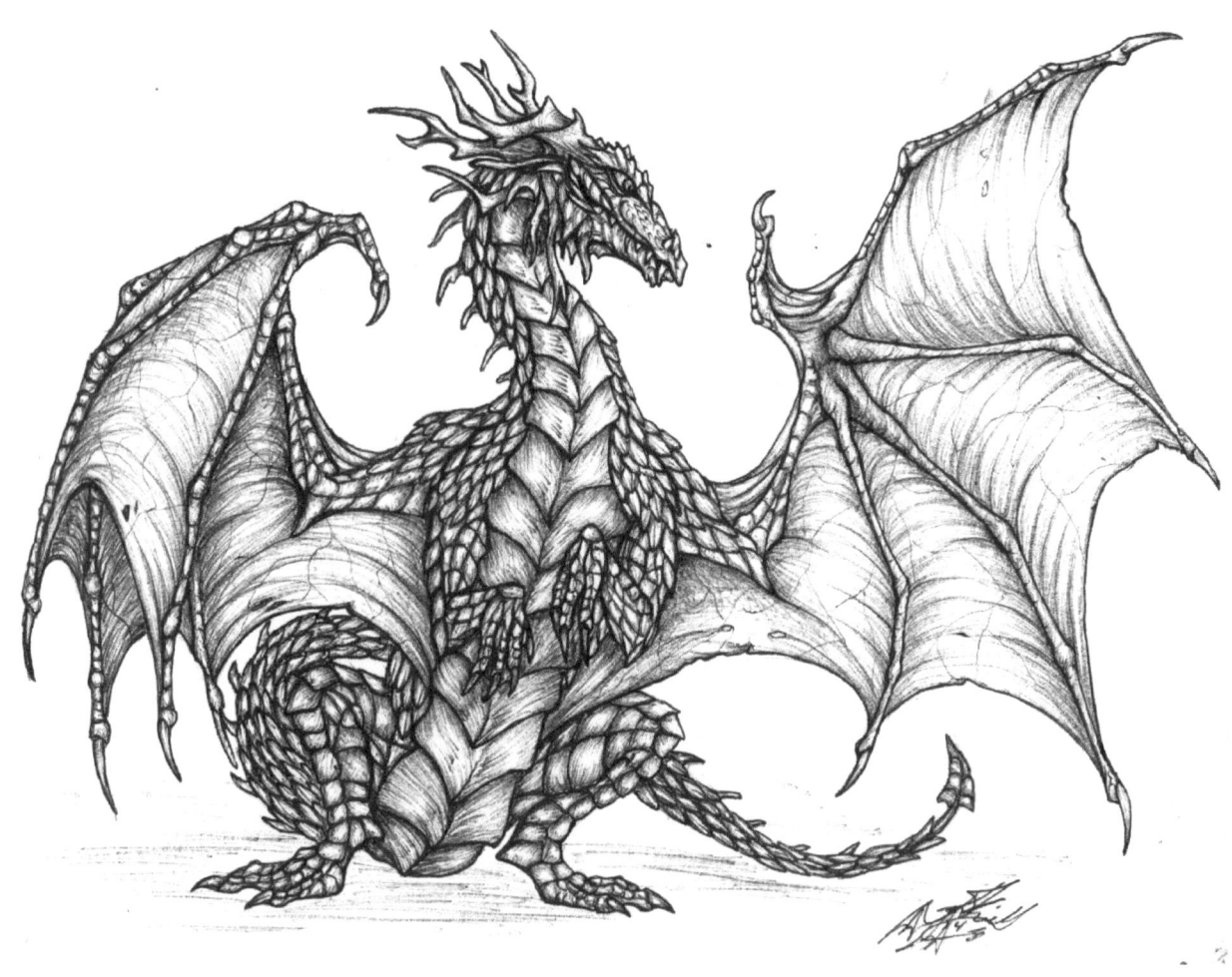

Forest Dragon

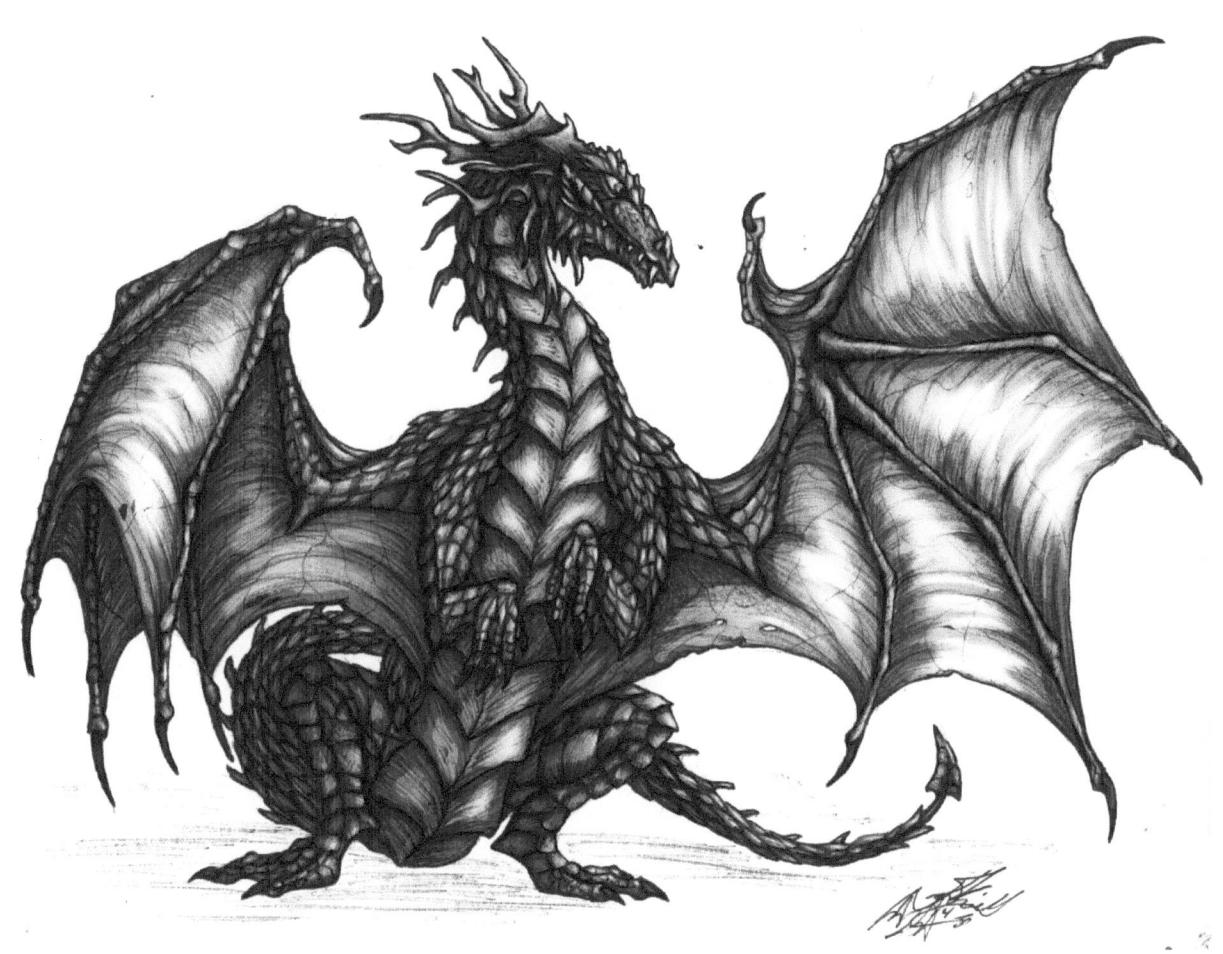

About the Author

Ever since she could hold a pencil, Kelin Beth Kiell has been an artist. With a unique imagination and a desire to show it, she taught herself to draw. For over twenty three years she has been drawing and writing. Dragons are her favorite subject, and everything strange comes next...

Part 4

Artwork done from age 13-16

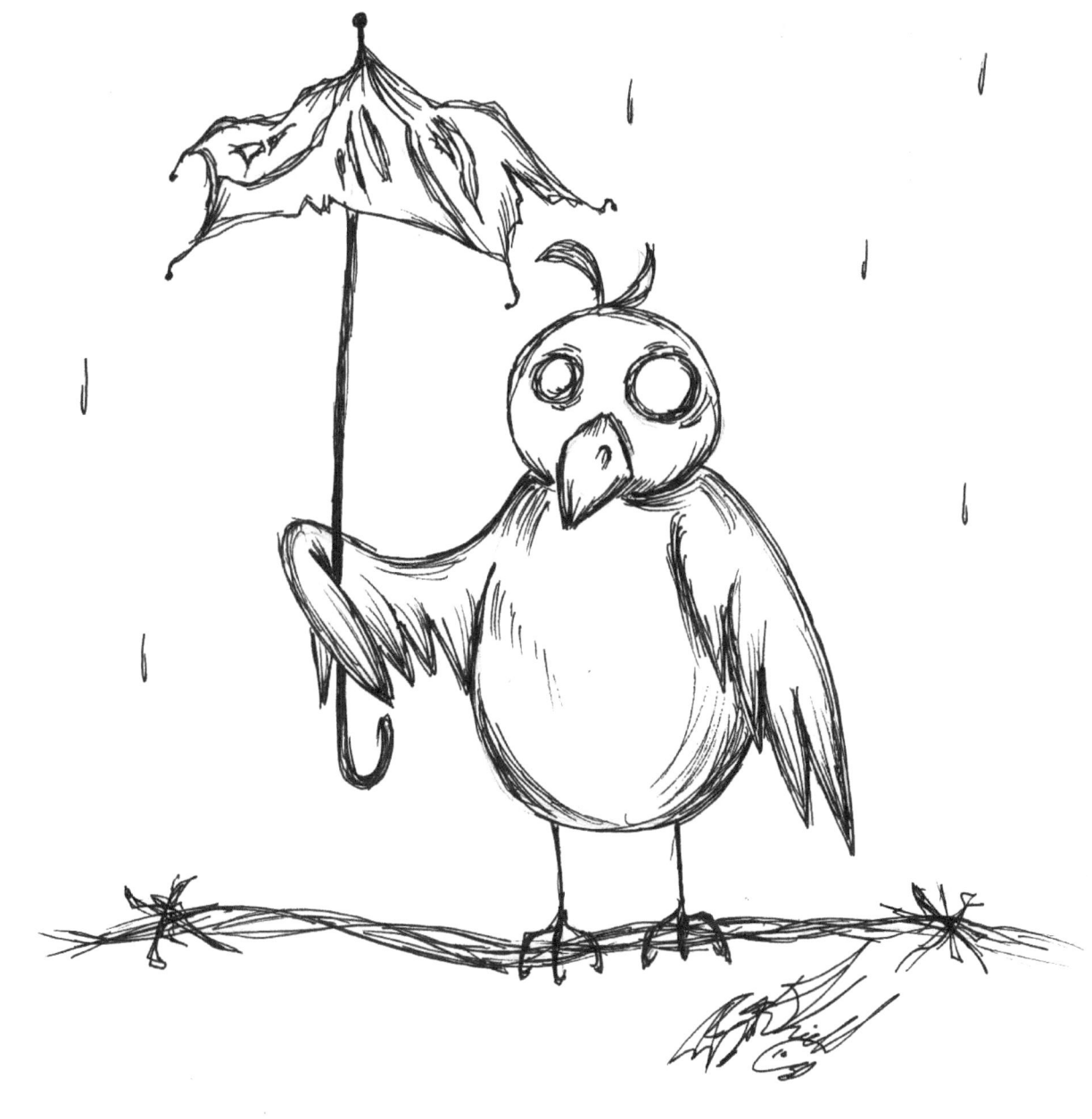

Bird

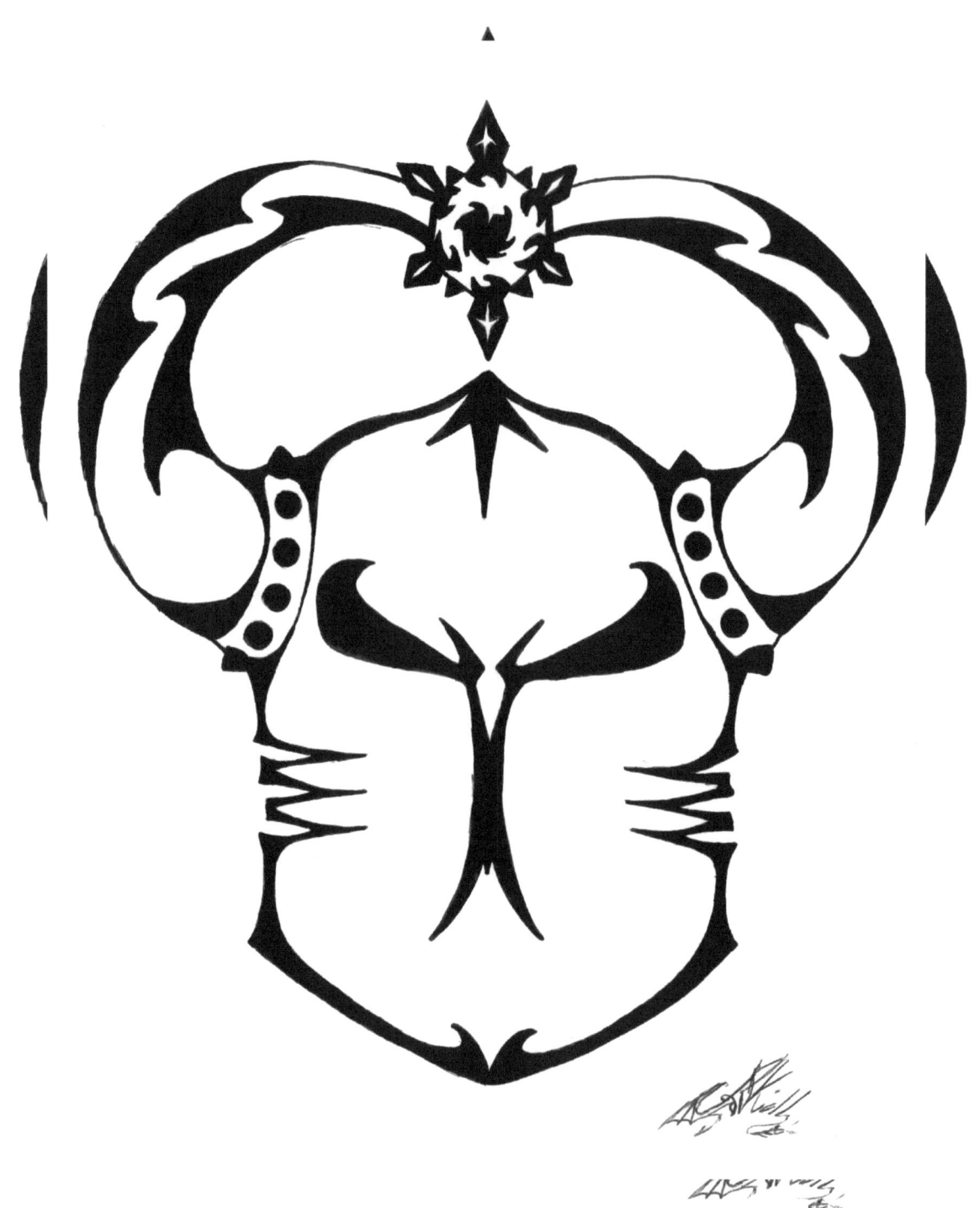

Chaos Helmet

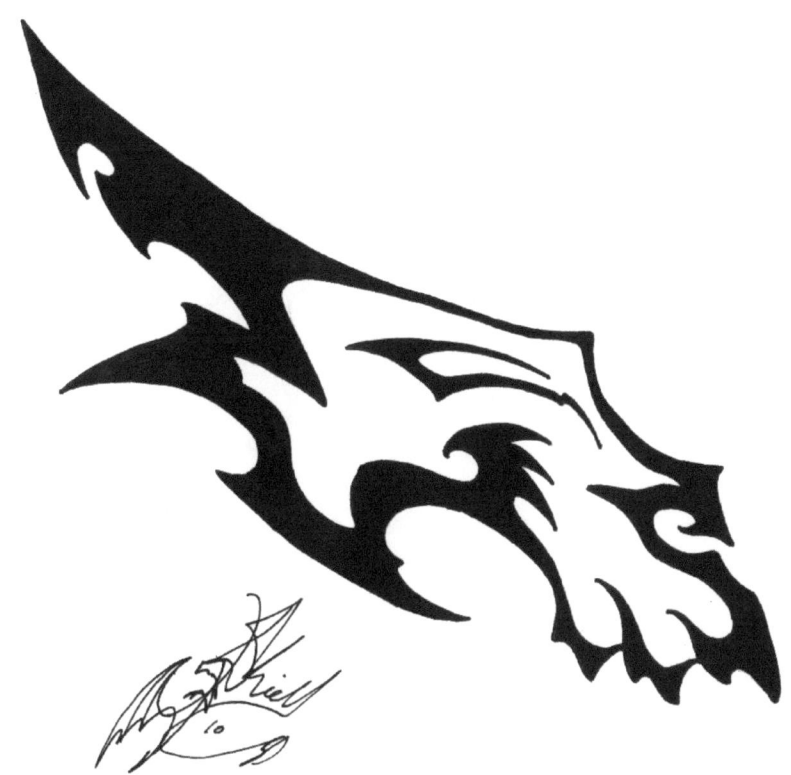

Dragon Skull

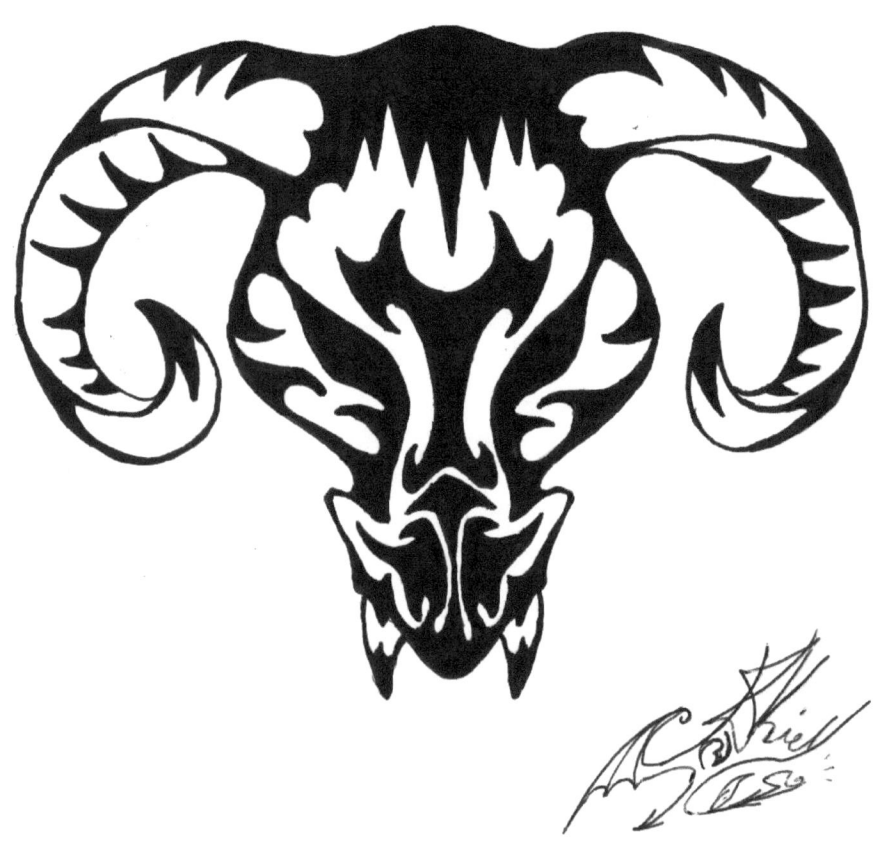

Aries Dragon

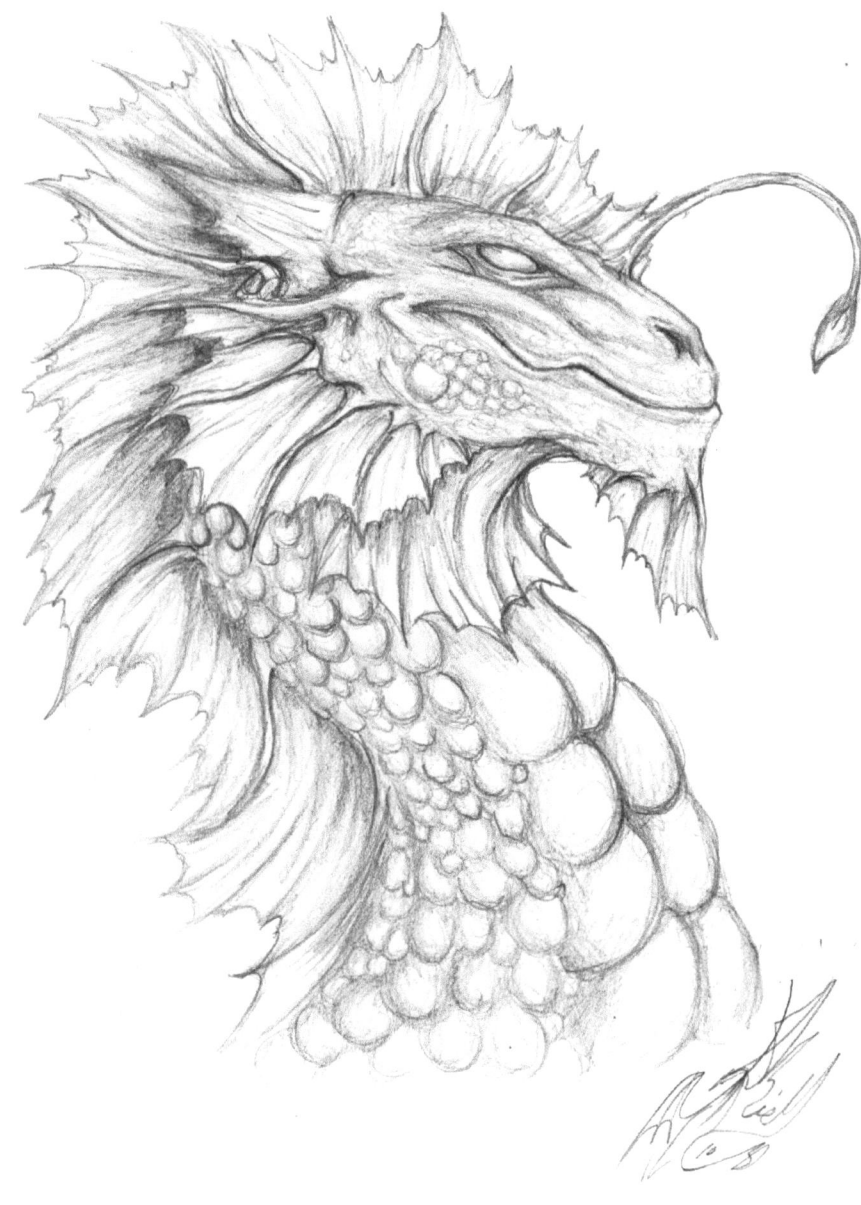

Sea Dragon

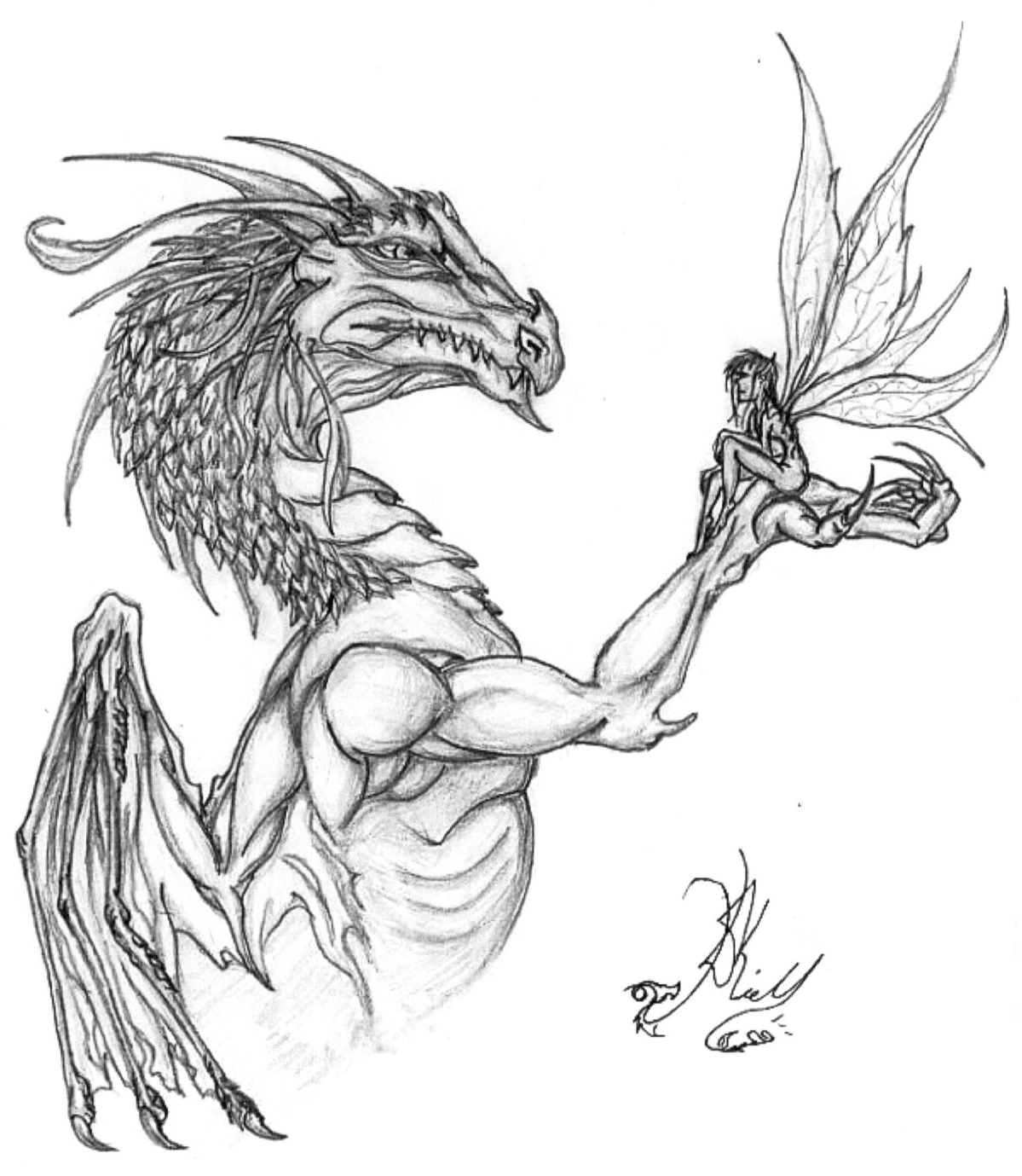

Dragon and Fairy

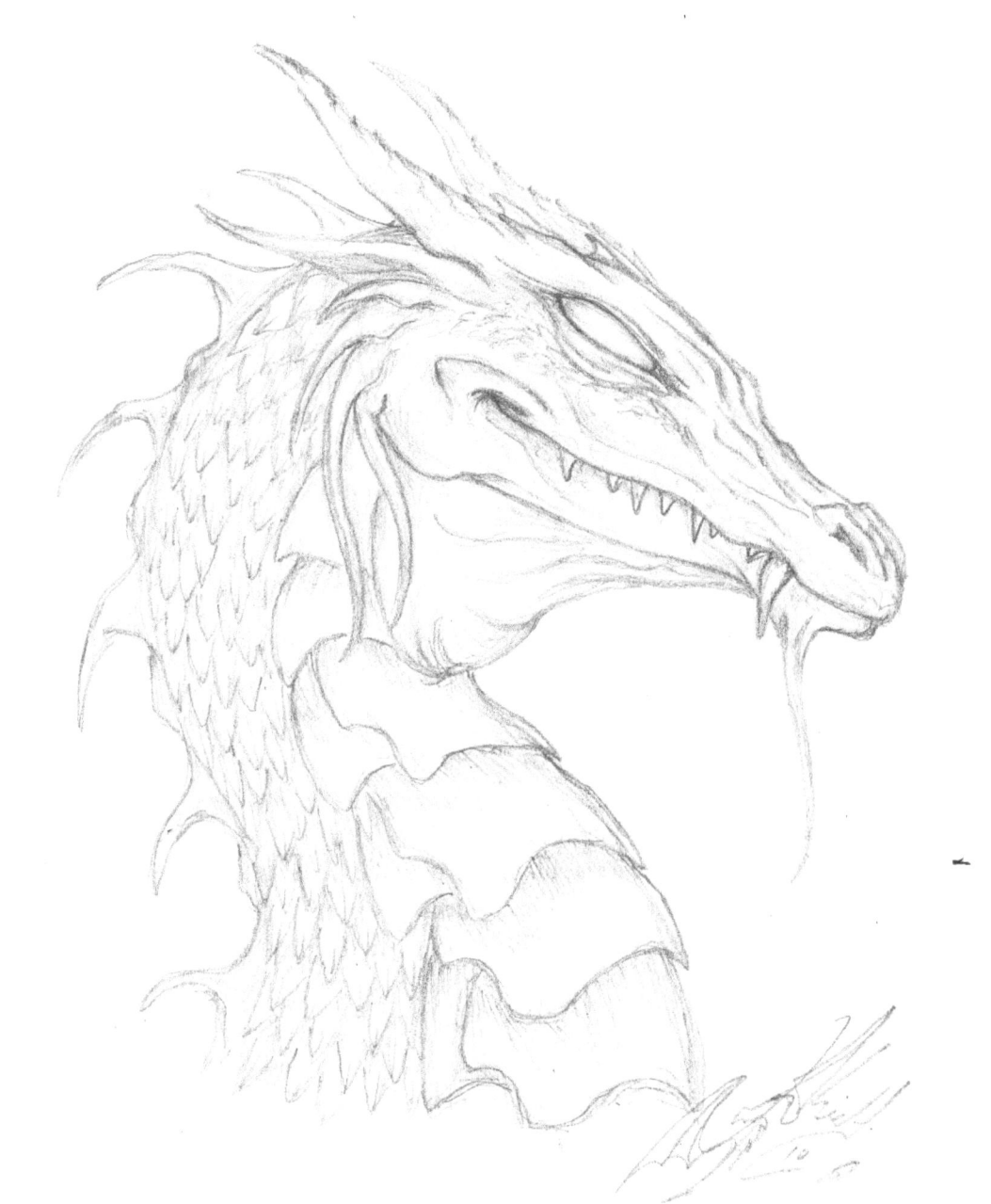

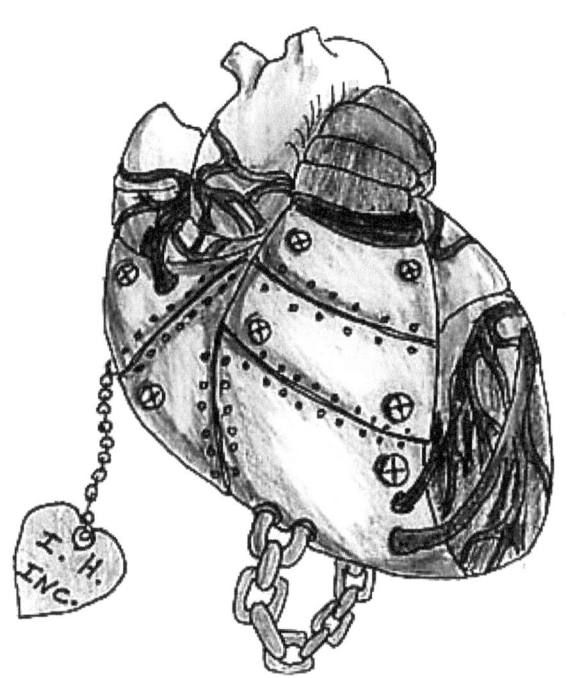

Iron Hearts, Inc.

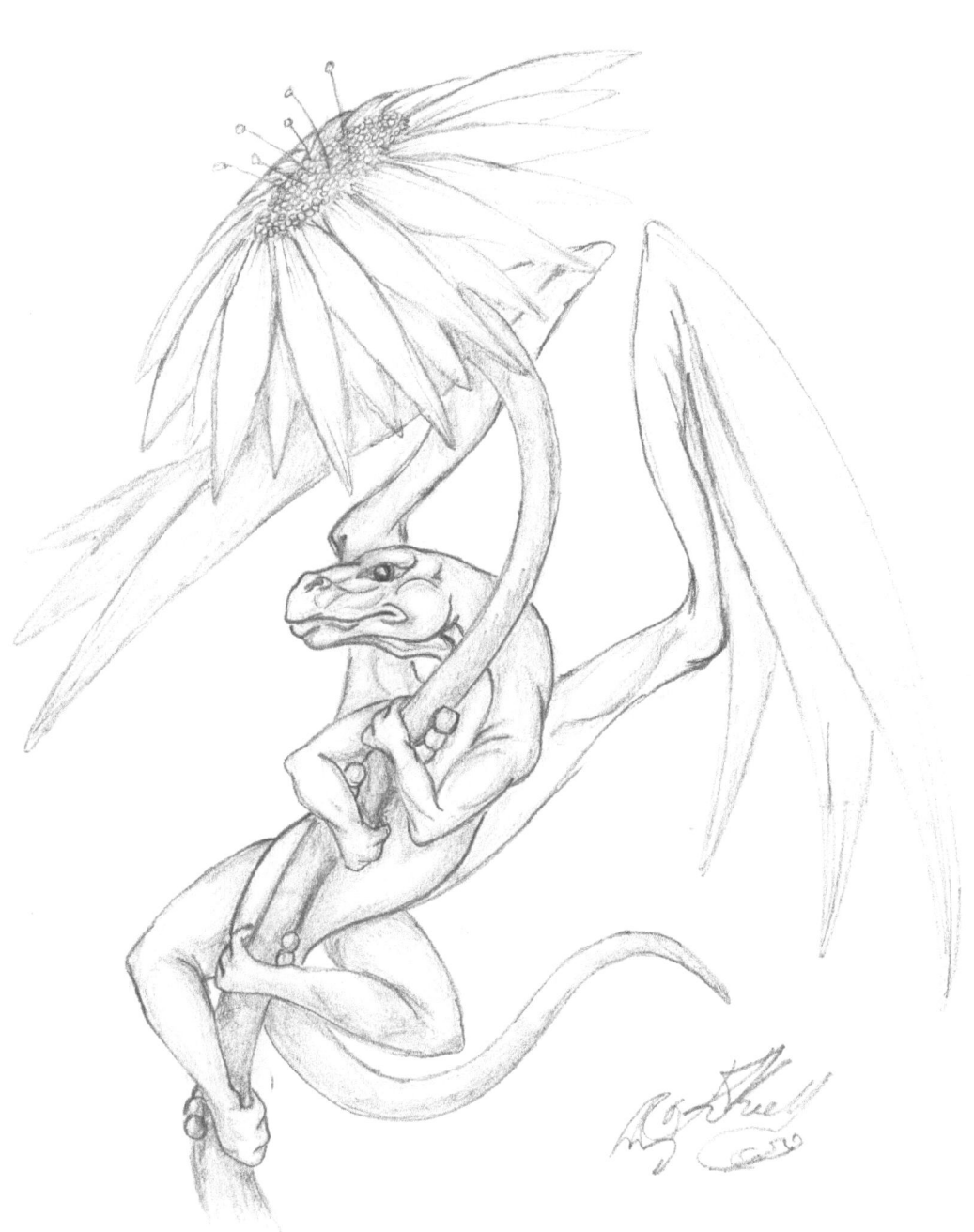

Daisy

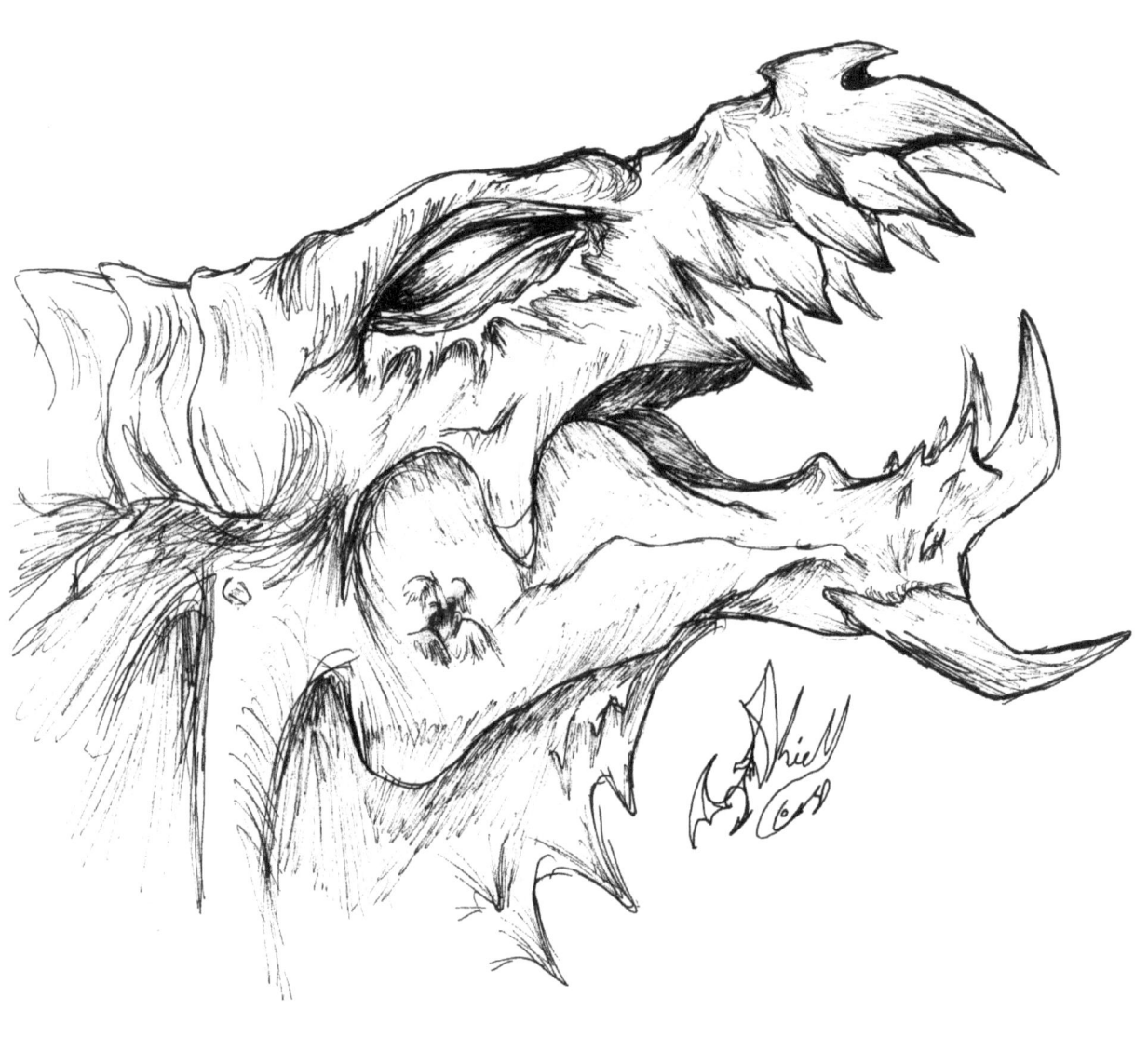

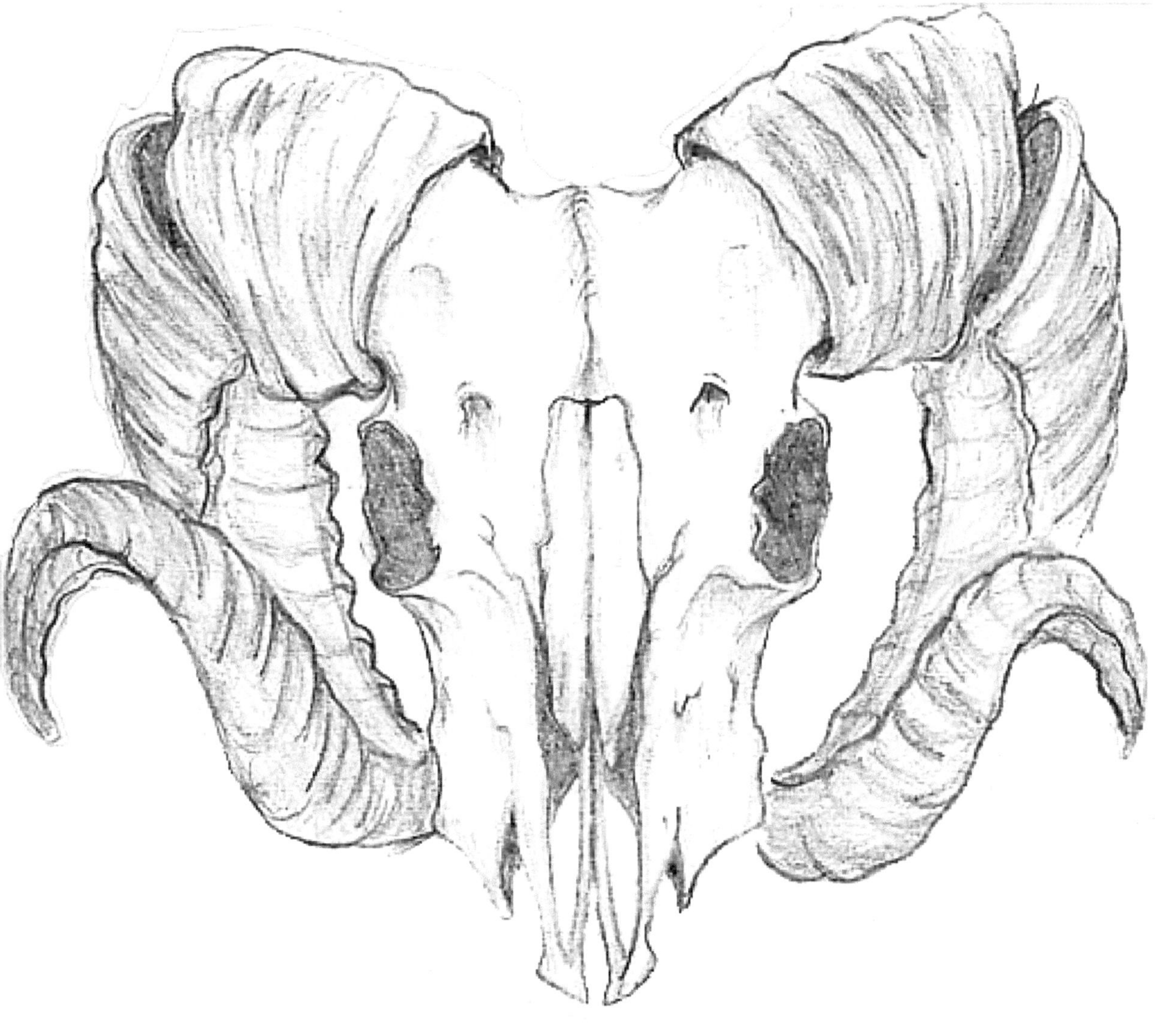

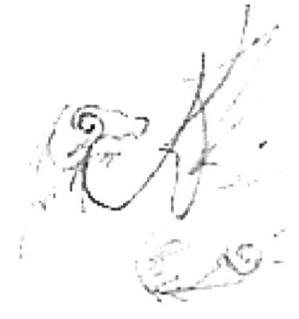

Ram Skull

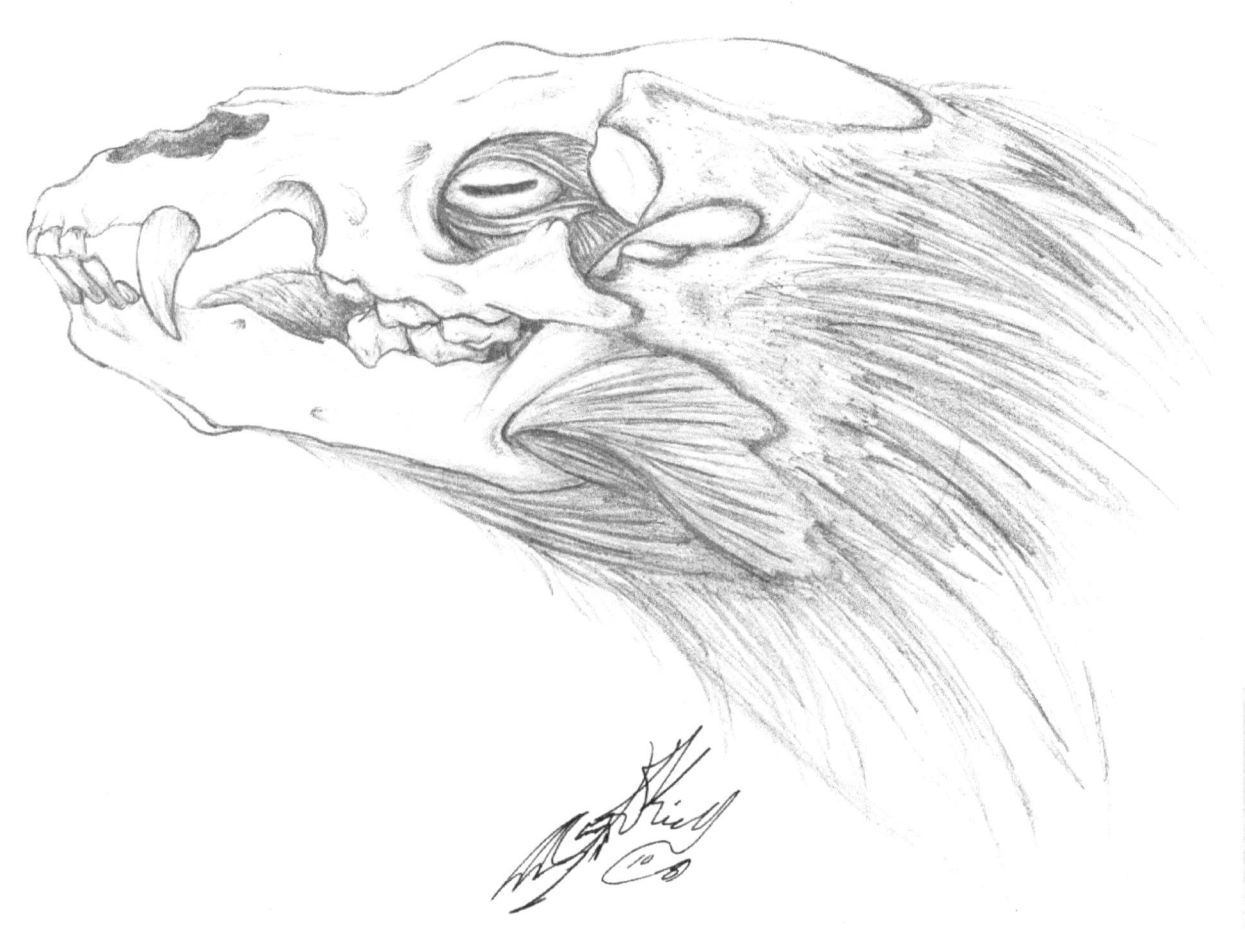

Monster

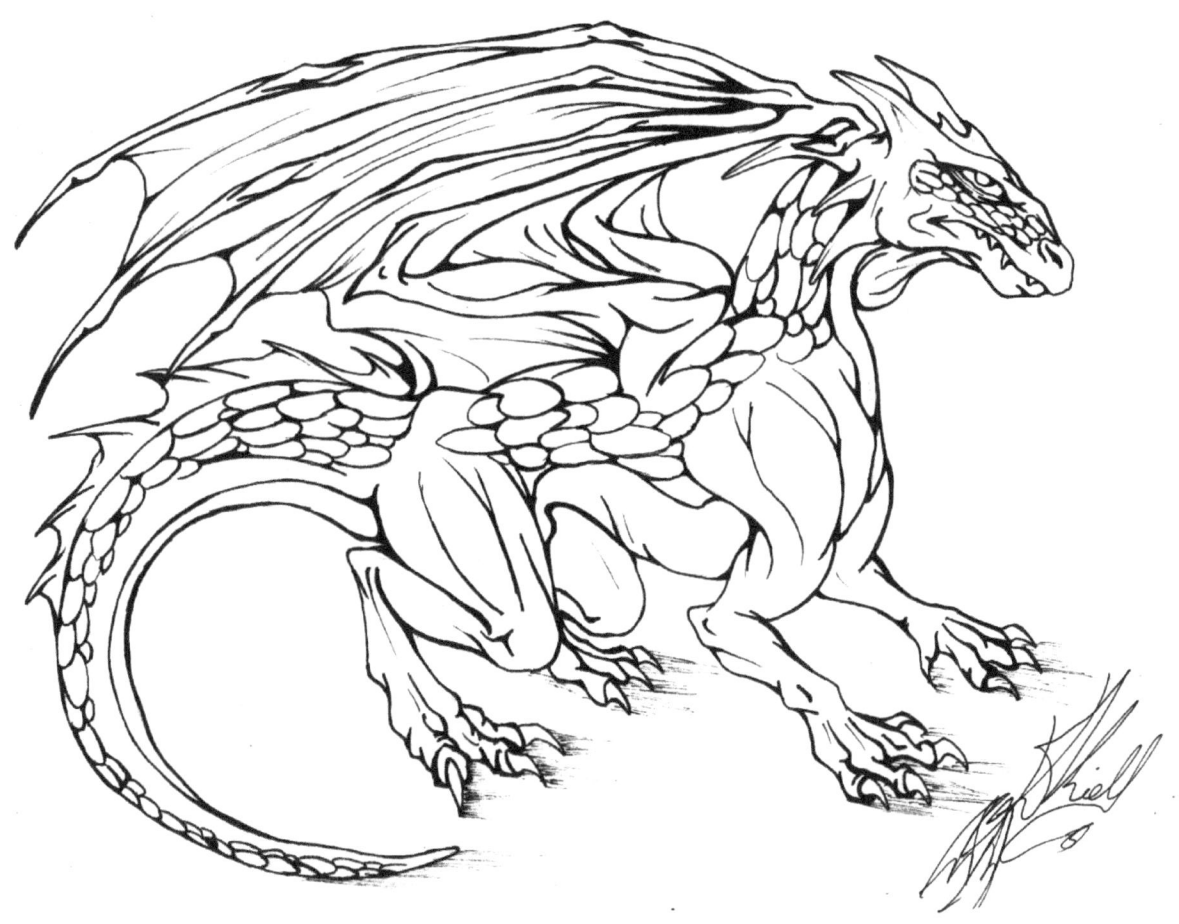

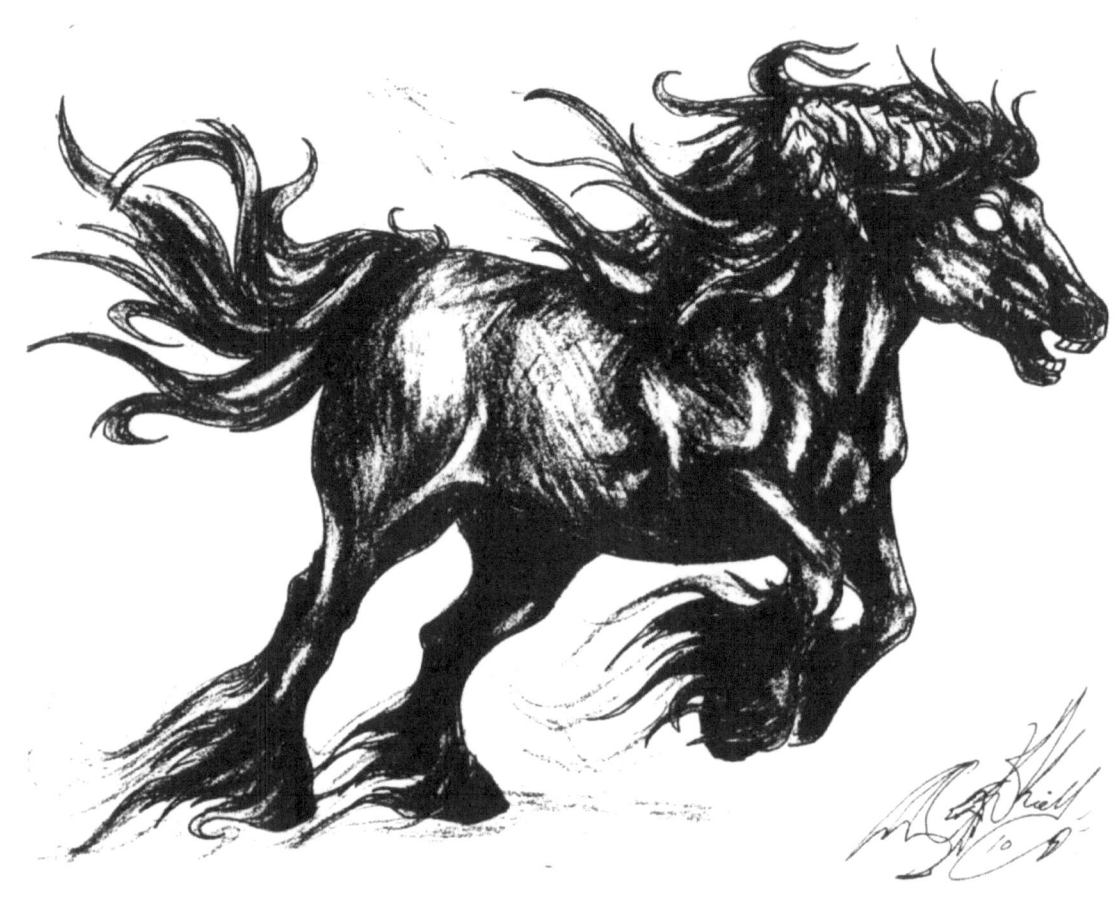

Dark Horse

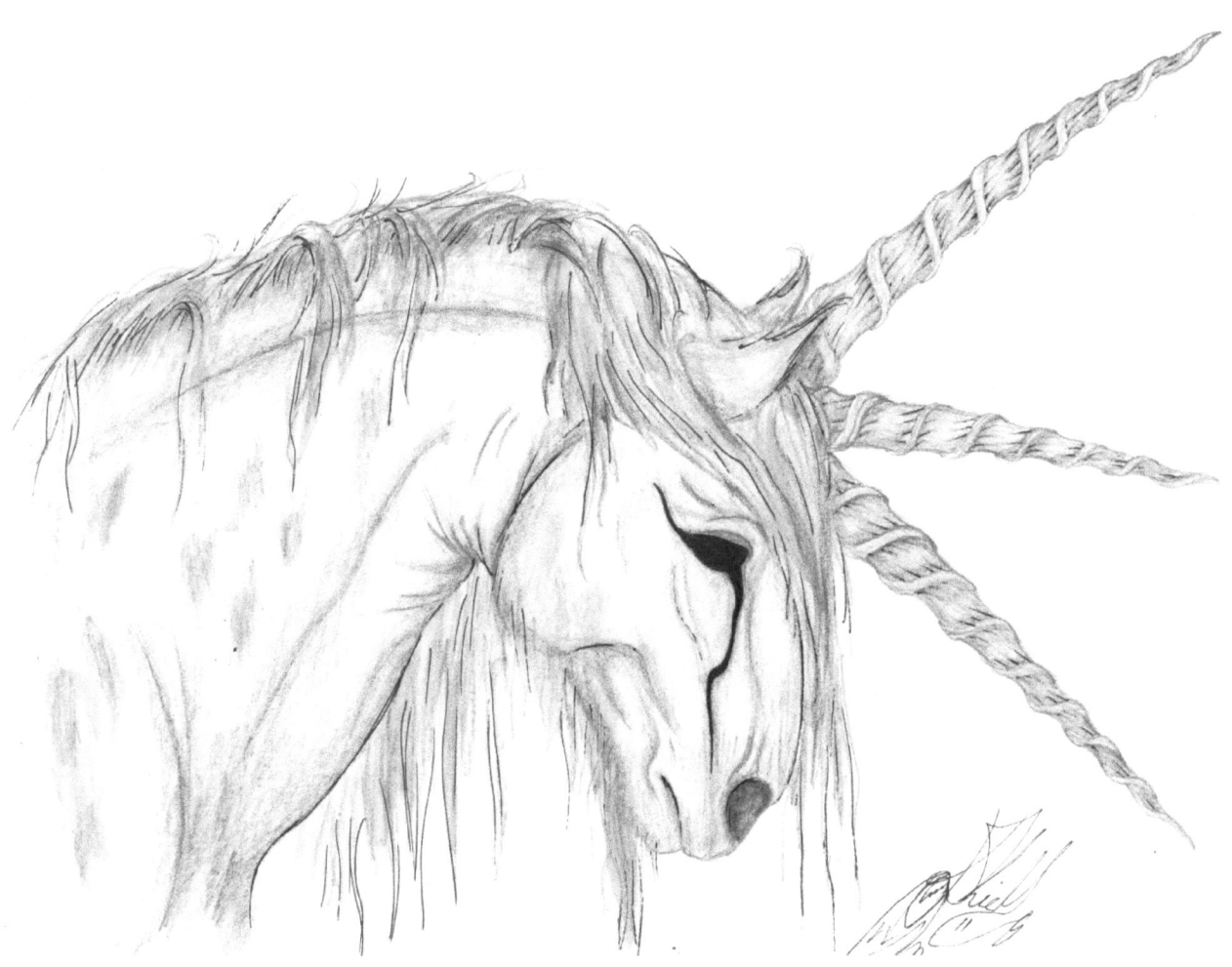

Trihorn

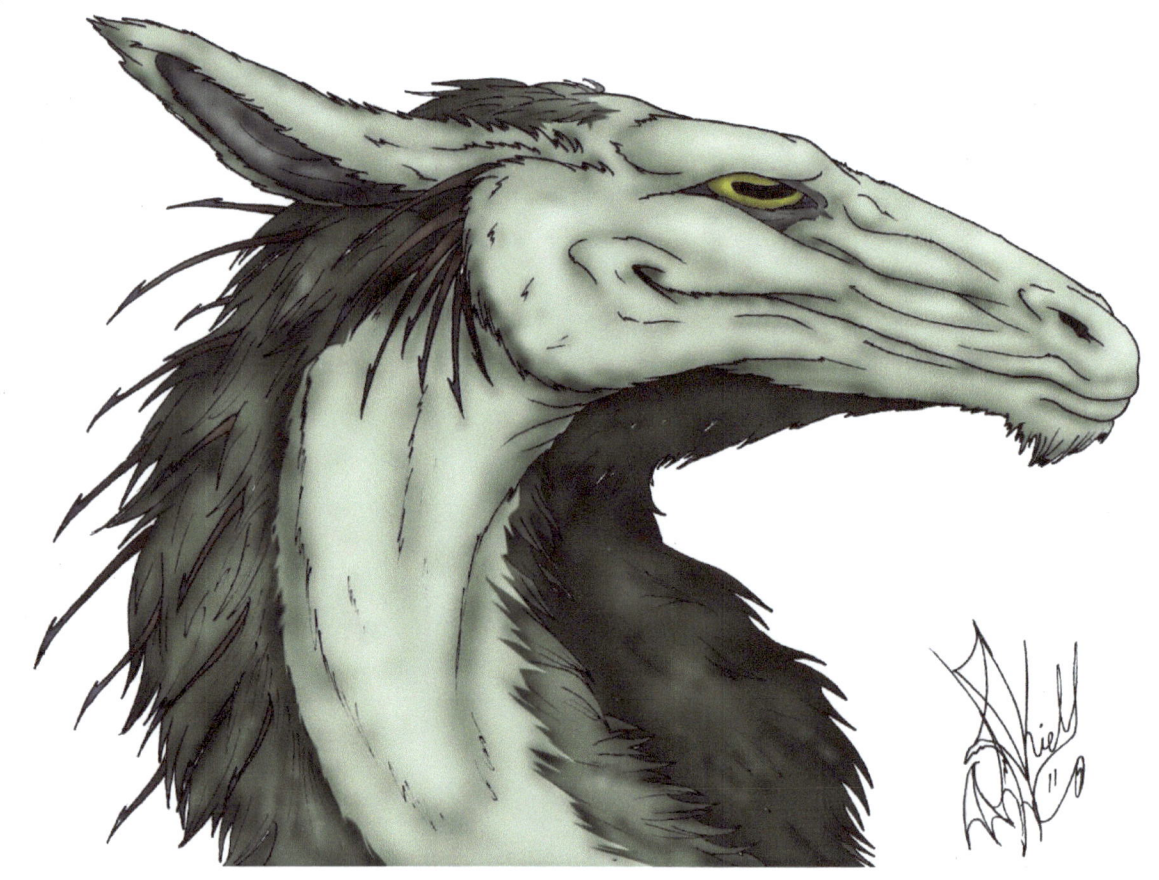

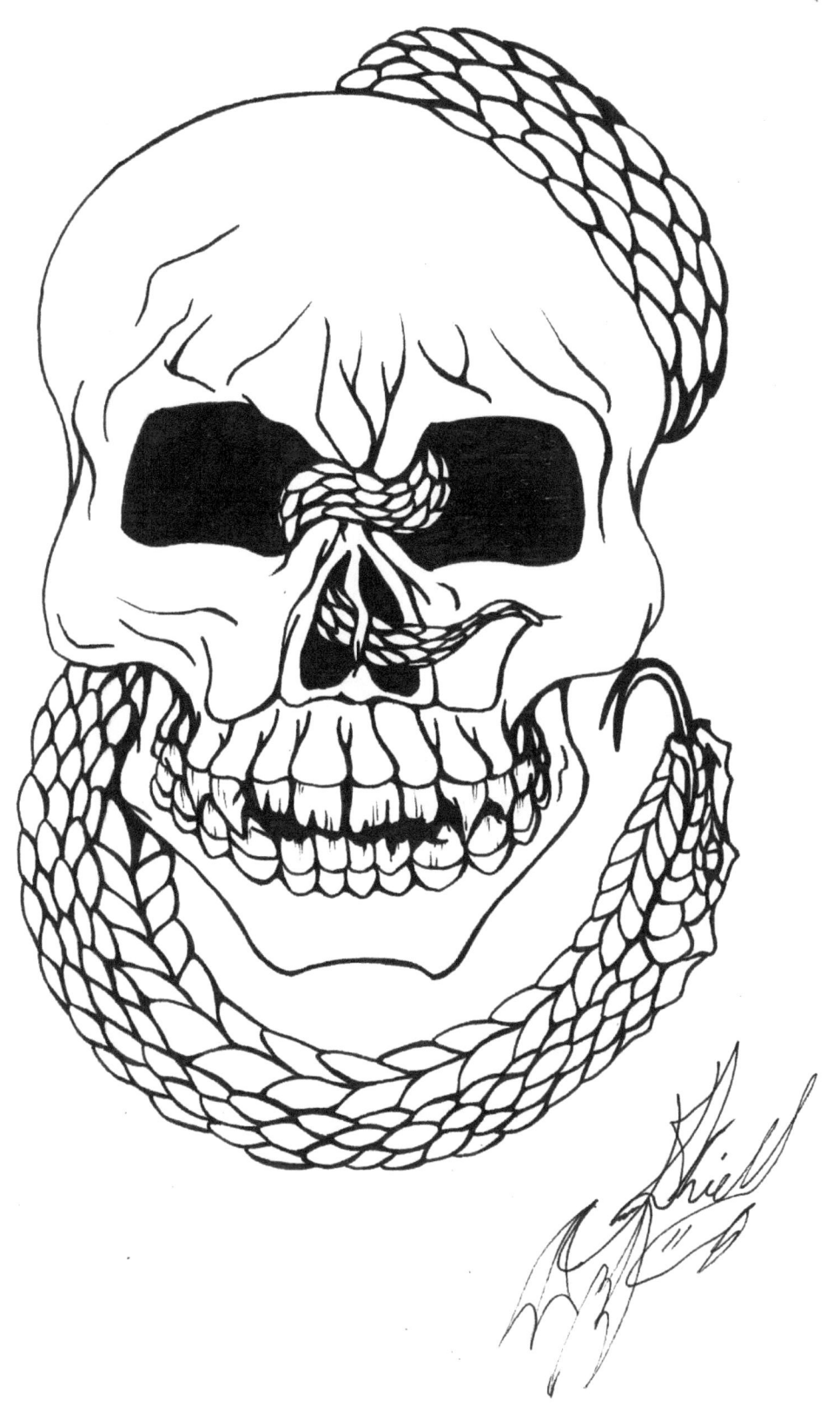

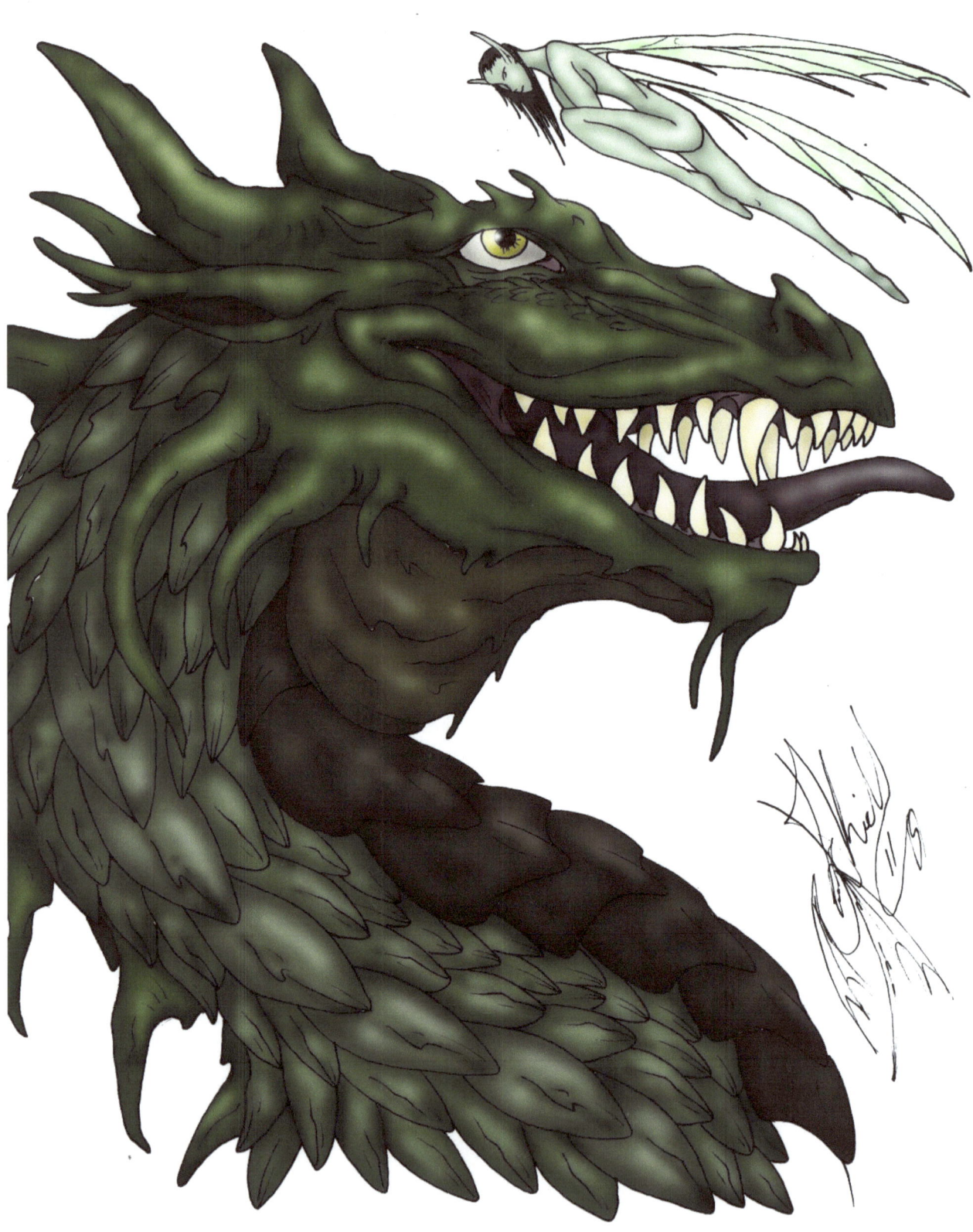

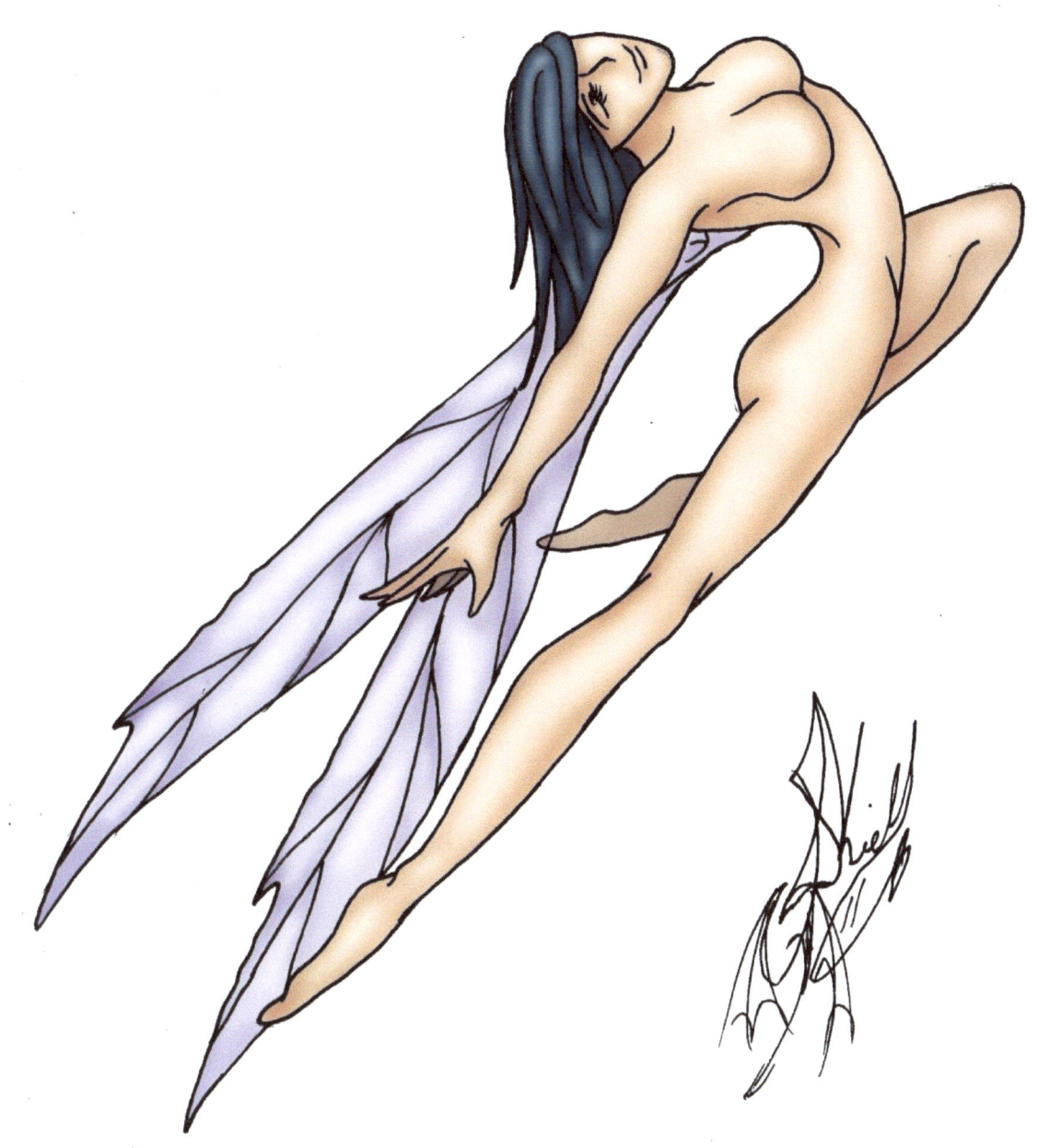

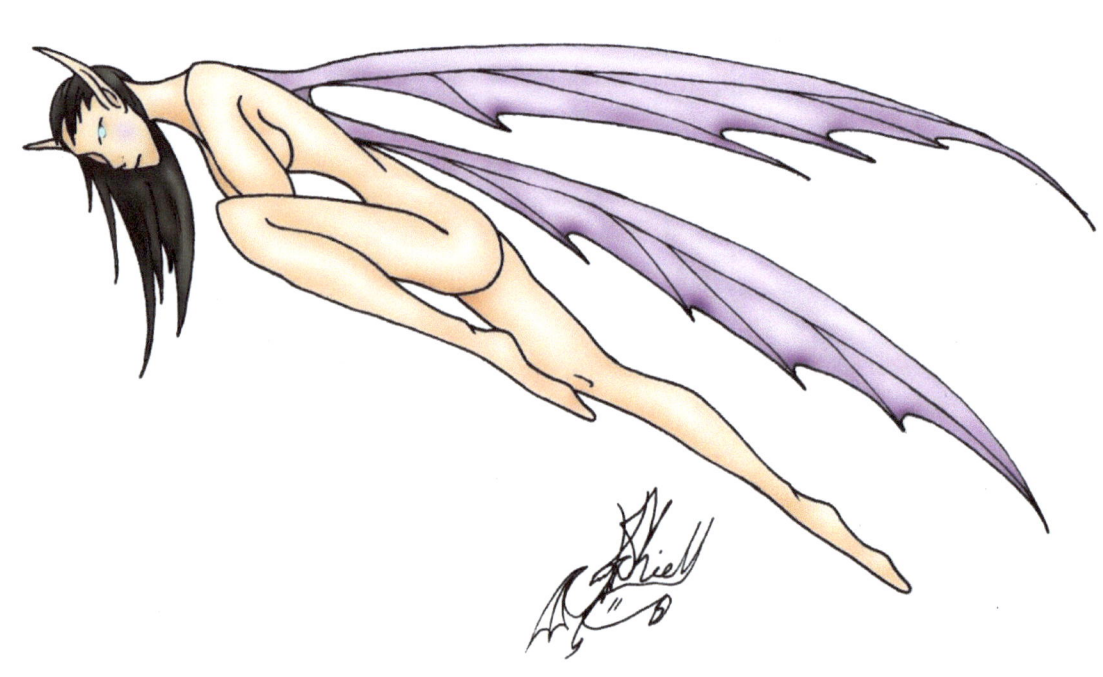

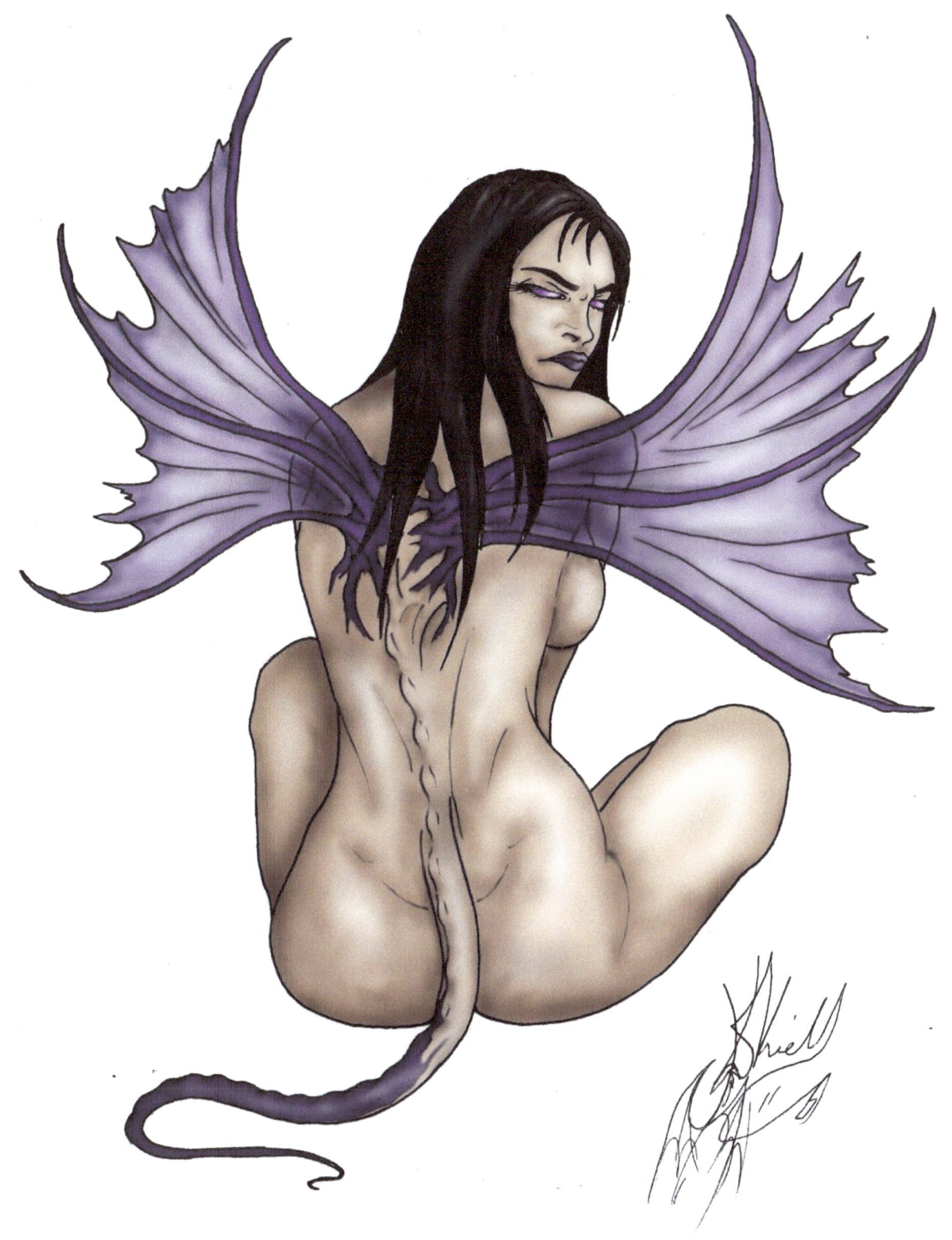

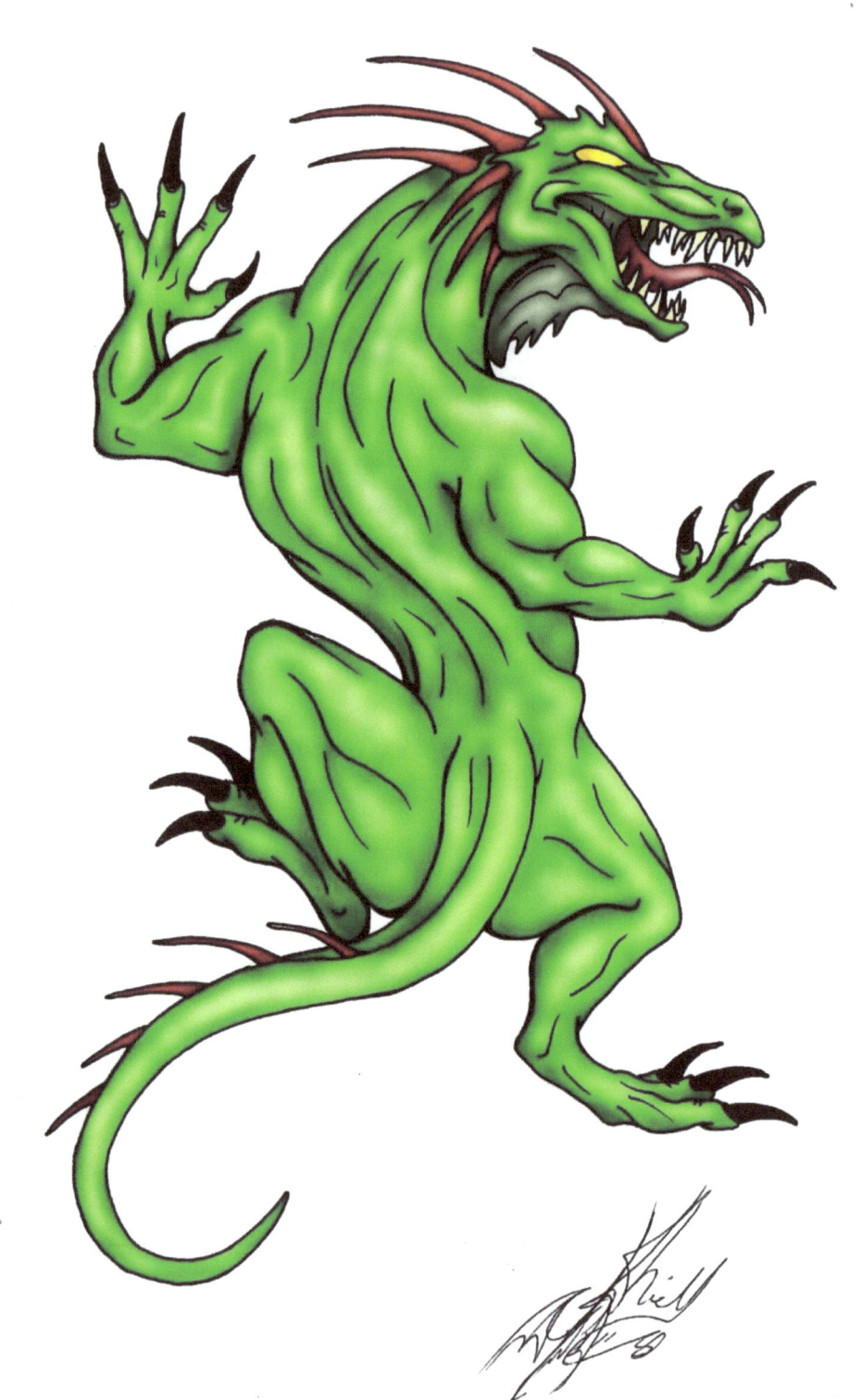

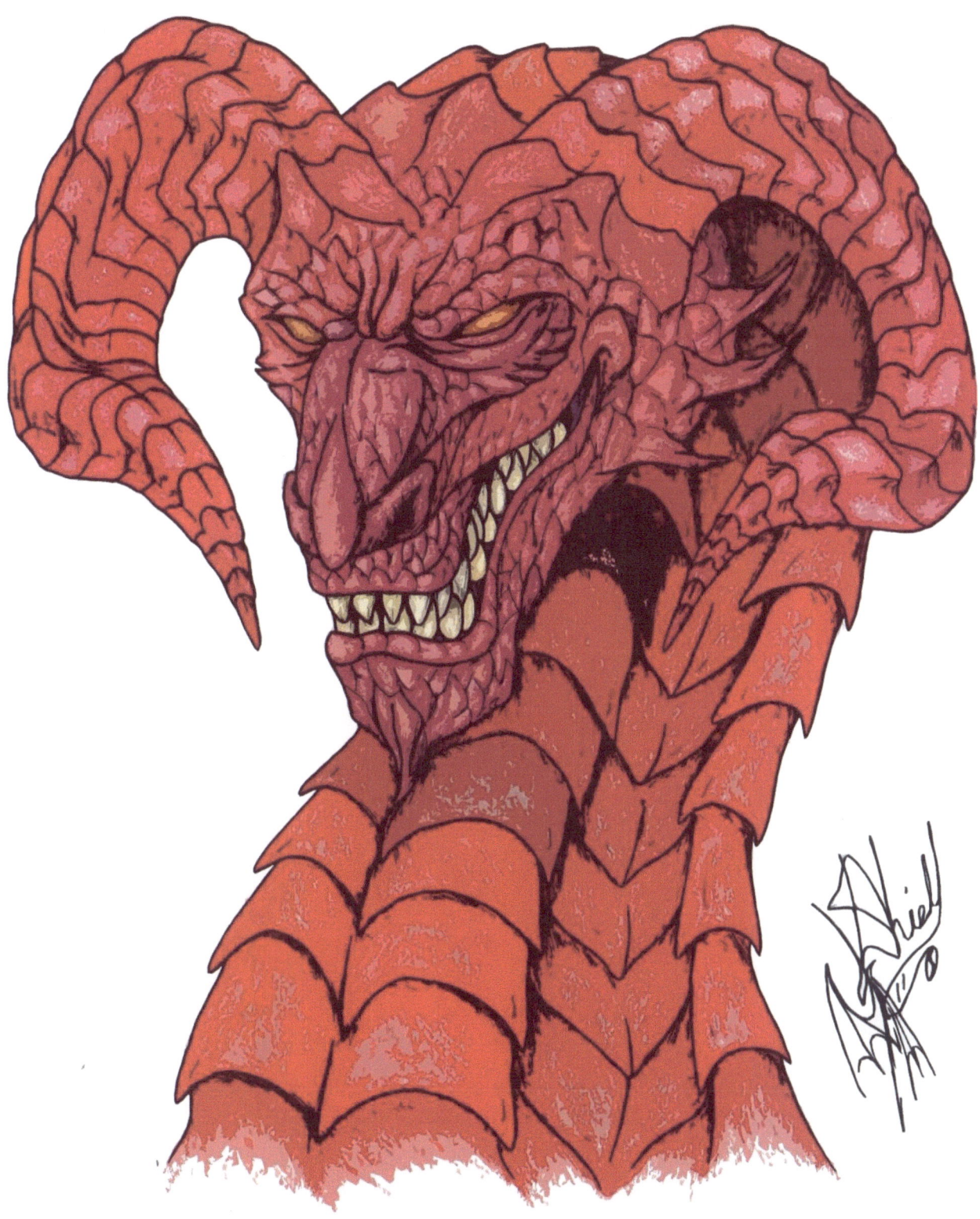

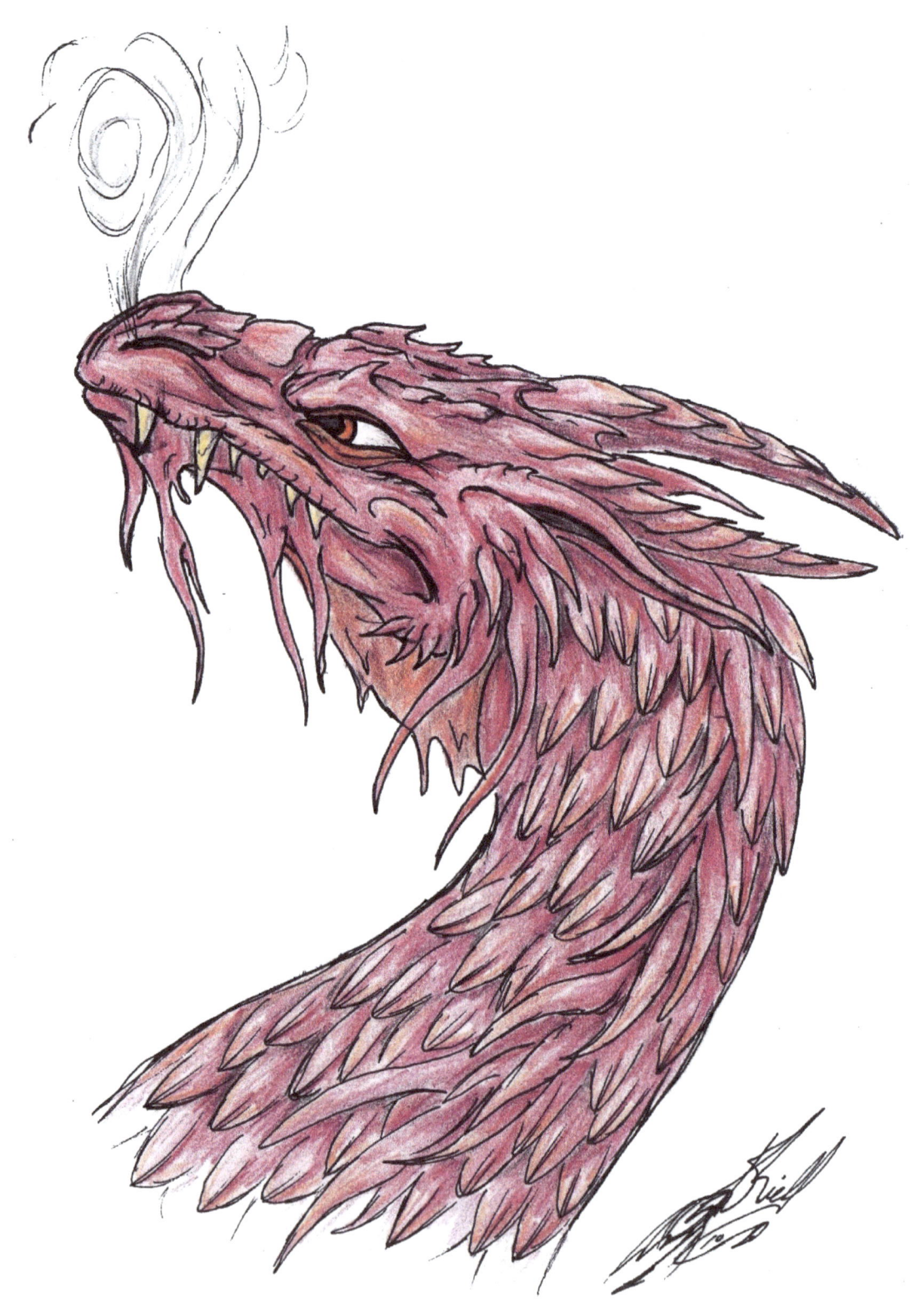

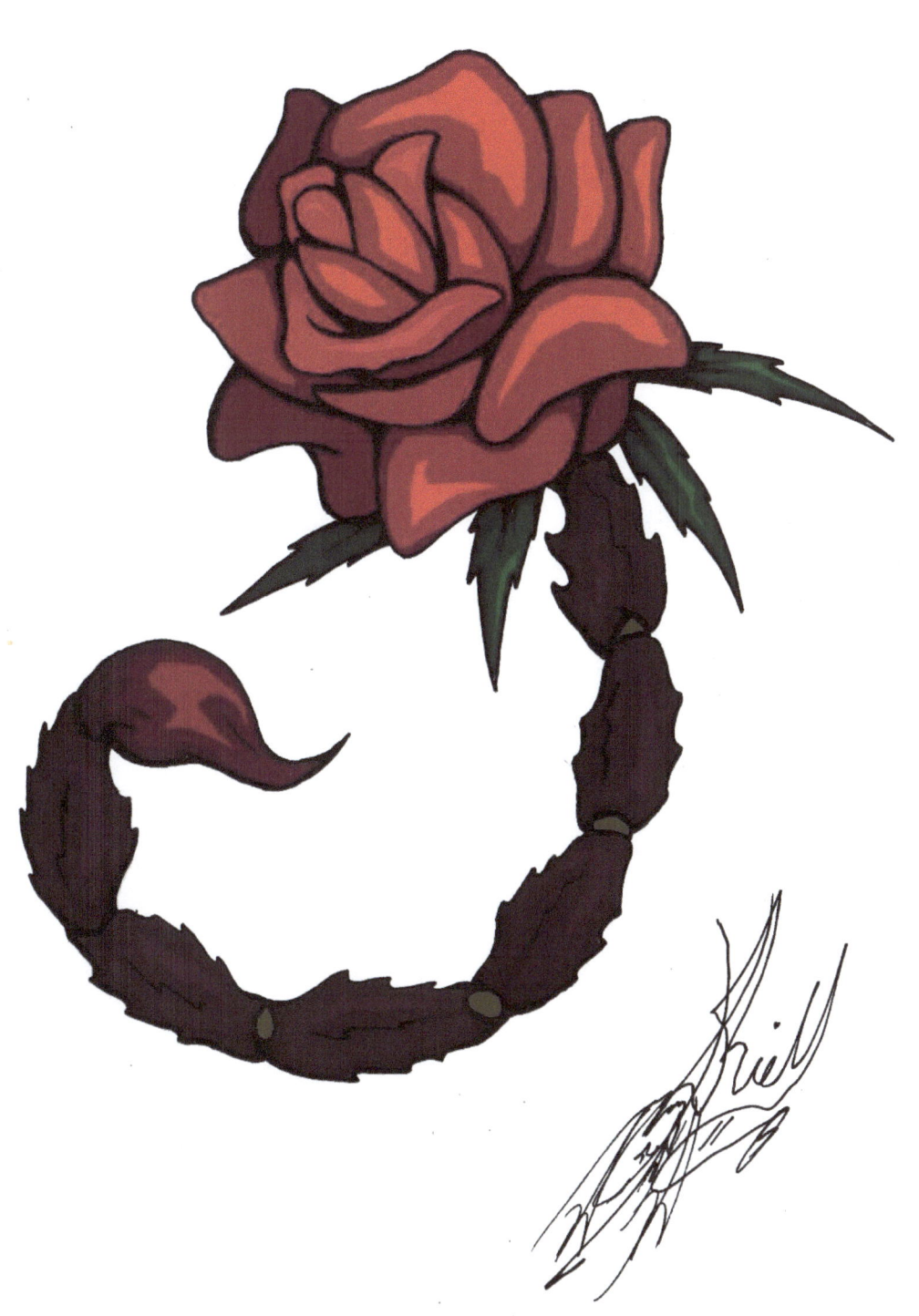

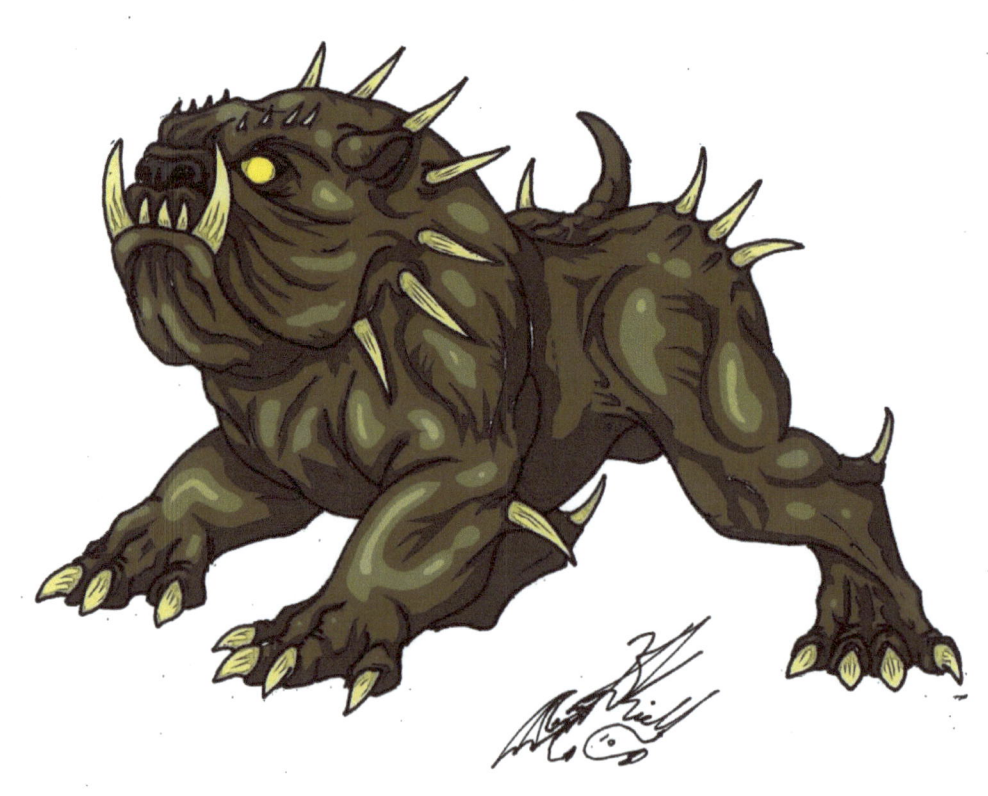

Bulldog

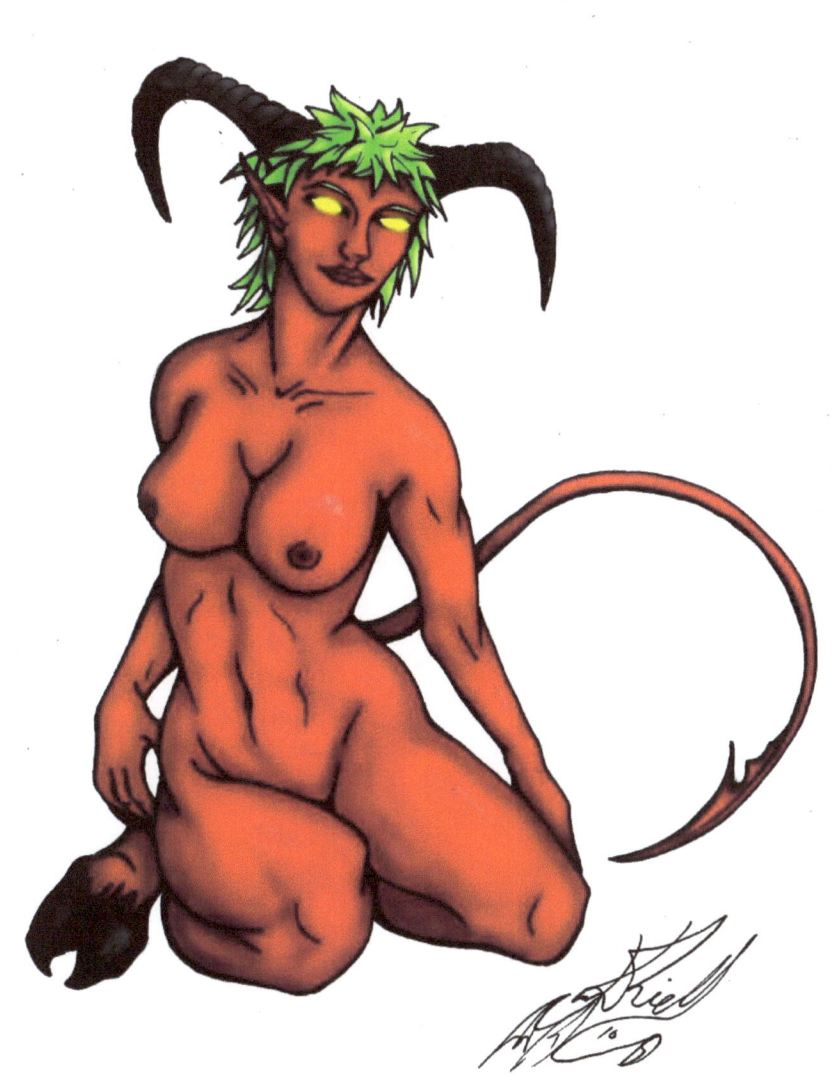

Succubus

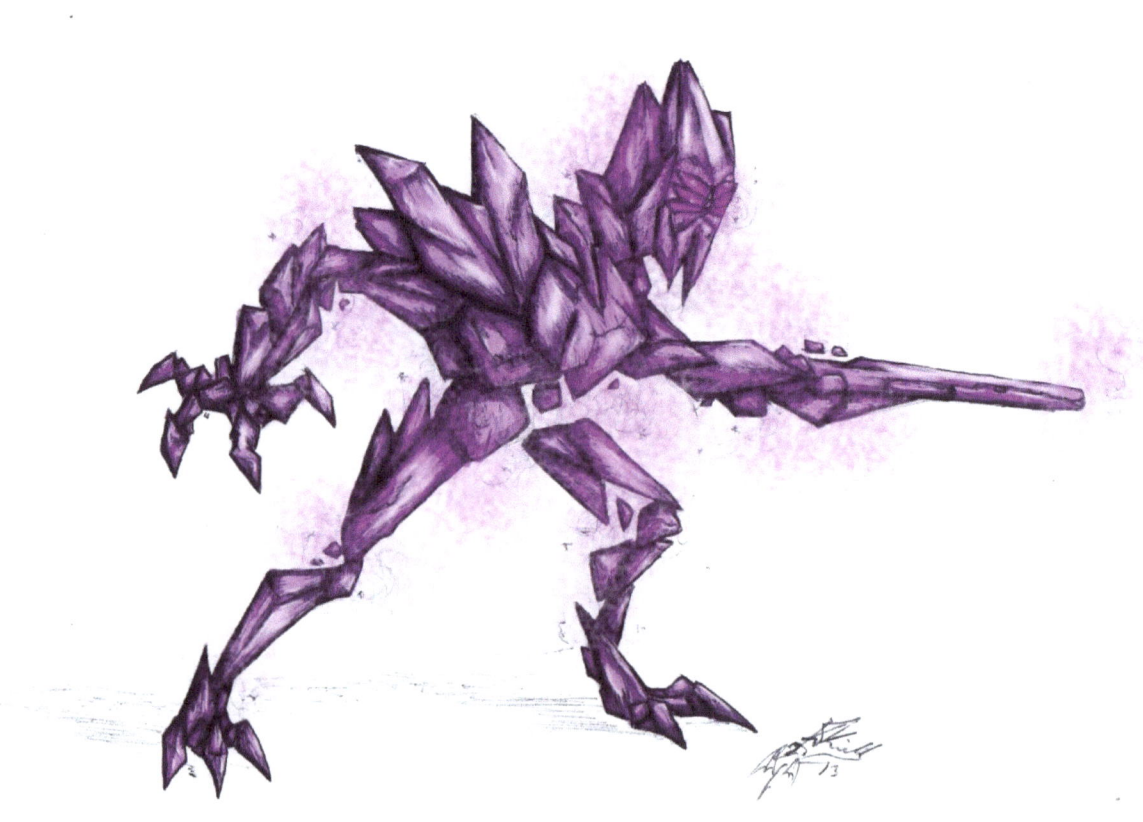

Jade Attacker

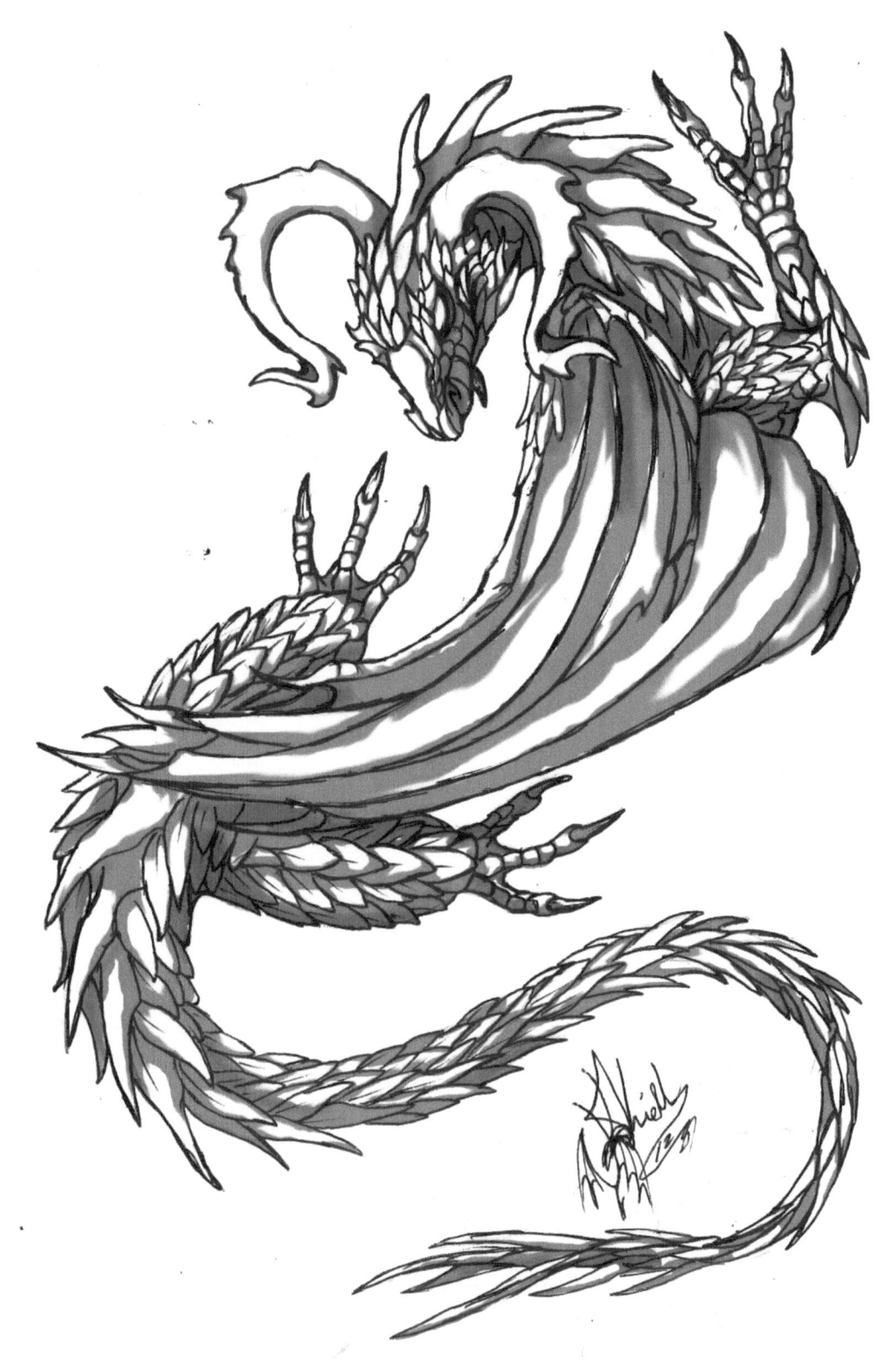

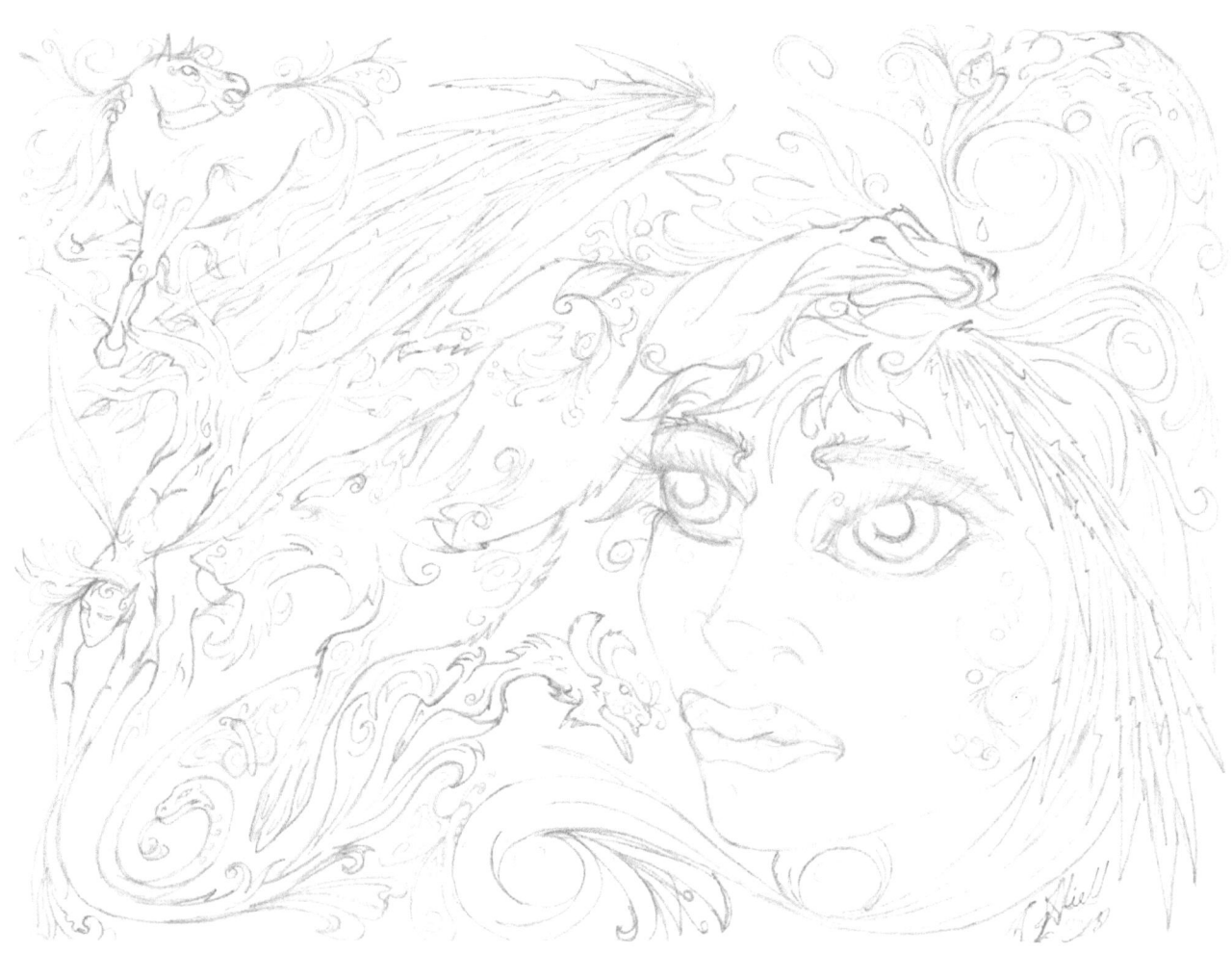

Imagination